# Jean-Claude Paye

*Translated by James H. Membrez*

# GLOBAL WAR ON LIBERTY

Telos Press Publishing

Printed in the United States of America.

10 09 08 07 06 05 04 03 02 01

Typeface: Spectrum

Originally published in French as *La fin de l'État de droit*
by La Dispute, Paris, November 2004
Revised and updated through December 2006.


ISBN-10: 0-914386-32-8
ISBN-13: 978-0-91438-632-2

Telos Press Publishing
431 East 12th Street
New York, NY 10009

www.telospress.com

# Table of Contents

# GLOBAL WAR ON LIBERTY

# Global War on Liberty

## INTRODUCTION

The real meaning of the war on terrorism is not self-evident. It appears to be a struggle between two equal adversaries, the State and terrorist organizations, "legitimate" violence against redemptive violence. This religious discourse of the struggle of "good against evil" must be overcome in order to bring out the real issue: a profound change in the organization of power, a transformation of the political system itself. In order to do that, it is necessary to lift the veil on this virtual reality and return to the facts. We must bring out all of the changes that have taken place in the relation between society and State. This transformation is manifested at the level of criminal law. The latter has a double function: it formalizes and legitimizes the changes that have occurred and it is a privileged instrument of this transformation.

### SEPTEMBER 11

The attacks of September 11 were the occasion for a tremendous acceleration in the transformation of codes of criminal law and procedure, already underway for several years. In the months, and sometimes days, that followed, governments adopted measures that restricted public and private liberties.[1] The speed with which these various laws were adopted is striking. This can be understood more easily if it is kept in mind that most of these changes had been made or anticipated well before the attacks. In the European Union, of the eleven proposals immediately brought in after the attacks, six had al-

---

1   Two organizations dedicated to the defense of privacy and public liberties, one English and the other American, Privacy International and the Electronic Information Center (EPIC) published a report of 393 pages that reviews the laws that were passed and proposed laws in 50 countries following the attacks of September 11: *An International Survey on Privacy Laws and Developments*. This report can be viewed online on ZDNet from the notes to Declan McCullagh's article "Report: Anti-Terror Efforts Pinch Privacy," September 3, 2002, http://news.com.com/Report+Anti-terror+efforts+pinch+privacy/2100-1023_3-956286.html .Also read "Internet en liberté surveillée," *Reporters sans frontières*, http://www.rsf.org/article.php3?id_article=3668.

ready been considered before September 11 and four others had been in preparation. Only one new item was added, which aimed at modifying the laws on the right of asylum and immigration for the antiterrorist struggle.[2]

What is at stake in these measures is symbolized in the content of an email message sent by an adviser to the British Minister of Commerce to his colleagues in the ministry immediately after the attack: "This is a very good day to bring up and adopt, on the quiet, all the measures that we must take."[3]

The measures adopted as a result of the attacks complete the transformation of criminal law and legitimize it. One may speak of a true transformation here because it is the very existence of the rule of law that is called into question. What had happened, in the absence of any publicity, appeared clearly in hindsight and was retrospectively justified. This is not to say that the decision-making process became transparent. On the contrary, all of the laws were passed without debate, either in civil society or in Parliament. The absence of any challenge to the content of these laws gives rise to a paradoxical discourse: these measures are justified by an emergency, but actually are part of a long-term war against terrorism.

The state of emergency exists for the long term. It emerges as a new type of political system, dedicated to defending democracy and human rights. In other words, the citizen must be willing to renounce his/her concrete freedoms for a lengthy period of time in order to maintain a self-proclaimed and abstract democratic order.

The fact that most of these acts assume the form of law indicates clearly that the ruling authorities are committed for the long term, seeking a new legitimacy and the consent of the people to the dismantling of their constitutional guarantees. The example of the United States confirms the effectiveness of these policies. Polls indicate that a growing number of people are ready to tolerate increased

---

2    Statewatch Observatory, "In Defense of Freedom & Democracy: New Laws & Practices Affecting Civil Liberties and Rights after September 11," www.statewatch.org/observatory2b.htm, 30 July 2002.

3    "Un très bon jour pour," *Le Monde diplomatique*, septembre 2002, p. 10.

2

surveillance[4] and inclined to make concessions concerning the rights that secure their privacy.

As Didier Bigo writes, "to define terrorism is to define what is democratic and what is not."[5] Established regimes that collaborate with an internationally organized antiterrorist policy are considered democratic. On the other hand, any political movement radically opposed to a regime that is part of the international struggle against terrorism can be criminalized. For example, the list of terrorist organizations issued by the Council of the European Union includes the PKK, a Kurdish party that advocates armed struggle against the Turkish State. Hence an armed opposition movement is criminalized and a government known for its systematic violations of human rights is legitimized.

The war against terrorism becomes a special instrument of legitimation for all established governments. Any government, regardless of its policies, takes on the mantle of defending fundamental freedoms if it joins "the camp of good against the camp of evil" and thus can pass itself off as essentially democratic. The introduction of a European arrest warrant is a good example of this reciprocal and automatic recognition on the part of the Member States of the European Union.

A CONSTITUTIVE ACT

Traditionally, war is a sign of sovereignty and the same thing is true for the "war against terrorism." It is simultaneously a police operation, management of society through force and an act of war. The fight against terrorism abolishes the distinction between enemy and criminal. War is reduced to a simple police operation against delinquent States. Likewise, any social movement can be criminalized in the name of acting against terrorism. The new laws allow the pros-

---

4  John Borland and Lisa Bowman, "Politics: Weighing Security against Liberties," CNETNews.com, August 27, 2002. http://news.com.com/Politics+Weighing+security+against+liberties/2009-1001_3-954565.html.

5  Daniel Herman and Didier Bigo, "Les politiques de lutte contre le terrorisme," in Fernando Reinares, ed., *European Democracies against Terrorism: Governmental Policies and Intergovernmental Cooperation* (Abington: Ashgate publishing, 2001), p. 75.

ecution of any radical activity on the part of a movement whose objective is to influence governmental policies or put pressure on an international organization. The antiterrorist fight is a long-term war against a potential enemy that is constantly redefined. Its objective is to redesign the organization of society. Criminal law takes on a decisive role in this process as an act of supreme authority.

The intent of antiterrorist laws is to establish exceptional procedures at all levels of criminal proceedings, from investigation to trial. They sanction the primacy of formal procedure, particularly exceptional procedures, over law. As far as other related measures are concerned, they establish control over private life by retaining data from Internet traffic and infringing on the secrecy of email. The transformation is so significant that it leads to a reversal of the norm: the exceptions become the rule. As a form of political organization, the exceptional procedure substitutes itself for the Constitution and the law.

Unlike earlier legislation, the latest antiterrorist laws are no longer the result of relatively independent national initiatives, but are promoted by international institutions, such as the G8, the Council of Europe or the European Union. As a result, all States, even those that have never confronted a terrorist menace, end up adopting laws of this type.

The latest legislation is a response by national States to their international obligations, that is, essentially to American demands. The place occupied by the United States in this process is, moreover, unique to the current situation. The fight against terrorism is constitutive of its imperial management of the world.

The most recent laws closely meet the specifications demanded for many years by the FBI concerning the legal interception of communications. In the area of computer crime, the FBI is also able to directly organize the police forces of most other States. The ability of the United States to closely influence the laws of other States concerning the antiterrorist struggle confirms its leading role in modernizing political authority on the world level.

The measures taken following September 11 allow the American executive power to intensify the subordination of European police and judicial apparatuses to the American political system. The agreements for extradition and judicial cooperation recently signed between the United States and the European Union make the special American tribunals the basis on which the new world order is constructed. These agreements, most of which remain secret, are, as far as one knows, designed so that the American authorities can continually and successfully lay down new demands. Police cooperation with the United States also authorizes the exchange and uncontrolled use of personal information.

The antiterrorist measures reveal yet another aspect of the role played by the United States, that of a superpower directly dominating other States. The first element of this power relationship is found in the legal capacity to favor American nationals by granting them particular rights. This is clearly evident in the different treatment citizens have been accorded by American legislation compared to residents of foreign nationality. American courts grant themselves universal power, as well as extraterritorial rights, in matters concerning terrorism and organized crime. The right that the United States confers on itself to overthrow any nonconforming regime, such as Iraq, constitutes the military aspect of this relationship.

The development of transatlantic cooperation within the context of the struggle against terrorism reveals the organic character of criminal law in the formation of the imperial structure. The European Union is placed under American hegemony as far as organizing control over its populations is concerned. As for the United States, its demands are focused on the ability of its police and judicial institutions to circumvent the formal structures of European executive and judicial powers. Thus the United States claims particular rights because of its status as the dominant power.

The war against Iraq and the fight on terrorism represent two complementary aspects of the organization of power on the world level. The deployment of a unified command, the Empire, is a complex question. It takes the form of a contradiction between the domination exercised by a particular national State, the United States, and the ability of this State to represent politically the dominant fraction of multinational capital.

The Empire has not caused the national form of the State to disappear. Imperial management is exercised by the American State, the only one to have all the prerogatives, i.e., army, money, police, judicial apparatus, which are specific to this type of State. Other national States remain, but are transformed, left with no more than the means to maintain order and control over their societies. They are integrated as subaltern structures into the imperial order.

This complex articulation is not without problems, notably concerning the preventive wars necessary to ensure the continuity of the unified command. It is at this level that differences between nations appear. For example, the petroleum interests of the United States are different than those of French companies. All States do not share the desire of the Bush administration to destabilize the entire Middle East and occupy conquered territories directly. The success of imperial policies assumes that, as in the 1991 Gulf War, national States abandon their specific interests in favor of those of the United States.

The development of the second aspect of imperial management, control over national populations, poses fewer problems to the various States and thus creates fewer tensions in the exercise of a globalized command. Although it has received far less media coverage, this process is quite widespread. Over the last ten years, the United States has put forward a group of demands concerning the fight against organized crime and terrorism. These demands have gradually been accommodated by other States and have profoundly transformed the approach to criminal law in these countries.

## MARCH 11

On the occasion of the March 11, 2004 attacks in Spain, we saw on our television screens a number of "specialists" on terrorism lump together Al-Qaida, the ETA and various political refugees. They made terrorism into a generic term that could be used in various concrete situations.

The immediate implementation of a European arrest warrant was one of the measures unanimously demanded in order to ward off this multiform danger. This arrest warrant permits one Member State to hand over almost automatically a person wanted by the judicial authority of another Member State. As opposed to extradition procedures, this warrant eliminates all the political and judicial checks on the substance and legality of the request, as well as any possible recourse against it. The request is unconditionally satisfied and legitimized by other countries, regardless of its legality or its conformity to the principles of the rule of law. The warrant was to come into force on January 1, 2004. Though adopted at the European Union level and already integrated into most national laws, this measure has hardly been implemented. One of the first consequences of the March 11 attacks was the end of the last resistance to the use of this procedure as well as the strengthening of unverifiable measures adopted within the context of judicial and police cooperation among European countries. One can thus fear that the process of suspending constitutional guarantees, begun after September 11, will be accelerated.

The first measures contemplated concern the strengthening of police and judicial cooperation. An "intelligence capacity" will analyze intelligence information supplied by the secret services and police forces of Member States. Also involved is the adoption of legislation permitting investigators from several countries to work together in teams and the ratification of a convention on judicial cooperation in criminal matters.

There is also a provision facilitating the exchange of fingerprints and biometric surveys. The Council of the Heads of State and Government also want to authorize the issuance, before 2005, of passports and identity cards containing such data as a photograph of the iris of the eye and fingerprints. Air carriers would also be obliged to communicate all information on their passengers to European customs authorities and police. Implementation of this measure was already underway to assist American authorities for transatlantic flights.

Different measures, such as passports and identity cards with microchips containing biometric data, have been under discussion for a long time. The attacks were simply the occasion to overcome resistance to such liberty-killing measures. Looking at the Madrid attacks, it is clear the effectiveness of these measures is largely uncertain, since the arrested people had been living in Spain for a long time and had not crossed any borders.[6] They could not have been found by such means. On the other hand, these measures are perfectly adequate for policing populations.

Statewatch has pointed out that, of the 57 measures considered by the Council of Heads of State and Government on March 25-26 2004, 27 had very little or nothing to do with terrorism.[7] Their purpose was to maintain surveillance, not of specific groups, but of entire populations by controlling communications.

## THE LONDON ATTACKS

Following the attacks of July 7, 2005 and the failed attacks of July 21, the British government presented a whole series of measures designed to deal with the terrorist threat. As The Guardian[8] wrote, the response of the politicians and police was to create panic and hysteria. Armed patrols walked the streets and arrested dozens of people. An innocent man was shot with eight bullets, seven of them in the head. While justifying its action by the fact the individual in question was allegedly running away, the spokesperson for the police claimed the right to shoot any presumed terrorist on sight. The "shoot to kill" claim of the police will be maintained even after surveillance cameras revealed the authorities had openly lied and that the person who was shot not only was not running away, but was immobilized on the ground.

With respect to terrorism, the government proposes to undertake judicial hearings without a jury, in the course of which a suspect could be detained without being accused of a crime. "What is suggested is a sensible period of detention of suspects in order to carry out the investigation successfully," Lord Falconer, Minister of Constitutional Affairs pointed out.[9] It would be a question of establishing a safe place,

---

6   Gérard Davet et Pierre Stroobants, "Après Madrid, l'Europe cherche une riposte au terrorisme," *Le Monde*, 26 mars 2004.

7   "Scoreboard on post-Madrid counter-terrorism plans," http://www.statewatch.org/news/2004/mar/21eu-terr-scoreboard.htm.

8   Louise Christian,, "Stay calm, the government says, in a mad panic itself," *The Guardian,* July 30, 2005.

9   "Tony Blair envisage de créer des tribunes déception," *Le Monde AEC AFP et Reuters*, le 12/8/2005.

shielded from the media and the public, in which sensitive information could be divulged. Suspects would be represented by attorneys who had successfully passed security checks, that is, were accepted by the prosecution. The rights of the defendant would be especially restricted, since these attorneys would not be able to reveal to their client the evidence upon which they are being detained.

This "sensitive" information would be examined only by a specialized judge. Thus, the government's proposal would be to set up a "pre-trial" procedure using an exceptional court, presided over by a judge who is a specialist in terrorist matters, but has no investigative authority. The latter is the exclusive jurisdiction of the police. This procedure would allow an extended police custody of up to at least three months. The latter would only be a first step, since the government already envisages the possibility of establishing police custody of indeterminate length.[10]

Extending police custody is also one of the measures contained in the new proposed antiterrorist law, "The Terrorism Bill," presented on September 15, 2005 by Charles Clarke, Home Affairs Minister. The proposed law calls for creating new crimes such as "glorifying" terrorism or "distributing" terrorist publications. This latter crime would be aimed at Islamist bookstores, but could also be used more widely. The bill also considerably increases the penalties attached to acts that are already prosecuted. Thus "preparing" attacks would be punishable by a life sentence, "indirect incitement" of terrorist acts would be punishable by a seven-year sentence and "training" for terrorism by a ten-year sentence.

British legislation on human rights would be changed in order to facilitate the expulsion of foreigners suspected of having a relationship to terrorism. On August 24, the Home Secretary, Charles Clarke, ordered a list of unacceptable behaviors to be published that would justify an expulsion from British territory. This list is not exhaustive and is likely to be completed by the government at any moment. Unacceptable behaviors include, among others: "foment, justify or glorify terrorist violence"; "seek to provoke others to terrorist acts"; or "foster hatred which might lead to inter-community violence in

10   *Ibid.*

the UK." Also, "writing, producing, publishing or distributing material," "public speaking including preaching," "running a website," or "using a position of responsibility such as a teacher or community or youth leader" to promote terrorism could also lead to expulsion.[11]

Such measures make it possible to go after any person who displays any violent action against any constituted government, no matter what the nature of the regime.

Occupying the Presidency of the European Union, the British Government attempted to speed up and, above all, direct police and judicial cooperation within the EU. It has announced, on several occasions, its intention to challenge the decisions of the European Court of Human Rights on the protection of refugees. The Court, charged with applying the European Convention on Human Rights that prohibits torture and inhuman and degrading treatment, has consistently been opposed to the return of refugees when they are threatened with such treatment. Charles Clarke considers this interpretation of the Convention prevents European States from expelling foreigners suspected of terrorism under the pretext they would run the risk of being tortured or mistreated in their country of origin.[12] This interpretation of Article 3 of the European Convention on Human Rights conflicts with the plan of the British government to deport foreigners who are accused of justifying or supporting terrorism to their country of origin or to third world countries where they would risk torture.

The intent of the government is not to make a frontal attack on the Convention but to make it ineffective by "readjusting" the decisions of the Court to consider the new situation created by terrorism, what Minister Clark calls the "circumstances of the modern world." The British Minister has found allies: the governments of Italy, Lithuania, Portugal and Slovakia.[13] These countries hope to persuade the Court at Strasbourg to reconsider the decisions that stipulate that the right of a person not to be tortured is absolute and that it cannot be weighed against the question of national security.

---

11  "Tackling Terrorism-behaviors unacceptable in the UK, reference 124/2005," 24 août 2005.

12  Clare Dyer "Ministers seek to overturn torture rule in deportations," *The Guardian*, October 3, 2005.

13  Clare Dyer, "UK wins allies in challenge to torture ruling," *The Guardian*, October 18, 2005.

During a press conference on August 5, 2005 Tony Blair announced a set of measures that directly attack the guarantees of the rule of law and clearly proclaimed that "no one should doubt that the rules of the game have changed."[14] While he justified these reforms because of the attacks, the change in rules preceded these acts. The anticipation of change in the legal order is confirmed here as well.

What is specifically different about the London attacks in relation to those in New York or Madrid is that the alleged perpetrators are citizens of the country where the events occurred. In general, anti-terrorist laws, such as the USA Patriot Act or the British Anti-Terrorism, Crime and Security Act 2001, provide arbitrary measures of incarceration for foreigners named as terrorists by the executive power. However, The Prevent Terrorism Bill, which came into force in March 2005, authorizes the British government to take administrative measures, without any evidence, that deprive any person simply suspected of participating in terrorist activities of their freedom. This procedure does not relate only to foreigners but also to citizens. The law, which eliminates habeas corpus for English citizens, came into effect before the London attacks. It anticipates the acts that serve to justify it.

The measures that deprive persons of their freedom are the most spectacular aspect of the antiterrorist laws. They are, however, accompanied by measures that permit surveillance over the private and public life of all citizens.

We are witnessing the dismantling of the rule of law, in its form as "the hierarchical organization of juridical norms"[15] and in its content as a totality of public and private freedoms guaranteed by law. The challenge to the way in which society is governed by the State[16]

---

14  Marc Roche, "Tony Blair s'affiche déterminé à lutter contre le terrorisme," *Le Monde*, le 6/8/2005.

15  Jacques Chevalier, *L'État de droit* (Paris: Montchrestien, 1999).

16  According to Hegel, in the *Elements of the Philosophy of Right* (edited by Allen W. Wood; translated by H. B. Nisbet. New York: Cambridge University Press, 1991), the rule of law is the conceptualization of the manner in which civil society is organized by the State. This theorization supposes a clear distinction between the two levels, civil society and State, as particularity and universality. It is this articulation, the distinction between civil society and its relations with political society, that is called into question by various reforms at the national and world levels.

can be carried out only because of a reversal in the primacy of law over procedure. What is specific to the current situation is less the accentuation of the control exercised by the executive power over legislative authority than the narrow instrumentalization of judicial authority and, in fact, its subordination to the police.

It is no longer only a question of the suspension of the law or of restricting the mechanisms that protect the fundamental liberties of specific categories of individuals or social strata placed outside of society. The specificity of these latest laws lies in their general significance. They affect not only specific individuals and organizations but the whole population as well. We are witnessing a drastic change in criminal law. Contrary to what is usually offered as explanation, the terrorist attacks, whatever they may be, are not the basis for the change in the legal order. The transformation in the modes of organizing power cannot be explained by an external element, but only by an analysis of their internal structure. The change in the law reveals a global transformation in the relation between society and State.

If it is true that "the political today takes on the appearance of the juridical"[17] to concentrate on the study of changes in criminal law does not indicate a desire to remain at the level of the phenomenon. The law is not only ideologic, but also an effective mode of regulating society. Its transformation bears witness to the establishment of a new political structure. It is the legitimation of that new structure. Thus, juridical analysis concerns essentially, not the relation of domination in the strict sense, but the relation of hegemony.

The study proposed here is thus a contribution to the analysis of the current form of the State. While it is based on the analysis of laws, it is not founded on a conception of power that reduces the latter to the totality of legal relations. To take note of the increasingly juridical form of social relations is not to choose to overlook the social and political transformations effected by the globalization of economic power. On the contrary, it is to emphasize the magnitude of the drastic change that financial globalization brings about in the organization of politics.

---

17  Jean de Maillard, *Le marché fait sa loi* (Paris: Mille et une nuits, 2000), p. 63.

# 1

## THE FIGHT AGAINST TERRORISM IN
## THE UNITED STATES

Following the attacks on September 11, 2001, the United States was the first to take new antiterrorist measures. After the first proposed law, called "Anti-terrorism Act," was rejected by the Senate because it's liberty-killing undertones were too overt, representatives of the House and Senate quickly drafted a new version, the Patriot Act, acronym for Provide Appropriate Tools Required to Intercept and Obstruct Terrorism. The House Judiciary Committee discussed this new proposed law on October 2. At the first reading on October 12, the legislation, renamed "USA Act" ("Uniting and Strengthening America Act"), was passed by Congress and came into effect on October 26.[1]

### THE PATRIOT ACT

This law gives new powers to the police and intelligence services for the fight against terrorism. Notably, authorities can arrest and detain for an indeterminate period foreigners suspected of being in contact with terrorist groups. These measures were supposed to expire at the end of 2004.

### Political Incrimination

The text of the USA Act does not clearly define the acts that are considered to be terrorist, but we will see later, just as in the European laws or in the Council of the European Union's Framework Decision relative to terrorism, the terrorist character of an infraction is linked to the perpetrator's intention, to his/her political objective, i.e., to influence the government by intimidation or force. The law stipulates that criminal offenses can be considered as terrorist if they "appear to

---

1   The complete text of the law is available at: "Politechbot.com: Final Text of USA Anti-Terrorism Bill," http://www.politechbot.com/docs/usa.act.final.102401.html.

be intended to [...] influence the policy of a government by intimidation or coercion or to affect the conduct of a government [...]."

The notion of intimidation is particularly subjective. What does intimidate mean if not to want to influence? Every strike, demonstration or march that aims at putting pressure on the government could be affected by this accusation if, while underway, one of the offenses listed in the law were committed.

The concept of coercion is just as arbitrary since its forms are not made explicit. Any government that adopts measures or backs away from doing so under pressure from the street is submitting to coercion. Thus it would always be possible to denounce acts committed during demonstrations or protest actions.

However, social movements do not seem to be the primary preoccupation of the Bush administration. It is more concerned with controlling private life. Thus, in the objective part of the law, forty offenses are mentioned, but those connected with computing are especially targetted.

The USA Act also criminalizes "aid" given to terrorist actions. This concept, which makes no distinction between incitements to violence and promoting peaceful actions, is so vague that it was declared unconstitutional by a federal court[2] on January 23, 2003.

*Unequal Rights*

On November 13, 2001, President Bush made the decision to establish a special military tribunal to try all foreigners suspected of participating in or supporting terrorism. The trial may be secret and there is no provision for an appeal before a civilian jurisdiction. The Secretary of Defense has indeed allowed for a review tribunal that would play the role of a higher court, but the independence of the members of this tribunal is doubtful since the President selects them on a case-by-case basis. If the accused does not accept the defense attorneys selected by the army, he/she can request a civilian lawyer, but that person, just like the press, would have to leave the court when information classified as "official secret" is presented.

---

2  http://www.cnn.com/2004/01/26/patriotact.ap/

The absence of the possibility of recourse explains why the American government has not used the court martial system, which allows for an appeals procedure before a civilian court.[3] Another important difference lies in the weaker criteria of acceptable proof. It suffices for the latter to be "convincing for a reasonable person."

The decision made by President Bush to form a special military tribunal to try all foreigners suspected of participating in or supporting terrorism strengthens American domination. Such military tribunals could be established in any suspect country.[4]

More than 1200 persons were arrested solely on the basis of their origin (Arab, Muslim, or of South Asian descent) and detained without any charges being brought against them. Even if most of them were released, some remain in detention without an indictment.[5] These persons do not have the right to an attorney nor can they contest their detention. They must submit to conditions of incarceration (ill treatment, torture, prohibitions against practicing their religion)[6] that are flagrant violations of the "Convention against Torture and Other Cruel, Inhuman and Degrading Treatment or Punishment," ratified by the United States.

The Anti-Terrorism Task force also interrogated 5000 foreigners who had entered the United States during the preceding two years. They were selected for interrogation based on their nationality.[7]

The National Security Entry-Exit Registration System, a procedure established to register Muslim foreigners, made it possible to amass 13,000 files. It found only thirteen cases of suspected terrorism. This did not prevent the Attorney General from incarcerating, under degrading conditions, numerous people deprived of legal representation. Accused of being in violation of immigration laws, they were

---

3    François Sergent, "Les États-Unis réécrivent les lois de la guerre," *Libération*, 22 mars 2002.

4    Fabrice Rousselot, "L'armée américaine jugera les terroristes," *Libération*, 15 novembre 2001.

5    Marjorie Cohn, "The War on Civil Liberties in the US since 11 September," speech at the symposium "Législations antiterroristes européennes et protection des droits de l'homme," Progress Lawyers Network, Brussels, 27 February 2004.

6    "Group Reports Mistreatment of Detainees," *New York Times*, 15/3/2002.

7    Joanna Cattanach, "War on Terrorism still Rolling at Cost of Rights," *The Lariat* (Baylor University), 29 January 2002.

detained for months, even after the order for their release. The Inspector General of the Justice Department brought these facts to light in a report[8] issued in July 2003.

Many of the detainees were repatriated to their countries of origin, in contravention of international agreements that prohibit returning a person to a country "where there are substantial grounds for believing that he would be in danger of being subjected to torture."[9] The fact that these people were considered to be suspects by the United States placed them in a situation where they could be potential victims of new arrests, incarcerations and ill treatment in these countries. The suspension of law in which these persons were placed could well be prolonged indefinitely. The fact of being suspected of terrorism by an American administrative authority moves such a person into a world system of non-law.

A STRENGTHENED EXECUTIVE

The September 11 attacks considerably accelerated the process of strengthening presidential powers. By passing the Patriot Act, Congress granted the executive branch extraordinary prerogatives concerning the secret and unlimited detention of foreigners in breach of the regulations. As we saw, it was a presidential decree, the Executive Order of November 13, 2001, that set up the exceptional military tribunals delegated with trying foreign nationals accused of terrorism.

The new executive powers exist within the context of the imperial sovereignty of the U.S. These powers concern individuals who are not of American nationality. For citizens of the United States, the formal separation between executive and judicial powers is maintained.

The American President has also pointed out that the rule of law is not the juridical form in which the American State intends to manage a globalized society. On the contrary, the state of exception seems to be the form chosen by this administration. Does not President Bush

---

8   Office of the Inspector General, "Report to Congress on Implementation of Section 1001 of the USA Patriot Act," http://www.fas.org/irp/agency/doj/oig/patriot071703.html (July 17, 2003).

9   Convention Against Torture and Other Cruel, Inhuman or Degrading Treatment or Punishment, April 18, 1988, S. Treaty Doc. No. 100-20, 1465 U.N.T.S. 85, note 10, art. 3. http://www.hrweb.org/legal/cat.html. .

constantly remind us that the United States is engaged in a long-term war against terrorism, unlimited in both space and time? This concept of permanent war entails a prolonged restriction of the freedoms of U.S. citizens and the elimination of those freedoms for individuals suspected of terrorism or named as terrorists when they do not have the protection of American citizenship.

## A Super Agency of Internal Security

The strengthening of the executive power is not limited to these measures but extends equally to the establishment of surveillance services over the entire population.

On December 20, 2001, the American administration created an Office of Homeland Security with the aim of centralizing intelligence gathering and coordinating antiterrorist actions. On June 6, 2002, President Bush announced the creation of a new department of internal security, the Department of Homeland Security. Both houses of Congress adopted these measures on November 25, 2002.

This new department centralizes the resources of thirty already-existing organizations and services. The department has a total annual budget of 40 billion dollars and employs 170,000 people.[10] It restructures internal security by regrouping twenty-two current federal agencies. These include the Secret Service, Immigration and Naturalization Service, the Coast Guard and the Border Patrol.

The new Department of Homeland Security brings together the five federal agencies that shared in the "protection of critical infrastructures."[11] The objective is to ensure the centralization of information. Notably, the law contains provisions that mandate that all federal intelligence agencies, which include the CIA, the Department of Defense and the National Security Agency (NSA), to communicate "information relative to the vulnerability of the techni-

---

10   Un omniprésent ministère de l'intérieur," 14 juin 2002, http://www.samizdat.net.

11   These are the National Infrastructure Protection Center from the FBI, the National Communications System from the Department of Defense, the Critical Infrastructure Assurance Office from the Department of Commerce, the Energy Security and Assurance Program from the Department of Energy and the Federal Computer Incident Response Center.

cal infrastructure of the United States" to this new department.[12] Methods for protecting secrecy are strengthened by prohibiting any disclosure of information by employees of the new department "not usually pertaining to the public domain." Violations can result in a penalty of one year in prison.

Special treatment is given to computer data. The law provides for the creation of a special office for researching new technologies, the Homeland Security Advanced Research Projects Agency (HSARPA). It has a budget of 500 million dollars for the creation of tools to fight against electronic crime as well as develop technologies for identifying DNA.

This reorganization does not aim at strengthening the formal structure of executive power against autonomous agencies such as the police and intelligence services. It does not call into question the work of the FBI or the CIA. Rather it is a wide-ranging development of all means of surveillance.

The creation of this new structure leaves the FBI organization intact. The Attorney General even planned an expansion of its powers of investigation and surveillance. Moreover, the Director of the FBI, Robert Mueller, announced on May 8, 2002, the creation of a "cyberdivision" within the FBI. This new office was established at the same time as the new department, which has to have its own new division for information analysis. The Central Intelligence Agency (CIA) is not affected by the creation of the new department either.

*A Population Involved in the Organization of its Own Surveillance*

In 2002, Attorney General John Ashcroft had developed a project designed to involve the population in the organization of its own surveillance. He wanted to create a corps of federal informers, volunteers who would "help local communities respond following attacks against information systems and communications networks in order to return quickly to normal operation."[13]

---

12   Declan McCullagh, "Homeland Security's Tech Effects," November 20, 2002, http://news.com. com/Homeland+Securitys+tech+effects/2100-1023_3-966552.html.

13   *Ibid.*

Following reactions from American civil rights organizations, Congress abandoned this projected organization of informers. However, the executive power has not given up its intentions in this regard, as we will see later. It is thus not superfluous to comment on this first proposal.

The Department of Homeland Security would provide the infrastructure for Operation TIPS (Terrorism Information and Prevention System), placed under the authority of the Attorney General, by enrolling certain categories of workers to provide permanent surveillance of American citizens. According to the American Civil Liberties Union, these civilians would be "encouraged to spy for the government and denounce all suspect activity. The program would target volunteers who, because of their employment, for example, mail carriers, technicians or repair personnel, are in an excellent position to recognize unusual events, according to the White House.[14]

This plan, which would involve several hundreds of thousands of volunteers, is an application of the theory of "community policing" on a grand scale. The federal version of this idea orients it towards the search for intelligence. It is a preventative approach that develops in the absence of any observable offenses. This plan is part of a tendency that identifies maintaining order with social control.

In fact, in this doctrine, also intended for implementation in European countries, it is less a question of curbing infractions than of preventing them and of ensuring citizen participation in police action. Numerous American States, as well as some German Länder, already implement such collaboration.

This mobilization of the population integrates it into the work of repression. But it also has another objective, which is to establish a close link between citizens and the police. The hegemonic function is the principal stake in this policy. The police are at the center of a new "social contract" that makes security the center of collective relationships. Within this context, repression also has an ideological function.

---

14   Maurice Magis, "USA: les libertés civiles en danger," *Le journal du Mardi*, Bruxelles, n° 90, 3 décembre 2002.

*A Potential Threat*

After the failure of this first program, the Pentagon created a secret network to denounce "suspect activities," which brings together military personnel and "conscientious citizens." The idea is to build a very large database that essentially contains "raw and unsubstantiated reports," thereby creating an inventory of "suspect activities" and of "non-specific threats."

This database of intelligence information, called "Talon," makes it possible to "identify, report and analyze information on foreign threats." It permits the collection of unsubstantiated information, which is shared with analysts and incorporated into the anti-terrorist alert procedure of the Department of Defense.[15]

The Pentagon description of this program defines what it means by unsubstantiated intelligence: "this information includes, but is not limited to, any event or series of events ... that might indicate a potential threat against American forces, their equipment or their mission, whether this threat be deliberate or unintentional."[16]

Thus the "Talon" reports contain information that can be "fragmentary and incomplete" and "may or may not be linked to a real threat." Deputy Secretary of Defense, Paul Wolfowitz, emphasized that "generally and as much as possible, the Talon reports will be protected by the highest possible level of confidentiality in order to allow the maximum distribution of information."[17]

These facts confirm that, just like in the "Terrorist Information and Prevention System" plan, conceived to recruit millions of Americans to spy on each other and report any "suspect activity," the objective is not to collect reliable information so as to make it possible to face real problems, but to engage the population in a process of close surveillance and organized informing, thereby making it possible to harass people on the basis of simple rumors.

---

15 http://www.kitetoa.com/Pages/Textes/Textes/Texte9/talon.shtml.

16 Matthieu Auzannea, "Le Pentagone crée un réseau secret de dénonciation d'activités suspectes," www.transfert.net/a9034 , 26 juin 2003.

17 Brian McWilliams,"DoD logging unverified tips," *Wired*, June 25, 2003, http://www.wired.com/news/politics/1,59365-0.html.

*High-Risk Profiles*

These different measures made it possible to arrest large numbers of people suspected of maintaining relationships with organizations designated as terrorist. Some were arrested simply because they came from Arab countries or Pakistan. These measures also allowed the FBI to put pressure on groups supposedly linked to terrorism, such as the women's group "Women in Black, which struggles against violence in the Palestinian territories occupied by Israel. The FBI had, in particular, threatened to imprison those who refused to deliver information on this group.[18]

The attacks on public freedoms did not stop in the days following the September 11 attacks. In February 2004, the University of Iowa and four opponents of the war against Iraq were summoned to appear before a national grand jury to furnish information on the National Lawyers Guild, an association of jurists opposed to the military engagement in Iraq. Grand jury proceedings were used in the 1960's and 1970's during the war against Vietnam in order to intimidate opponents to the war.

The United States is a good example of population surveillance set up as a result of measures adopted in the context of the war against terrorism, particularly a series of exploratory controls designed to establish high-risk profiles.

In 2003, the private company Seisint, Inc., was asked by the government to manage a personal information program that makes it possible to detect potential terrorists. This system, called Matrix, deals with a set of raw data (unverified) from the police that it cross checks with information such as credit histories, proximity to addresses and telephone numbers already identified with criminal activity, as well as information from official documents such as a police records, drivers licenses or pilot's licenses. Matrix makes it possible to quickly and closely examine billions of computerized files. As a result of this program, the company has already supplied the government with a list of 120,000 persons achieving a "high score," identify them as potential terrorists.

---

18   Michael Ratner, "Les libertés sacrifiées sur l'autel de la guerre," *Le Monde diplomatique* novembre 2001.

According to the ACLU, Seisint would have developed this system on its own initiative shortly after the September 11 attacks and then offered it to the government, which then would have adopted it.[19] Despite reiterated requests, the ACLU has not been able to find out who is authorized to access this list of suspect persons: police, administrative authorities or private firms.

This system is a violation of the privacy of entire populations and forces "high-risk" persons to enter into a system of non-law, where administrative error is only one of the most visible aspects.

The only restriction that the Matrix system has come up against is its cost. Launched in 2002 in 13 States representing half of the American population, most have abandoned it for financial reasons. Only five States still use it: Michigan, Ohio, Connecticut, Florida and Pennsylvania.[20]

The plan developed by the American government to create a list of airline passengers is also a part of this logic. Here it is a matter of compiling computerized lists from airline companies in order to create a database combining information on all travelers with their respective profile.[21] This information, recorded at the time a reservation is made (name, address, telephone number, date of birth as well as destination), would be cross checked against that of those detained by the administration. As a result, it would be possible to detect individuals likely to present a risk for air traffic. The name of the air passenger is entered into a program designed to evaluate the risk represented by that person. These "high-risk" categories are very extensive since they can involve between 5% and 15% of the passengers.[22] These are social groups considered as potentially terrorist given their national origins, their prior travels, their religion or their political commitment. In light of the impossibility of closely monitoring such a large number of individuals in order to detect possible terrorists among them, this

---

19  "120000 personnes fiches comme terrorists potentials aux États-Unis," *Le Monde*, 22 mai 2004.

20  *Ibid.*

21  Etienne Wéry, "Les USA envisagent un mega-fichier des passagers aériens pour lutter contre le terrorisme," *Droit et nouvelles technologies actualités*, 4 février 2002.

22  "EU agree to adopt passenger name record scheme (PNR)," http://www.statewatch.org/news/2004/mar/27eu-pnr.htm.

procedure ends up ultimately stigmatizing these populations. It creates a mass scapegoat. The Computer Assisted Passenger Prescreening System II (CAPPS II) should come into force during the summer of 2004.[23] Its objective is to carry out investigations on 100 million air passengers in the United States.

GENERALIZED ELECTRONIC SURVEILLANCE

Since September 11, 2001, electronic eavesdropping on the Internet has developed very rapidly. Several access providers have indicated that they have been invited to install the electronic surveillance system Carnivore. Developed by the FBI, this system, since renamed DCS 1000, allows, among other things, the recovery of the content of email messages as well as connection data. Before the attacks, this system could be used only with the prior consent of a judge. The Combating Terrorism Act, passed by the Senate with extreme urgency on September 13, 2001, exempted the security services from this authorization.

Surveillance on the Net was permanently legalized by the Patriot Act, which authorized the FBI to connect the Carnivore system to the network of an access provider in order to monitor the circulation of email messages and retain the browsing histories of a person suspected of contact with a foreign power. The consent of a special court is sufficient to make such a connection.

Simplified procedures are set up and new rights granted to governmental agencies (CIA, NSA, INS and other civilian and military secret services) in order to make it possible for them to exchange and cross-check their information. These measures also authorize the "proactive" collection of information. Such investigations can take place apart from any offense and without the knowledge of the targeted individuals. Since these investigations have been legalized, the data can be reused later if these persons should be prosecuted.

Since the fight against terrorism is the declared aim of such investigations, the new measures make it possible to loosen judicial supervision of eavesdropping and even, most often, to eliminate it.

---

23 "Pre-Screening Jeopardizes Nation's Freedom," *Los Angeles Daily Journal*, February 20, 2004.

In fact, the USA Act includes a number of new measures concerning electronic surveillance. It authorizes the tapping of any communication device used by a person supposedly in touch with a presumed terrorist.

*Computer Crime and Terrorism*

The "Cyber Security Enhancement Act"[24] adopted by the House in July 2002 as a supplementary bill to the USA Act, was again approved by this body on November 13, 2002[25] as a rider to the law that regulates the scope of activities of the new Department of Homeland Security, the Homeland Security Act.[26] This law aims at increasing the involvement of the private sector in the defense of internal security. It also extends the powers of the police by allowing them to carry out telephone or electronic wiretapping without a legal warrant, while permitting the imposition of a sentence of up to life in prison for breaking into a computer system. Any act of computer piracy, understood as the simple unauthorized entry into a computer system, server or governmental web site, is classed as a terrorist act.[27] The same is true for the unauthorized use of a computer as well as the act of damaging it.

The purpose of this law is to amend the penalties incurred from computer attacks, such as a fraudulent intrusion or introduction of a virus, when these offenses "place national security in serious danger." It would also make it possible to expand police prerogatives in the area of telephone wiretaps or the reading of email messages by authorizing, without the consent of a judge, certain forms of communications interception.

The bill authorizes the police to carry out a limited surveillance, without a court order, in cases of "continuous attack" against a computer or if "a national security interest is confronted with an im-

---

24 Text of the law: http://thomas.loc.gov/cgi-bin/query/z?c107:H.R.3482.

25 Declan McCullagh, "House Considers Jailing Hackers for Life," *CNET News.com*, November 13, 2002, http://news.com.com/House+considers+jailing+hackers+for+life/2100-1001_3-965750.html.

26 http://thomas.loc.gov/cgi-bin/query/z?c107:h.r.5005.enr.

27 Thibault Verbiest et Etienne Wéry, "Terrorisme et Internet: vers un dérive sécuritaire?," *Droit et nouvelles technologies-Actualités*, 22 mars 2002.

mediate threat." Surveillance carried out in this context can only be concerned with the information about the identity of users, to the exclusion of the content of messages. Reading messages is only permitted in cases of "serious injury" or in the context of the fight against organized crime. There is also a provision for the cooperation of access providers and Internet service providers in order to facilitate the identification of their subscribers or clients during a criminal investigation.

The concepts of immediate threat, of "serious injury," of "continuous attack," or "seriously putting in danger" are intended to amend the nature of the offenses by considering them to be terrorist. They provide an appearance of seriousness to the prosecuted offense. They should, however, be read keeping in mind the particularly frenetic context in which these decisions were taken. In fact, the latter do not really add anything to the offense to make it dangerous. That is presupposed by the very nature of the act itself. The principal promoter of the CyberSecurity Enhancement Act, Republican Senator Lamar Smith, stated in the summer of 2002: "Until we make our 'cyberinfrastructure' secure, a few clicks and an Internet connection is sufficient to threaten the economy and put lives in danger. A (computer) mouse can be as dangerous as a bullet or bomb."[28]

## The Concept of Cyberterrorism

The concepts of cyberwar and cyberterrorism are central to the discourse of the American government on security questions. The unleashing of the Iraq war gave rise to an increase in alarmist declarations. Tom Ridge, Secretary of Homeland Security, announced that his department was going "to monitor the Internet to detect any possible sign of terrorist attack, of cyberterrorism, piracy and information war carried out between States."[29] For him, the cyberterrorists are as dangerous as the terrorists: "We will make no distinction between virtual and physical in this department," he affirmed.

---

28  Ibid.

29  Declan McCullagh, "Perspective: Cyberterror and Professional Paranoiacs," CNET News.com, March 21, 2003. http://news.com.com/Cyberterror+and+professional+paranoiacs/2010-1071_3-993594.html.

The Cyber Security Enhancement Act[30] was drafted before September 11. Thus it is not a question of a group of measures intended to respond appropriately to a particular situation, but a law meant to modify the exercise of fundamental rights on the Net on a long-term basis. It aims first to increase the full cooperation of access providers with police and administrative authorities. The USA Act already made it legal for the police or intelligence agencies to capture information otherwise protected by law as private if there is "reasonable grounds" to think that there is an offense. The Cyber Security Enhancement Act limited even more the possibilities for access providers to refuse to collaborate. Their cooperation is imperative when these companies believe in good faith in the existence of a crime.

The possibility of demanding such cooperation is no longer limited to judicial authorities but is extended to all administrative authorities, be they federal, state or municipal. That includes different police forces or intelligence services, but, as Declan McCullagh points out,[31] this possibility is also offered to a school principal, university president, the Centers for Disease Control and Prevention or just a municipal library.

*General Surveillance*

The new plan, Total Information Awareness, developed by the Secretary of Defense, is presented as the use of new technologies in order to fight against terrorism. It would involve cross-checking databases from diverse sources, such as files from banks, insurance companies or car rental agencies, with the aim of identifying terrorist activities. Investigations carried out in this context were assured of financing by a Congressional vote on February 20, 2002. In effect, then, this arrangement would assure the complete subsidizing of projects at the Pentagon's Defense Advanced Research Projects Agency (DARPA).[32]

---

30  H.R. 3482 CSEA.

31  Declan McCullagh, "House OK's Sentences for Hackers," July 15, 2002, http://news.com.com/2001-1001-955057.html?tag=politech.

32  Declan McCullagh, "TIA Proponents Defend Domestic Spy Plan," *CNET News.com*, April 2, 2003. http://news.com.com/TIA+proponents+defend+domestic+spy+plan/2100-1029_3-995229.html.

What is established by these laws and plans is indeed a widespread surveillance of the whole population by a coordinated group of administrative agencies and not targeted measures concerning specific organizations. Electronic investigations are not linked to an "imminent threat." An indeterminate risk or a virtual threat is sufficient to justify such investigations.[33] Judicial control is nonexistent, à priori or à posteriori. No warrant is required to begin investigations. There is no provision to inform a judicial institution or any other institution. The only obligation is to inform the Attorney General three months after the inquiry begins.

What is more, these techniques for intercepting electronic exchanges could be used to avert a risk having nothing to do with computers. It is sufficient that the Net could be used to transfer information about a crime. Such a possibility relativizes even more the legal justification for the capture of electronic information, i.e., "putting anyone's life in danger through the use of a computer by a hacker." This possibility, even if unintentional, justifies a sentence of up to life imprisonment.

This whole idea of putting life in danger through computer piracy immediately poses a problem since, logically, it would only concern piracy of particularly secure computer systems, such as those of a nuclear power plant, air traffic control center or military servers. These systems operate with a very high level of encryption[34] that is accessible only to a very small number of potential pirates. But it is each and every one who is monitored. This law's applications can cover an exponential number of uses since it can potentially concern any use of a computer connected to the Net.

The National Infrastructure Protection Center coordinates all defensive reactions following a computer attack, but also all preventative activities. This center was not established by a law but by gov-

---

33 Electronic Frontier Foundation Action Center, http://www.eff.org/Privacy/TIA/20030520_tia_report.php October 1, 2003.

34 This type of server operates with encryption RSA 1024 or 2048 bits. By comparison, "home banking" operates usually with 128 bits. The increase in encryption is exponential.

ernment decree. It is not responsible in any way for the information collected, either at the criminal or civil levels.[35]

## Net Police

American companies dominate the market of the new economy. They have always been opposed to the idea of regulating it. However, the organizations that represent them, such as the National Retail Federation, are demanding increased monitoring of crime on the Web.

In response to this demand and to the aspirations of the executive branch, American courts were given universal jurisdiction concerning prosecution of computer crimes. The Department of Justice gave itself the right to prosecute computer pirates regardless of their nationality and the place the crime took place. American laws became universal in so far as the largest part of world traffic on the Internet passes through the United States and is thus under the jurisdiction of this country.

The nature of the crimes prosecuted is very wide and imprecise. The concepts of hacker or pirate can cover multiple activities. The scope for action on the part of the police and the possibilities of interpretation for the judge are huge, so that "the perpetrators of any basic crime on the Internet, stealing computer data, petty pirating from sites containing pornographic images, could thus be harassed by American authorities."[36]

The United States has the power to disconnect a country from the network. This happened with Somalia for two months. In November 2001, the only access provider, Somalia Internet Company, and the main telecommunications company, Al-Barakaat, were forced to cease operations.[37] These two companies were placed on a list of organizations suspected of financing terrorism.

---

35 Anita Ramasastry, "The Cyber Security Enhancement Act's Good Faith Disclosure Exception: A Serious Threat to Individual Privacy," March 28, 2002 http://writ.news.findlaw.com/commentary/20020328_ramasastry.html.

36 Explanation of Mark Rasch, expert in Internet security, "Internet en liberté surveillée," p. 7, *Reporters sans frontières*, http://www.rsf.org/article.php3?id_article=3668.

37 *Ibid.*

The police function exercised over the Net by the United States makes it possible to maintain both the dependence of the huge number of Internet users and information systems on the dominant American companies and the domination of American imperial power. On this "occasion," it is thus all of the data and information exchanged on the network that is under the control of the American State. This police function is fundamental to its hegemony over globalized society.

## THE PROPOSED PATRIOT ACT II

The American Civil Liberties Union (ACLU) revealed[38] that the Department of Justice drew up a new proposed antiterrorist law, the "Domestic Security Enhancement Act of 2003"[39] that accentuates the tendencies of the "USA Patriot Act." This proposal is already known under the name of "Patriot Act II." Combined with the earlier law, it finalizes measures that deviate from common law with regard to non-citizens and strengthens the powers of the executive to the detriment of the judiciary. What is more, this proposal forms a significant advance in the establishment of a state of exception. It takes the suspension of law to which foreigners are subjected and generalizes it to all Americans accused of collaborating with organizations considered to be terrorist. Thus the procedure that departs from the law becomes the norm, the exception becomes the rule.

### A New Step in the Relinquishment of the Rule of Law

The proposed law would prohibit the release of information on detained foreigners incarcerated as part of a terrorist investigation. It proposes to expand the exceptions allowed to the Freedom of Information Act so that access to information relative to detained individuals is prohibited up to the filing of an indictment.

---

38  ACLU, "ACLU Says New Ashcroft Bill Erodes checks and Balances on Presidential Power," February 12, 2003 http://www.aclu.org/safefree/general/17189prs20030212.html.

39  Domestic Security Enhancement Act of 2003, http://www.eff.org/Censorship/Terrorism_militias/patriot2draft.html.

It is necessary to point out, however, that the USA Patriot Act authorizes unlimited incarceration of foreigners without any obligation to bring them to trial and thus without the obligation to bring an official indictment. In the latter case, the prohibition on divulging their incarceration would also be indeterminate in length. The same thing applies to foreigners imprisoned as simple witnesses. Secrecy concerning their imprisonment will depend on the good will of the executive authorities.

Section 503 would also allow the carrying out of summary expulsions of non-citizens, permanent residents of the United States, without the latter having committed a crime or having had the intention of doing so, if the Attorney General designates them as a threat to national security.

The proposed law also envisages an expansion in the applicability of the death penalty. It would apply it to crimes committed during protest movements, when the latter "undertake violent acts or acts dangerous to human life."[40] The ACLU concludes from that that protesters could be subjected to the death penalty if they violated the law during a demonstration that involved the death of an individual.[41]

The measures proposed in this new law are part of the tendency already laid out by the earlier antiterrorist law of strengthening executive authority and dismantling judicial monitoring of criminal law procedures. It gives new means to the police to carry out increased surveillance on the political and religious activities of citizens. Federal agents engaged in "undercover" surveillance activities without a judicial warrant would see their acts legalized, if they are officially dispatched by an agency of the executive branch.[42]

It will be easy for the government to organize surveillance over Americans and proceed legally to capture their telephone and computer messages. To do that, all that is necessary is to include these

---

40   Section 411.

41   ACLU, February 12, 2003, *op. cit.*

42   Ibid..

actions in a vague plan for surveillance of and acquiring intelligence on foreigners.[43]

Measures in the Foreign Intelligence Surveillance Act (FISA) of 1978 will be profoundly changed. While the surveillance of nationals was exercised under cover of the law, that concerning non-citizens depended on statutory measures established by the executive. If Patriot II is adopted, this distinction will no longer exist.

Section 101 amends the Foreign Intelligence Surveillance Act. It broadens the scope of the definition of a "foreign power" and extends the possibilities of surveillance accorded to executive authorities in the absence of any judicial supervision to "any person who is engaged in international terrorism, even if that person is not part of an international terrorist group."

Section 102 proposes to modify the definition of "agent of a foreign power" contained in the FISA by removing the condition that criminal activities "involve or can involve a violation of a criminal law." As a result, "any person engaged in clandestine activities to collect information for a foreign power can be qualified as an agent of a foreign power, even if these activities are not federal crimes."

The link between these two amendments makes it possible to put under surveillance, without an order or judicial supervision and in the absence of criminal activity, any person suspected of supplying information to an organization designated as terrorist by the Attorney General.

Here we come upon the originality of the new plan in relation to the existing antiterrorist law: the legal capability to treat American citizens with the exceptional procedures reserved for foreigners up until now. The final element of this process is the withdrawal of American citizenship.

### A Generalized Suspension of Law

The right to a fair trial is easily flouted by extending to the prosecutor the possibility of resorting to "palpable proof." Section 204 modifies the current conditions imposed by the Classified Information Proce-

---

43  Sections 101, 102 and 107.

dures Act (CIPA) for using secret evidence. The prosecutor must always demonstrate before the court the necessity of resorting to such means, but with the new amendment, this procedure takes place separately, where the secrecy can be protected from the unauthorized, but also from the accused, and no longer in open court, where the rights of the defense can be exercised.

The proposed law provides for taking away citizenship from American nationals who give aid to an organization designated as terrorist by the Attorney General. This measure breaks with earlier measures, such as those contained in the USA Patriot Act, which clearly distinguish between procedures reserved to foreigners and those applicable to nationals. With Patriot II, the suspension of law no longer applies just to non-citizens but also to all Americans.

Formally, the proposed law still distinguishes between citizens and foreigners. However, in fact, the legal protection reserved to American citizens can be taken away from them by a simple administrative decision. For supporters of this proposal, it would be the suspected person who would demonstrate his intention to abandon his citizenship by supporting a terrorist group. Thus it is assumed "that his intention can be presumed from his conduct"[44], even if the person never made this claim nor announced this intention.

Simply being involved in an activity, even a legal one, with an organization that is singled out as terrorist by a simple note from the Attorney General could be considered an act presumptive of abandoning citizenship. This could, among other things, lead to the expatriation of the person.

According to the ACLU, this measure would even offer the possibility of harassing individuals who are part of organizations fighting against vivisection or experimenting on animals, such as Operation Rescue or People for the Ethical Treatment of Animals.[45]

The possibility of taking away citizenship from American nationals means that the latter will no longer be treated according to the law, as restrictive as it may be from the point of view of individual liberties, but according to the goodwill of the administration. Given

44  Section 501.

45  ACLU, February 12, 2003, *op. cit.*

that they can become non-citizens, Americans can then fall under the measures provided for foreigners suspected of terrorism in the USA Patriot Act of 2001. They can thus be imprisoned without a legal indictment for an indeterminate length of time.

The scheme for suspending the law is thus potentially applicable to the whole population of the United States and to the entire world since, within the context of the antiterrorist struggle, the U.S. gives itself the right of intervening outside of its national territory and capturing foreigners suspected of terrorist activities.

The scheme for suspending the law is also extended to nationals who are not even suspected of terrorist activities. Sections 101 and 102 provide for the possibility of wiretapping any American and capturing his/her telephone and electronic communications for a period of 15 days without any judicial order. This measure would be applicable by a unilateral decision of some part of the executive branch that concludes "that an attack created an emergency situation."

The emergency situation is not defined and can be declared in the absence of any declaration of war. Judicial authorities are informed only after this period of fifteen days. Then it is necessary to have judicial consent to pursue the surveillance legally.

The proposed law aims at imposing important restrictions on judicial injunctions that are intended to limit surveillance activities on citizens by the police and intelligence services. Section 312 would abrogate all judicial orders and consents passed before September 11, 2001 that prevented these agencies from collecting information on nationals and social and political organizations.

Sections 301-306 would also authorize the creation of a DNA database consisting of persons suspected of terrorism. The latter would consist of those who have aided a group designated as terrorist as well as non-citizens suspected of certain crimes or of having been in contact with a group recognized as terrorist.

*A Generalized State of Exception*

While the proposed law follows in the path of the original Patriot Act concerning the fate of foreigners and of the individual and public liberties of American citizens, it breaks new ground by modifying the very form of the State. The rule of law becomes increasingly formal, not only because its content, the protection of private life and the defense of individual and public liberties turns out to be very limited, but also by the practical possibility offered to the executive power to free itself completely from the last safeguards of legal order. The strengthening of the executive relative to the other powers makes possible the general and permanent suspension of the law. It is thus the instrument for setting up a state of exception, a state in which procedures that are exceptions to the rule become the norm.

The USA Patriot Act is still based on the existence of a double legal system. On the one hand, there is protection of the law for nationals, even if it is increasingly restricted. On the other, there is suspension of the law for foreigners. Thus there coexists a reduced rule of law for American citizens and a method of organizing pure violence against non-citizens.

This double legal order tends to disappear with the new proposed law that allows the executive branch to take away citizenship from American citizens and to transfer them from a system of legal protection to an order devoid of law. The procedure of exception prescribed for foreigners can thus be applied to citizens. Exception to the law becomes the norm and a state of generalized exception replaces the rule of law.

The proposed Patriot II act was not adopted. Only some measures restricting the rights of non-nationals were established. The possibility of taking away the citizenship of an American designated as a terrorist is the heart of this proposed law. The possibility of removing British citizenship was taken up in Great Britain in a proposed law presented by the Attorney General.

This issue is the center of gravity of a change in the political system. Such a reform would mark a point of no return in the dismantling of the rule of law. Its adoption in the United States would facilitate its spread in Europe. Usually, antiterrorist measures have been set up first in the United States before being adopted on the European continent, with Great Britain playing the role of intermediary. The Framework Decision of the European Union relative to terrorism is, moreover, strongly influenced by English law which, this time, also anticipated the provisions included in the Patriot Act.

## THE PATRIOT ACT REAUTHORIZATION

The Patriot Act, established after the attacks of September 11, 2001, is known above all for the provisions that authorize the imprisonment, for an indeterminate period of time and without trial or even indictment, of foreigners simply suspected of terrorism. However, the law also authorizes widespread surveillance of the population. Some of the measures are permanent, while others were adopted for a period of four years. The latter, contained in 16 articles, expired at the end of 2005.[46]

The Patriot Act does not actually contain all the statutes that are the most inimical to the freedoms and privacy of American citizens. Some statutes that are part of other legislation are even more restrictive. Challenges are focused on this law because of its symbolic character, referring to September 11, and because of the systematic character of the measures undertaken. The intent of the government when it introduced the Patriot Act was to point to a rupture that had occurred, to establish a boundary between a before and an after September 11, 2001. The crossing of this boundary on September 11 thus, in effect, compels the population to consent to the relinquishment of its individual liberties.

While the original Patriot Act was adopted very rapidly, this was not the case for the reauthorization. It was only on March 9, 2006 that President George Bush signed "The Patriot Act Improvement and Reauthorization Act."[47] It was in the Senate that resistance was organized. Some senators even carried out a filibuster, a parliamentary procedure in which long speeches, the introduction of irrelevant issues and the like, are used to obstruct the passage of a bill. However, while this process made possible, for the first time, a Congressional

---

46 "USA Patriot Act Sunset," Electronic Privacy Information Center, http://www.epic.org/privacy/terrorism/usapatriot/sunset.html.

47 H.R. 3199, final version, http://thomas.loc.gov/cgi-bin/query/D?c109:6:./temp/~c109wRyCSR. The PDF file: http://frwebgate.access.gpo.gov/cgi-bin/getdoc.cgi?dbname=109_cong_bills&docid=f:h3199enr.txt.pdf.

discussion on the content and issues of the law, in the end, the government's bill was adopted. After ten months of debate, the government successfully avoided the imposition of restrictive judicial controls in connection with the permanent measures. It also was successful at having 14 of the temporary measures, adopted in 2001 as emergency procedures, made into permanent clauses.

The whole process, from the Patriot Act to its reauthorization, can be summarized as follows: with the Patriot Act, the exception becomes the rule; with its renewal, the temporary becomes permanent.

*The Extension of Permanent Measures*

The opponents of the Patriot Act wanted to take advantage of the extension procedure in order to set up control measures that would guarantee individual liberties, while the government wanted to increase the prerogatives of the FBI. The Administration did not succeed in realizing this objective, but it hung on to the most important thing: the modifications to the original legislation do little to enhance judicial authority.

Article 213 was extended. It permanently establishes very intrusive investigative techniques called "sneak and peek." The FBI is authorized to enter a home or office in the absence of the occupant. During this secret investigation, the federal agents are authorized to take photos, examine the hard disk of a computer and put a digital espionage device, called "magic lantern," into the hard drive. Once installed, this device records all computer activity, without transmitting it over the Net.

This possibility already exists in standard criminal procedure, but it is subjected to the authorization of a court and the agents must immediately tell the person concerned about the action. Under the original Patriot Act, the notification was delayed for three months or more if a court authorizes it. Moreover, the government had the possibility of indefinitely postponing it for reasons of "national security." The agreement made during the reauthorization discussions was to establish this delay absolutely at thirty days.[48] It is important

---

48   Sen.John E. Senunu, "Patriot Act deal balances liberty, security, *Washington Memo*, February, 12, 2006.

to note that this intrusive measure has almost never been used in terrorism cases. Up to January 31, 2005, it was used 153 times, only 18 of which concerned cases of terrorism.[49]

Another permanent procedure extended is that established by clause 505, which expands the possibilities granted to the FBI and administrative authorities to obtain "National Security Letters." This is a form of administrative subpoena giving access to personal, medical and financial data, information from travel agencies, car rental agencies and casinos, as well as library files.

Prior to the Patriot Act, National Security Letters were used during investigations concerning spies, presumed terrorists, or persons "in contact with a foreign power." An authorization from a judge was necessary. The Patriot Act eliminated this condition. Henceforth, the FBI simply has to declare that a NSL is "pertinent" within the context, for example, of an investigation concerning terrorism.[50]

Section 505 extends the ability of the FBI to obtain such an authorization outside the context of a counterespionage investigation. The applicability of this procedure is thus greatly expanded for any supposed criminal activity. During the Congressional debates, it was revealed that the government has used 30,000 national security letters per year since the September 11 attacks.[51]

The Patriot Act Reauthorization formally restricts the applicability of National Security Letters in relation to libraries. This administrative summons can no longer be granted to obtain data from libraries that do not offer Internet access as a part of their patron services. Those libraries that "are providers of Internet services" remain objects of possible National Security Letters.[52] In effect, then, this changes nothing in relation to the original version of the Patriot Act, since almost all American libraries offer Internet access.

---

49  DOJ, Letter to Rep. Bobby Scott, July 5, 2005, in USA Patriot and Terrorism Prevention Reauthorization Act of 2005, Report of the Committee of the Judiciary, House of Representatives, July 18, p. 463, http://judiciary.house.gov/media/pdfs/109-174p1.pdf.

50  "National Security Letters" and your Privacy, ACLU, http://action.aclu.org/reformthepatriotact/nsl.html.

51  "Senators Question Terrorism Inquiries," Associated Press, *Washington Post*, November, 7 2005, p. A 10, http://www.washingtonpost.com/wp-dyn/content/article/2005/11/06/AR2005110601038.html.

52  Charles Babington, "Patriot Act Compromise Clears Way for Senate Vote," *Washington Post*, 10/2/2006.

By imposing silence on the recipients of a NSL and making recourse to legal counsel difficult, these administrative subpoenas impede efforts to organize an effective defense for the suspect. Several courts have ruled against these impediments and the pressure exerted by the administration. Thus, in a decision dated September 28, 2004, Judge Victor Marrero of the southern district of New York decided in favor of an Internet access provider subjected to such an administrative subpoena. The decision prohibits the issuance of National Security Letters that demand personal information on subscribers from Internet access providers, such as personal address, past telephone calls, content of email messages, and web sites visited. The judge emphasized the unconstitutionality of the measure, notably the violation of the first amendment (freedom of speech) and the fourth amendment (the right not to be subjected to arrests, searches or seizures without a warrant). Marrero ruled against a clause that results in a situation in which "all but the most mettlesome and undaunted NSL recipients would consider themselves effectively barred from consulting an attorney or anyone else who might advise them otherwise."[53]

*Strengthening Police Prerogatives*

All of the measures contained in the first version of the Patriot Act result in a strengthening of the power of various police forces to the detriment of citizen rights and judicial authority. Article 209, another permanent measure that was renewed as such, widens the power of the police legally to seize vocal messages. Prior to the Patriot Act, capturing such messages on an answering machine installed in a private residence required a judicial warrant. Seizing vocal messages sent via a service provider required a court order. Such authorizations offer more protection than an ordinary search warrant, which is granted upon notification that there is "reasonable presumption" to believe that a crime is going to be committed.

---

53  Declan McCullagh, "Judge disarms Patriot Act proviso," *CnetNews.com*, September 29, 2004, http://news.com.com/Judge+disarms+Patriot+Act+proviso/2100-1028_3-5388764.html.

Article 209 amends the law to the effect that vocal messages are treated as ordinary electronic messages. Thus the possibility of seizing them is considerably expanded. Any prosecutor has the possibility, at any moment, of granting such authorization. If the seizure is carried out on sent messages, and not on an answering machine placed in a residence, it can be done without notifying the person concerned.

Article 220, already permanent in the first version of the Patriot Act, authorizes an ordinary court to issue a search warrant for collecting electronic evidence. This warrant has a federal scope, since it is valid on all of American territory. Article 220 solely concerns criminal investigations such as, for example, the prosecution of a "hacker." This article considerably strengthens the prerogatives of the police in relation to judicial authority. It allows police officers to obtain a warrant from a judge who has nothing to do with the case in question. For example, an investigation in New Jersey can be undertaken with a warrant obtained in Florida. In fact, it allows the police to choose the judge and thus obtain a warrant that corresponds to their needs. This measure makes it impossible for judicial authorities to have any control over police work. The balance of power between the judiciary and the police is permanently shifted to the advantage of the latter.

While the attempts of the government to increase the prerogatives of the FBI through the reauthorization of the Patriot Act failed overall, it did succeed in imposing, amidst an almost general indifference, the establishment of a new police force whose function is quite openly to take away public freedoms, such as the freedom to assemble or demonstrate. Section 605 of the Patriot Act Reauthorization creates a new federal police force, which has the power to "make arrests without warrant for any offense against the United States committed in their presence, or for any felony cognizable under the laws of the United States if they have reasonable grounds to believe that the person to be arrested has committed or is committing such felony."[54]

This new police force, which is directly under the authority of the Secretary of Homeland Security, is assigned a variety of jurisdictions,

54  House Report 109-333 USA Patriot Improvement and Reauthorization Act of 2005, Sec. 605.

including "a special event of national significance." These terms are not defined. They do not imply the presence of a "protected person," such as a president. It is thus the administration, more specifically the police, which designates the event as having a "national significance." Consequently, the police can proceed with arrests at its pleasure.

The terms used, such as "offense against the United States" or "reasonable grounds to believe" are particularly vague. Their meaning effectively depends on the interpretation given to them by the police itself.[55] The arbitrary actions of the administration's agents are justified by the meaning that they themselves give to the events that precipitate their intervention.

FROM THE STATE OF EMERGENCY TO THE PERMANENT
STATE OF EXCEPTION

The renewal of the Patriot Act made possible the re-establishment, for an indefinite period of time, of a whole set of surveillance measures which had initially been justified by the state of emergency that developed after the September 11 attacks. This development illustrates the change that has occurred in the legitimation process for government decisions. The executive power lays claim to a permanent concentration of power in its hands. Hence, the abandonment of any protection for liberties has to become a permanent feature because it would allow all parts of the government to fight against terrorism. Symbolically, in terms of the organization of political hegemony, we leave the state of emergency and enter the permanent state of exception.

Article 212, which became permanent, authorizes telephone companies and Internet access providers to disclose to the government the content and record of communications if these companies believe that such communications contain information that presents a danger of death or serious physical injury to any person. There is no à posteriori judicial monitoring, such as examination by a court, of the results of the operator's transmittal of the information. There is no notification to the person concerned of the transmittal of such information. This information could be used in investigations of

---

55 Paul Graig Roberts, "Unfathomed Dangers in Patriot Act Reauthorization," http://antiwar.com/roberts/?articlied=8434.

criminal matters and not only in terrorist cases. There are no longer any sanctions provided for criminal or negligent behavior on the part of a police officer in applying the law, such as, for example, gaining access to the content of communications without first having obtained a warrant.

While Article 212, originally a temporary clause set to expire at the end of 2005, was the object of Congressional debate during the reauthorization process, that debate was purely formal. Section 225 of the Homeland Security Act (HSA) of 2002 already makes permanent the same measure, i.e., authorizing the disclosure, by Internet access providers or telephone companies, of the content of transmitted messages. It is also worth pointing out that the exceptional measures contained in the HSA are even more intrusive than the ones contained in Article 212 of the Patriot Act. Purely administrative "control" is substituted for the judicial control normally exercised over measures undertaken in connection with a criminal case. The HSA only requires that each administrative entity that has received such disclosed information must inform the Attorney General within 90 days. The latter must, in turn, report the information to Congress. To date, that has never been the case.[56]

Section 214 of the Patriot Act, which also became permanent, makes it easier for the FBI to obtain pen register and trap and trace data from electronic and telephone connections within the context of the "Foreign Intelligence Surveillance Act" of 1978. The seizure of such data does not require a judicial warrant. Prior to the Patriot Act, the government had to prove that the monitored person was an agent of a foreign power. Now, it simply has to indicate that the information seized is in "connection" with an investigation concerning terrorism. The vague character of this qualification makes it possible to justify any kind of investigation.

Thus, Article 214 modifies the measures that permit connection data to be obtained. This article makes it easier for the FBI to obtain telephone and Internet data under FISA "for any investigation to

---

56 USA Patriot and Terrorism Prevention Reauthorization Act of 2005, Report of the Committee of the judiciary House of Representatives, July 18, p.457, http://judiciary.house.gov/media/pdfs/109-174p1.pdf.

gather foreign intelligence information"[57] without demonstrating that the operation is against a foreign agent or a person engaged in international terrorism. The elimination of any reference to the idea of a foreign power modifies the very nature of the procedure, since it now permits it to be applied to American citizens.

Article 204, a temporary clause also reinstated for an indefinite period of time, establishes that surveillance conducted for the purpose of collecting counter-espionage intelligence is exempt from the restrictions set up to control the seizure of telephone or electronic connection data. This section exempts the government from legal restrictions concerning the capture of wire and oral communications. The government can thus intercept electronic vocal communications by means of an ordinary search warrant, much less restrictive than an interception warrant. Section 202, which authorizes the interception of oral, electronic, or telephone communications relative to computer piracy, was also reinstated for an indeterminate time period.

Article 218, which expired at the end of 2005 and became permanent, authorizes secret searches of a residence or office, without notification, if there is "reasonable presumption" to believe that the residence or office contains information relative to the activity of an agent of a foreign power. The existence of any proof or indication of a crime is not required. Agents obtain a warrant from a secret court, established by the FISA. Prior to the Patriot Act, federal agents had to certify that the primary objective of the search concerned obtaining intelligence in connection with the suspect foreigner. Article 218 lowers this standard in a significant way, since now the agents no longer have to state that the seizure of information in connection with the suspect foreigner is a "significant objective" of the search.[58] Hence this law permits secret searches of anyone's home, foreigner or American citizen, on the mere suspicion that this individual is more or less linked to terrorism.

---

57  "USA Patriot Act Sunset," Electronic Privacy Information Center, http://www.epic.org/privacy/terrorism/usapatriot:sunset;html.

58  "Memo to interested Persons Outlining What Congress Should Do About the Patriot Act Sunsets," ACLU, March, 28, 2005, http://www.aclu.org/SafeandFree.cfm?ID=17846&c=206.

Article 207 extends the time from 30 days to 6 months during which connection data relating to intelligence about the foreigner under investigation can be used without court authorization. There is a possibility of extending it up to one year before having to obtain a court authorization. This measure also became permanent, as did Article 216, which allows a federal judge or a judge from another jurisdiction to issue a warrant to record incoming and outgoing data from an electronic connection without having to specify the IP number concerned. The warrant can be issued anywhere on American territory.

Article 216 also modifies the criteria for accessing the numbers of incoming and outgoing telephone calls. The agent simply has to certify that the sought after information is "pertinent for the investigation of a crime in execution." The level of proof required is less stringent than that contained in probable cause, in which "a crime was committed or is on the point of being committed."

Article 216 does not permit the capture of the content of intercepted messages. While the content of telephone messages is separate from incoming and outgoing connection data, this is not the case for electronic messages. This information is communicated by "packets." It is the FBI, or another administrative agency undertaking the interception, which, in principle, is responsible for separating the communication data from the content. In other words, the agents are expected to read the former and ignore the latter. This is a veritable blank check given to federal agents. In order to obtain authorization, the agent simply has to certify that the sought after information is "pertinent for the investigation of a crime in execution." The judge must issue the authorization at the moment the agent's certification is received, even if he or she is not in agreement with the procedure involved.

*Renewal of the Most Contested Temporary Measures*

Attacks against the Patriot Act, from the Senate or civil liberties organizations, were concentrated around two articles, clauses 215 and 206, which contain particularly outrageous measures. The existence of this challenge made it almost impossible for these clauses to be made permanent. This did not prevent the House, before the opposition was organized in the Senate, from extending these statutes for ten years by a vote on June 21, 2005.

In the end, Article 215 was extended for a new period of four years. It allows the FBI, after obtaining a secret authorization from a court, to have access to medical data, bank account information, library borrowing data or "any tangible thing" without any necessity on the part of the investigators to demonstrate that this investigation concerns facts related to terrorism or a foreign power. While the FBI has to specify that the order is being requested for an inquiry concerning counterespionage or terrorism, it does not have to establish that there exists a "probable cause" link between the requested records and a foreign power.

The persons concerned cannot speak to anyone concerning this seizure of information. Article 215 stipulates that "no one should reveal to another person that the FBI sought to obtain or has obtained 'tangible things" under this section." The agreement reached in the Congressional debate allows such persons to challenge this procedure after one year. There is thus introduced a formal process to contest an order which gives to the person subjected to it the right to refer the case to a FISA judge[59] for the purpose of modifying or annulling the non-disclosure requirement.[60] It also removes the requirement that the person subjected to such an order must provide to the FBI or other relevant government authority the name of the attorney consulted for legal advice.

However, the government has the possibility to override this challenge procedure for national security reasons. Thus the new law makes it almost impossible to modify these "gag orders." For Congressman John Conyers "this is far worse than current law under

---

59 The Foreign Intelligence Surveillance Act of 1978 establishes a special court responsible for authorizing surveillance of "agents of a foreign power." This is a secret court composed of eleven judges appointed by the Chief Justice of the U.S. Supreme Court, Electronic Privacy Information Center, http://www.epic.org/privacy/terrorism/fisa/.

60 USA Patriot Act Additional Amendements Acts of 2006 (s.2271), February 17, 2006.

which the federal courts have rejected numerous certifications which failed to provide sufficient facts to justify the 'gag order'."[61]

The Department of Justice has consistently stated that Article 215 of the Patriot Act has never been used to obtain library records. The Attorney General has affirmed that "the reading habits of ordinary Americans are not of interest to those investigating terrorists or spies."[62] However, since 2001, federal agents or local police have visited libraries in order to obtain records, 178 of which were received by FBI agents. The real number of these demands can only be much higher, since the Patriot Act makes illegal any disclosure on the part of the institutions concerned.

As for Article 206, it authorizes the use of "nomad" connections, which move from one monitored device to another. FBI agents do not need to identify the suspect in order to obtain the authorization to install their communications surveillance devices. An "undercover" connection is installed on all the telephones in the neighborhood of the targeted individual or on the telephones of his or her relatives. It is not necessary to demonstrate that the individual under surveillance even uses these telephones. That explains why such a measure is called a "John Doe" connection. Since the person in question does not have to be named before being subjected to surveillance, the government can legally monitor the telephone of any individual, without having to show that that individual is connected, in some manner or other, with a foreign power, with terrorism or any criminal activity.

Prior to the Patriot Act, "nomad" connections were used solely in criminal investigations, including terrorism cases, but were not allowed in intelligence investigations. A criminal inquiry includes a series of measures to safeguard the protection of privacy. Such a connection must specify the identity of the person under surveillance or the telephone proposed for surveillance. To move from one device to another, the government must make sure that the object of the sur-

---

61  "Conyers calls Patriot Act reauthorization 'dangerous'," February, 28, 2006, http://www.rawstory.com/news/2006/Conyers_calls_Patriot_Act_reauthorization_dangerous_0228.html.

62  Testimony of Alberto Gonzales, Attorney General, before Senate Select Committee on Intelligence, April, 27, 2005.

veillance identified by the warrant currently uses that device. With the Patriot Act, "nomad" connections are authorized for intelligence gathering as investigations under FISA without including these measures of protection.

The change initiated by the Patriot Act was then integrated into other laws. The Intelligence Act for FY 2002, a law organizing intelligence investigations, authorizes nomad connections that mention neither the name of the person under surveillance nor the apparatus involved. Since the connections become "John Doe" interceptions, they can follow any unknown person from telephone to telephone on the basis of a vague physical description. Thus the door is open to an extended surveillance of anyone who more or less corresponds to such a description or who uses the telephone. Intelligence obtained in this manner could be used in a criminal case.

The reauthorization of Section 102 of the Patriot Act extended Section 6001 of the Intelligence Reform and Terrorism Prevention Act of 2004 for four years. This authorizes surveillance of isolated persons suspected of being terrorists. These individuals are called "lone wolves." They are part of international terrorism but act alone. This article redefines the concept of "agent of a foreign power" by including persons engaged in "international terrorism" or in "preparing for terrorist actions." Thus to be considered an agent of a foreign power, it is no longer necessary to be in contact with such a power. This measure applies to individuals who are not American citizens. The consequence of this reform of the FISA is that any foreigner can be placed under surveillance as a result of procedures that are designed for spying on agents of a foreign power. In effect, this means that the law considers any person who is not an American citizen to be potentially in the service of a foreign power.

This article of the Intelligence Reform and Terrorism Prevention Act establishes measures that are reminiscent of the proposed Patriot II legislation. The latter aims at generalizing the possibility of spying on anyone, regardless of nationality, as a potential agent of a foreign power. If the Patriot II legislation were passed, Section 6001 would be applicable to the whole American population.

*Conflation of Intelligence Work and Criminal Investigation*

Connections for the purpose of intercepting communications in relation to criminal cases, called connections under Title III because they were first authorized by Title III of the Omnibus Crime Control and Safe Streets Act, require a judicial warrant based on a "reasonable presumption" that the communications intercepted might reveal an activity constituting a federal crime. A connection in relation to a criminal investigation must specify the identity of the person under surveillance or the telephone number put under surveillance. In order for the connection to pass from one apparatus to another, the government must be sure that the object of the surveillance identified by the warrant actually uses this apparatus.

The Patriot Act eliminates the difference between criminal inquiry and intelligence work by permitting the FBI to conduct investigations under Title III and obtain the necessary authorizations under the procedures and with the reduced guarantees of the FISA, the 1978 law regulating counterespionage investigations. In fact, the Patriot Act, through such measures that ensure control over the population, erases the boundaries between police functions and intelligence work in a double sense. On the one hand, it expands to criminal cases the applicability of the criteria authorizing surveillance and the seizure of information that were established in relation to counterespionage by the Foreign Intelligence Surveillance Act of 1978. This law gives exceptional prerogatives to the administration by removing acts undertaken by the latter within the context of FISA from any true judicial control, other than the preliminary authorization from exceptional, often secret, courts without any further monitoring. On the other hand, it allows the intelligence services to use particularly intrusive measures, formerly reserved to criminal investigations, such as the use of the "magic lantern" device. Formerly, the use of such techniques was accompanied by guarantees for the protection of freedoms.

Finally, evidence obtained by investigations under the mandate of FISA, whose authorization is easier to obtain and which is governed by lower standards for the protection of freedoms, can be sent to criminal courts, normally guided by a higher level of protection for privacy. Thus the Patriot Act also creates permanent authorizations for a widespread exchange of information between intelligence agencies and the police by allowing them to bypass the administrative barriers impeding such cooperation. Article 905, renewed for an indefinite period, authorizes the Attorney General to get from the Director of National Intelligence evidence obtained by intelligence work for use in a judicial proceeding.

Section 203b, which became permanent, authorizes various governmental agencies in national security, immigration and counterespionage to share information obtained in the fight against terrorism. Article 504, also permanent, authorizes the transfer of FISA intelligence to the criminal division of the Department of Justice.[63] The Department admitted having sent around 4500 FISA dossiers to the criminal division. The number of prosecutions underway is unknown.[64]

The absence of boundaries between criminal inquiries and counterespionage investigations is an important element in the subordination of judicial power to the executive. The concentration of power in the hands of the President and the government was a demand laid down by the executive branch after the September 11 attacks. The renewal of the Patriot Act makes it possible to make measures permanent that were initially justified by an emergency situation during their first adoption in 2001. As a result of their permanent status, these freedom-killing surveillance measures become the basis of a new political order that gives to the administration prerogatives belonging to the judiciary. However, contrary to the first version of the Patriot Act Reauthorization passed by the House in June 2005, the juridical form adopted in the final version remains that of a permanent state of exception and not directly that of a dictatorship. In effect, the resistance of the Senate made it possible to maintain and introduce some formal possibilities for judicial control and recourse, without, of course, actually weakening the prerogatives of the FBI and the government. It should be recalled, however, that the House

---

63  Kate Martin, "Why Section 203 and 905 Should be Modified," American Bar Association's Patriot Debates, http://www.patriotdebates.com/203-2#opening.

64  Oversight answers, submitted by Jamie E. Brown, Acting Assistant Attorney General, May 13, 2003, on file with the House Judiciary Committee.

of Representatives, which had passed the first version of the Patriot Act Reauthorization in June 2005 by a large majority, had shown no doubts about the judicial prerogatives granted to the administration almost permanently.

It was the war in Afghanistan that provided the opportunity for prisoners to be arrested and held at Guantanamo. Around 500 people from forty-odd countries are still detained at the American military base; only 9 have been charged. According to the Executive Order, these prisoners will be tried by a military court specially set up for foreign nationals accused of terrorism.

The Pentagon has always been against Guantanamo detainees challenging their confinement. It has denied them POW status, and hence the possibility of exercising rights guaranteed by the Geneva Convention. The administration has been careful not to resort to U.S. criminal law, which would have placed the prisoners under the protection of the Constitution. Instead, detainees are being held without trial and generally without being charged. They have no legal status, being neither POWs, common law detainees, or political prisoners. They form an anomaly.

## Violence, a Cornerstone of Imperial Order

The government justified its policy by claiming that Guantanamo Naval Base lies outside sovereign U.S. soil. The United States obtained what it claims to be an indefinite "lease" of the base by force in 1902, as one of the conditions for ending its occupation of Cuba. This 1902 treaty is by current governing norms of international law invalid, as contrary to jus cogens, self-determination, and the doctrine of "unequal treaties." The administration chose the base to escape the legal clutches of the U.S. courts, and so hold detainees indefinitely, entirely at the mercy of the U.S. government. The Executive has granted itself extraordinary powers that go against the Constitution of the United States, and against international law.

These claims of special dispensations are repeated far and wide by the U.S. authorities in an attempt to have their self-arrogated right to violate the common rule of law accepted by international opinion. The privilege that the U.S. is arrogating to itself has been broadly defended by the European Union. Cuba, as a result, was forced to ditch a vote on its April 2004 resolution to the UN Commission on Human Rights demanding that the United States "clarify the living conditions and legal status" of detainees. After a non-action motion (one that allows a resolution to be indefinitely put aside) was prepared by the United States and their allies, including the European Union, and several Latin American countries, the Cubans were obliged to withdraw the resolution.[65]

The "war against terrorism" is characterized by the refusal of governmental authorities to acknowledge the opposing forces as combatants. The thesis that the Geneva Conventions cannot be applied to prisoners captured in Afghanistan is based on the fact that these prisoners are not soldiers in a regular army, that they did not wear uniforms and they had an unknown command structure. The administration thus calls them "irregular combatants." Note, however, that American special forces soldiers operating in Afghanistan wore neither uniforms nor recognizable insignia.

The antiterrorist struggle would not then be a campaign in a war, but a police action. It does not combat soldiers of a constituted State, but undertakes to bring to heel insurgents against a recognized order. By taking the entire population hostage and by denying combatant status to individuals carrying out armed resistance, this military operation effaces all distinctions between soldier and civilian. In fact, it makes the latter disappear altogether by enlarging the concept of combatant to include an insurgent's family, neighbors or entire populations, as in Palestine or Chechnia. Thus, "there exists an absolute symmetry between the status of combatant and civilian: if one disappears, then so does the other. The non-recognition of the status of

---

65  'Guantanamo: la Commission des droits de l'homme ne condamne pas les Etats-Unis', *Le Monde*, 22/4/2004.

the adversary leads to his demonization and his treatment outside of all legal status.[66]

The non-distinction between combatants and civilians is equally part of the organization of the American military. Numerous operations are carried out by companies whose personnel, of different nationalities, are under private contract. These combatants also stand outside of any legal order. "The question of what responsibility a private company has for acts committed by its contract employees against third nationals while on a mission with the American army in a foreign country is an insoluble legal headache."[67]

The concept of "irregular combatant" and the privatization of military engagement indicate that the possibility offered by the fight against terrorism to isolate itself from any legal order indeed rests on calling into question the separation between public and private, questioning the very foundation of the rule of law.

The resolve expressed by the United States to seize people in other countries and detain them at its pleasure, coupled with the other countries' recognition of America's self-appointed right, heralds a new international political order. Out-and-out violence —acts of war or policing without regard for legality— is the cornerstone of this brave new imperial order.

## A New Political World Order

The Washington Post disclosed on January 2, 2005[68] that, at the request of the Pentagon and the CIA, the White House is in the process of establishing permanent rules concerning the treatment of prisoners suspected of terrorism and against which there is insufficient evidence to bring them before a court. That would include the prisoners incarcerated at Guantanamo, those detained in military centers or under surveillance by the CIA, but also all persons likely to be apprehended in the course of future antiterrorist operations.

---

66  Françoise Bouchet-Saulnier, "Combattants illégaux, un faux débat," *Le Monde*, 30/6/2004.

67  *Ibid.*

68  Dana Priest, "Long-Term Plan Sought for Terror Suspects," *Washington Post*, January 2, 2005, p. A01.

Since the United States Supreme Court granted the Guantanamo prisoners the right to bring their cases before American courts, the administration has to set up other procedures permitting the indefinite detention of arrested persons. They would be transferred to camps established in foreign countries, in Afghanistan, Jordan, Egypt or Iraq. Local authorities and Americans would jointly manage these camps, built by the American army. The prisoners are thus directly put into an international system of exception to the law, coordinated by the administration of the United States.

This system does not contradict the decision of the Supreme Court since the latter does not oppose the concept of incriminating illegal combatants invented by the Executive. The decision specifies only that persons detained under this term have the right to contest the facts leading to their incarceration before a civilian jurisdiction when, as at Guatanamo, they are detained on territory under the "full jurisdiction" of the United States. By transferring prisoners to places that are partially outside American sovereignty, the administration can bypass the judgment of the Court.

The Administration is thus creating a status of exception permitting the indefinite detention of these prisoners without an indictment and without the right of the prisoners to have recourse to American or international law. "In view of the fact that we are engaged in a long-term effort, engaging in a global war against terror, it is normal to look for long-term solutions,"[69] stated Bryan Whitman, spokesperson for the Pentagon.

Thus, the Administration wants to set up lasting solutions and, in order to accomplish that, formalize relations between the United States and affected countries that were established in the emergency. Detention centers set up by the CIA already exist in the countries mentioned above. The method employed is to transfer captives to a third country in order to keep them in detention indefinitely without any public procedures of supervision.

The transfers, called "rendering," depend on agreements between the United States and these other countries. The security services of the latter, well known for their systematic violation of human

---

69  *Ibid.*

rights, are supposed to create a climate of terror among the detainees, thereby facilitating the interrogations. Little is known about the prisoners detained by the CIA and the procedures determining the duration and conditions of incarceration. The Administration argues that "the details concerning the system must necessarily remain secret."

The actual objective, however, is to legitimize these practices by including them in a legal concept created by the executive power. It is part of a larger strategy aimed at establishing, at the international level, a legal system of exceptions to the law. The new Attorney General, Alberto R. Gonzales, indeed stated at his nomination that "the protections of the Geneva Convention would not be applied to presumed terrorists."[70] He also suggested that the United States would have to renegotiate international treaties in order to fight more effectively against terrorism.

In this context where the administration can create and interpret the law, legal decisions are the result of a sheer show of strength.

This creates an unstable and kaleidoscopic legal regime. The President reserves the right to appoint the judges who try any foreign nationals accused of terrorist activities in the special military commissions. If arrested on American soil and suspected of being part of a terrorist organization designated as such by the Attorney General, these people can be held indefinitely under the 2001 Executive Act. However, the Supreme Court ruling grants prisoners captured abroad the right to show before a civil court of law that the enemy or illegal combatant charges brought by the Executive do not factually apply to them.

We are in a period of transition, with the Executive trying to restructure the legal regime around extraordinary powers granted by Congress, or by itself. This is a process that leads to the establishment of a new kind of political regime.

---

70  Dan Eggen and R. Jeffry Smith, "Gonzales Defends His White House Record," *Washington Post*, January 7, 2005, p. A01.

After a wait of two and a half years, the United States Supreme Court finally pronounced on the appeals of 16 Guantanamo prisoners on June 28, 2004. As guarantor of the Constitution, the Supreme Court ruled on two important matters. In the first ruling in Rasul v. Bush, the petitioners were UK and Australian citizens apprehended on foreign soil in the "War Against Terrorism." They were imprisoned at Guantanamo without charges being brought, or evidence provided, and with no way of pleading their innocence. The U.S. government claimed it can detain the petitioners indefinitely under these conditions, and that no court has jurisdiction to examine the reasons for their detention.

The question presented was "Whether United States courts lack jurisdiction to consider challenges to the legality of the detention of foreign nationals captured abroad in connection with hostilities and incarcerated at the Guantanamo Naval Base, Cuba."[71]

The Supreme Court replied that U.S. courts have traditionally been open to nonresidents, and may test the legality of holding foreign detainees captured abroad during the hostilities, and imprisoned at Guantanamo.[72] "The District Court has jurisdiction to hear petitioners' habeas challenges under 28 U.S.C. §2241, which authorizes district courts, 'within their respective jurisdictions' to entertain habeas applications by persons claiming to be held in violation with the … laws … of the United States. Such jurisdiction extends to aliens held in a territory over which the United States exercises plenary and exclusive jurisdiction, but not 'ultimate sovereignty.'"[73]

The Supreme Court states that "irregular combatants" (a term used by the US administration for non-US nationals captured in Afghanistan) may challenge their confinement in a civil court by claiming that such charges do not apply to them.

The Court clearly states that detainees may contest the legality of their detention by petition, arguing that they are being held indefi-

---

71 CA DC, 321 F.3d 1134, 03-334 RASUL v. BUSH, www.supremecourtus.gov.

72 www.supremecourtus.gov/opinions/03pdf/03-334.pdf, Syllabus.

73 www.supremecourtus.gov/opinions/03pdf/03-334.pdf, Opinion, pp.4-17.

nitely by the Executive, without trial. In other words, it would appear that the Supreme Court has not called into question the U.S, claim to punish at its total discretion those charged with the supposed offense of being "illegal combatants" – that is, of daring to oppose U.S. forces anywhere in the world. A trial merely gives the petitioner a chance to challenge the charge that he was "engaged [neither] in combat [n]or in acts of terrorism against the United States."

The second ruling on Hamdi v. Rumsfeld affects U.S. nationals detained as "enemy combatants." Before the Supreme Court judgment, the government line had been backed by the Court of Appeals for the 4th Circuit, which ruled that the petitioner's detention was legal. The court "was in entire agreement about the fact that he did not have the chance to contest his designation as an enemy combatant."[74] The judgment allowed the government to claim recent jurisprudence ratifying indefinite custody for American citizens.

The following questions were presented to the Supreme Court:

"Does the Constitution permit Executive officials to detain an American citizen indefinitely in military custody in the United States, hold essentially incommunicado and deny him access to counsel, with no opportunity to question the factual basis for his detention before any impartial tribunal, on the sole ground that he was seized abroad in a theater of the War on Terrorism and declared by the Executive to be an "enemy combatant"? [...]

In a habeas corpus proceeding challenging the indefinite detention of an American citizen seized abroad, detained in the United States, and declared by Executive officials an 'enemy combatant', does the separation of powers doctrine preclude a federal court from following ordinary statutory procedures and conducting an inquiry into the factual basis for the Executive branch's asserted justification of the detention?" [75]

The second ruling recognizes the Executive's power to incarcerate an American citizen accused of terrorism without trial, and even without charges. However, unlike the Court of Appeals, the Supreme Court does not sanction the unlimited detention of prison-

---

74   www.supremecourtus.gov/opinions/03pdf/03-6696.pdf, Opinion of the Court, p. 1.

75   CA 4, 316 F.3d 450, 03-6696 HAMDI v. RUMSFELD, www.supremecourtus.gov.

ers. It reaffirms "the fundamental nature of a citizen's right to be free from involuntary confinement by his own government without due process of law." The Court concluded that "although Congress authorized the detention of combatants in the narrow circumstances alleged here, due process demands that a citizen held in the United States as an enemy combatant be given a meaningful opportunity to contest the factual basis for that detention before a neutral decision-maker."[76]

Judge Souter was in partial disagreement with the judgment since, according to him, the detention is illegal. He aligns himself with the majority decision by concluding that it gives the petitioner a wonderful opportunity to prove he is not an enemy combatant. Again, the concept of legality advanced in the judgment is not about the charge itself, but only about its applications, the unlimited nature of the detention, and the right to challenge its factual basis before a neutral tribunal.

### Legitimation of Illegal Incriminations

The decision by the highest legal authority in the land was hailed as a victory by human rights organizations. For Steven Shapiro, director of the ACLU (American Civil Liberties Union), the rulings called back into question "the administration's argument that its actions in the war on terrorism are beyond the rule of law and unreviewable by American courts."[77] The view of Human Rights Watch was that "the Supreme Court's decisions will force the Bush administration to comply with the law rather than the whims of the Executive."

But things are not unilateral. The Supreme Court's finding does not reject the Executive's claim of power to seize and incarcerate anyone it calls a "terrorist." Rather the decision rejects the claim to detain such persons indefinitely without judicial review of the basis for the detention. If the Supreme Court's decision clearly underlines that the Executive may not act outside the rule of law, the Executive itself is a long way from complying with the concept of a legal State.

---

76  HAMDI v. RUMSFELD, pp. 14-15.

77  'Satisfaction chez les défenseurs des droits de l'homme' *Le Monde*, 30/6/2004.

Though the pseudo-legal terms "enemy combatants" (used for U.S. nationals captured in the War against Terrorism), or "illegal combatants" (used by the administration to justify the indefinite detention of those captured) are unknown in military or criminal law —be it American or international— the rulings do not oppose such ideas. By granting anyone so charged the right to challenge the factual basis of their detention, the Supreme Court rulings are effectively endorsing an exceptional right conjured up by the Executive out of the blue. The Court's rulings clear the way for the Executive's operations. Instead of opposing the anomaly they make it law.

The Supreme Court merely gives the prisoners the right to appeal to a federal judge, and does not guarantee them formal access to a lawyer, thus endorsing exceptional procedures at the detention and the trial stage. At trial it establishes a veritable regime of exceptionality, and reverses the burden of proof, for it is the prisoners challenging their detention who are to present the evidence proving they have been improperly detained — albeit under unlawful charges.

The Supreme Court may have reminded the Executive it cannot by fiat abolish the most minimal notions of judicial review. But it does not oppose the government's self-conferred legal privileges —principally the implementation of an exceptional right in its relations with the rest of the world. It confirms the "legal specificity" of the United States by not opposing the Executive's tendency tacitly to repudiate the Geneva Conventions and override the statutes of the International Criminal Court. It gives new legitimacy to the idea that U.S. political and judicial authorities can grant themselves global extraordinary powers where "terrorism" is concerned.

### A Permanent Show of Strength

The point at which this claim of a novel global police power becomes enshrined in law is not set in stone. The Supreme Court's decisions leave room for interpretation —such as the idea of a "neutral court"—, a fact that the administration will exploit. To counter the rulings, the Pentagon decided on July 7, 2004, to institute an examination procedure that goes beyond any legal civilian or military bounds. The procedure involves military created "Combatant Status Review Tribunals," specially set up to determine whether the prisoners' detention as "enemy combatants" is justified. They comprise three officers to be called "neutral," at least one of whom is a military judge. The prisoner is assisted by an interpreter and an officer to help him put his case together. Yet he is still denied access to a lawyer. To comply with the Supreme Court ruling these special courts must inform the prisoners of their right to challenge their detention before a federal court. The administration can therefore argue before civil courts that the plaintiffs' demands have already been examined.

The current administration is doggedly resisting the Supreme Court's decision, and is determined to set up new exceptional procedures to counter any fallout from the ruling. A good example of this process is the constraints the Pentagon wants to impose on the detainees' lawyers. It authorized three civilian lawyers to meet Guantanamo prisoners for the first time on August 20, 2004. It also tried to force them to accept conditions such as recording their clients' interviews, and their notes being read by the prison administration. Having refused to accept the detainees' option to be represented by civilian lawyers as a right, but rather a privilege resting on its goodwill, the Bush government also refused to tell lawyers the reasons for their clients' imprisonment. It has also refused to commit itself to letting lawyers see their clients again at some stage in the future.[78] The lawyers have simply stopped visiting.

The Pentagon's attempt to impose a discretionary power on legal representation for detainees is unwavering. Since February 2004, the government has allowed one of the petitioners, the U.S. national Yaser Hamdi, to consult a lawyer, but by no means does it concede this as a right.

On August 24, 2004, four prisoners from the Guantanamo camp appeared before a military commission. Instituted by presidential decree (the Executive Order of November 13, 2001) the mission of these ad hoc courts is to try foreign nationals accused of terrorism —or in the Bush administration's terminology, "enemy combatants." Such courts are a departure from the entire body of American criminal

---

78  'Washington a autorisé des avocats civils à se rendre à Guantanamo', *Le Monde*, 31/8/2004.

and military law. They are composed of five military judges appointed by the Executive. The accused have access to an officially appointed military lawyer. They later get access to a civilian lawyer but one whose role is limited. He does not have access to all the facts of the case, and any information classed as a "defense secret" is withheld from him. He also has to leave the hearing whenever such classified evidence is presented. The level of proof is drastically reduced: it is good enough that it "be convincing to a reasonable person."

This mockery of legality is a real test of whether any constraints at all can be imposed upon the government. Nothing is defined in concrete terms. Procedure is made up from one day to the next, and evolves with public reaction.

## Incorporation of Anomie into Doctrine

The Supreme Court judgment reinforces the Executive's initiatives by claiming that "the detention of these persons for the duration of the particular conflict is fundamental, and is accepted as an episode of the war, that it is a consequence of the exercise of the necessary and appropriate force which Congress has authorized to be employed."[79]

The detentions are founded on the congressional act that stipulates "That the President is authorized to use all necessary and appropriate force against those nations, organizations, or persons he determines planned, authorized, committed, or aided the terrorist attacks that occurred on September 11, 2001, or harbored such organizations or persons, in order to prevent any future acts of international terrorism against the United States by such nations, organizations or persons."[80]

According to Supreme Court Judge Scalia, who opposed the majority ruling, Congress's authorization cannot be considered a simple suspension. The suspension clause in the Constitution carefully defines the conditions under which the rule of law may be suspended, as with rioting or invasion. Scalia is the most overt reactionary on the Court, a member of the right-wing Catholic Opus Dei, an or-

---

79   www.supremecourtus.gov/opinions/03pdf/03-6696.pdf, Opinion of the Court.

80   Authorization for Use of Military Force, Pub. L. 107-40, §§1-2, 115 Stat. 224.

ganization that served for most of its shadowy existence as a central prop of the fascist Franco regime in Spain.

For Judge Scalia, "the role of habeas corpus is to determine the legality of the detention pronounced by the Executive, not… to render it legal." He believes that "it is not the role of a habeas corpus court to legalize an illegal detention,"[81] and asserts that "if civil rights have to be reduced, it must be done openly and democratically as required by the Constitution, rather than by silent erosion, by a judgment of this Court." According to Judge Scalia, the true suspension of the rule of law rests not so much on vague Congressional authorization as on this ruling, which gives it a legal application. For Judge Scalia, a fierce opponent of "judicial activism," the most elementary of civil rights are being suspended in the wrong way. A suspension of law should rather take place within the framework laid down by the Constitution, which limits the option to war or insurrection.

Congress's authorization is highly abstract. It does not state precisely what the "appropriate measures" are that the President is to take. Nor does it mention the suspension of habeas corpus in any way, shape or form. Without explicitly stating the conditions, this authorization hands the Executive the power to grant itself extraordinary privileges. The Supreme Court ruling specifically enacts the suspension of the rule of law, and it is the Supreme Court that lays down the conditions of this suspension, and makes it law. For the arch-reactionary Scalia this is sloppy thinking. Far better for Scalia would be a simple state of war and military emergency, under which habeas corpus could be suspended constitutionally without further ado.

These judgments endorse the unlawful 'enemy combatant' and 'illegal combatant' charges by making them a part of criminal procedure, which is again central here. They bring such charges into constitutional territory by tying their applications in with habeas corpus.

They alter the legal regime by legalizing the government's right to arrest someone and hold him indefinitely, unless he can prove before

---

81   Scalia, J., dissenting, p.24.

a neutral court that the facts negate the government's accusations. And so they reverse the burden of proof.

The Executive has a very potent arsenal of legal privileges at its disposal in the War against Terrorism. Their scope changes with the latest show of strength as result of the links between laws and decrees granting the administration exceptional powers on the one hand, and rulings that make such abstractions part of the legal order of things, on the other. This morphing of the legal order is significant. Bringing the illegal charges into criminal procedure legalizes the Executive's self-proclaimed judicial powers, and lays the foundations of a new kind of political regime.

## THE INCORPORATION OF ANOMIE INTO THE LAW

Despite the Supreme Court's decision reversing the burden of proof, the government is still opposed to granting to Guantanamo detainees the right to request American courts to rule on the legality of their detention. From now on, the sole possibility for the government to eliminate the rights granted to the prisoners is to act at the level of the law itself.

### The Detainee Treatment Act

A last-minute amendment to the "Detainee Treatment Act of 2005"[82] proposed by Republican Senator Graham and passed by both Houses gave this opportunity to President Bush. This amendment gave him the legal possibility to prevent persons detained as enemy combatants from filing Habeas Corpus petitions before a civil court. Congress adopted this law, signed by President Bush on December 30, 2005, without any deliberation by Congressional committees. The Guantanamo detainees saw the opportunity to have the legality of their imprisonment examined reduced to nothing. This is the legal implementation of a space of non-law within the law. It allows the US administration to send whomever it likes to Guantanamo and effectively cause them to disappear without trial or the possibility of any recourse. The victims

---

82  Detainee Treatment Act of 2005, December 31, 2005, http://www.justicescholars.org/pegc/ detainee_act_2005.html.

of false imprisonment and torture are no longer authorized to appeal for justice. The Administration justified its freedom-killing measures by arguing that the detainees were dangerous, despite the fact that the military authorities have acknowledged the innocence of a great number of them. Most of them were turned over to American forces in exchange for financial compensation or were simply found in the wrong place at the wrong time.

While this law removes all competence from federal courts to examine the situation of the Guantanamo detainees, at the same time it provides, as a substitute, an exclusive review mechanism for decisions taken by the Combatant Status Review Tribunal. Prisoners designated as "enemy combatants" by this administrative tribunal can request a review of the proceeding only before the United States Court of Appeals for the District of Columbia Circuit. This procedure is permitted under two circumstances: an appeal related to the composition of the review tribunal and an appeal of the initial decision. The request is purely procedural and does not involve an investigation of the facts themselves.

There has been resistance to the new law in court decisions. The District of Columbia Court of Appeals, in a decision on March 22, 2006, reviewed the impact of the Detainee Treatment Act.[83] The Court had to decide whether this law was retroactive in preventing Guantanamo detainees from bringing an action under Habeas Corpus. It ruled that this law did not have the authority to eliminate actions already underway, basing itself on the Supreme Court decision in Rasul v. Bush. The latter states that the Guantanamo prisoners have the right to bring an appeal before a civil court. However, the government has had no difficulty, in other decisions, from asserting its view that the Detainee Treatment Act invalidates the Supreme Court decision.[84]

---

83 Christopher G. Anderson "Appeals court considers whether Detainee Act Gitmo bars habeas claims," Jurist, March 22, 2006, http://jurist.law.pitt.edu/paperchase/2006/03/appeals-court-considers-whether.php.

84 Oral Argument Scheduled for March 22, 2006, http:www.scotusblog.com/movabletype/archives/AlOdahSuppBrief-Final.pdf.

*The Supreme Court Decision in Hamdan v. Rumsfeld*

In a new decision issued on June 29, 2006,[85] the Supreme Court concluded that the Bush administration had exceeded its prerogatives. Judge John Paul Stevens wrote, in the Court's majority decision, that the military commissions do not have the power to issue legal decisions because their structure and procedures violate "the rights of the defense contained in the military code of the United States, the Uniform Code of Military Justice, and the Geneva Convention of 1949."

Judge Stevens thus rejected the claims of the White House that it has the right to create these special tribunals based both on the President's powers as Commander in Chief of the armed forces and the resolution that Congress passed after September 11, 2001. Nothing in that resolution, wrote the judge, "even suggests" that the extension of presidential powers is envisaged. The Court emphasized that it is Congress that has the power to declare war and organize legal proceedings relative to prisoners of war.

The Supreme Court took up the Hamdan versus Rumsfeld case in November 2005. Salim Ali Hamdan had been captured in November 2001 in Afghanistan and transferred to Guantanamo two months later. He was Osama Bin Laden's chauffeur. The Administration's military prosecutors charged him with "conspiracy."

Hamdan was to have appeared before a Military Commission in December 2004. In his Habeas Corpus petition before the Supreme Court, he maintained that these commissions did not have any authority to try him because there is no common law nor law of war that punishes such a crime. He further maintained that the military commissions violate military and international laws, notably because the defense is not able to see and hear the evidence presented against it. In its decision, the Court recognized the validity of the defense's arguments and added that the vague accusation of conspiracy cannot be maintained because only a clearly described act can be prosecuted.

The reaction of the American Civil Liberties Union (ACLU) summarized the reactions of others: "'Today's decision is a victory for

---

85 Supreme Court of the United States, Hamdan v. Rumsfeld (no. 05-184), http://www.supremecourtus.gov/opinions/05pdf/05-184.pdf.

the rule of law in the United States,' said ACLU Executive Director Anthony D. Romero. 'The Supreme Court has made clear that the executive branch does not have a blank check in the war on terror and may not run roughshod over the nation's legal system. This decision moves us one step closer to stopping the abuse of power that has become the hallmark of this White House.'"[86] The events which followed, the incorporation of anomie into the law and the legalization of the military commissions by the Military Commissions Act of 2006, demonstrate that, while the Supreme Court decision does indeed indicate a return to the role of the law, that role is no longer the basis of the rule of law, but of a totalitarian regime granting to the Administration the power to suppress Habeas Corpus for all foreigners. The majority decision of the Supreme Court has left the door open for the government to achieve its objectives. It does not modify the status of the Guantanamo prisoners. Nor does it order the closure of the prison. The decision authorizes the government, rather, to find another way to try the prisoners according to the law. A minority opinion, written by Judge Stephen Breyer, even points to the appropriate course of action: while "Congress has not given a blank check to the executive, nothing prevents the President from returning to Congress to seek the authority he believes necessary."

*The Military Commissions Act*

This is, in fact, the way in which the government has proceeded. It anticipated the response of the Supreme Court, so events moved quickly. The very next day after the Court's pronouncement, a preliminary bill called "The Unprivileged Combatant Act of 2006"[87] was brought by Senator Arlen Spencer to the Senate Judiciary Committee. It authorized the creation of special military tribunals by the executive branch. Another bill was concocted by the White House, "The Enemy Combatant Military Commissions Act of 2006."[88] It had the same ob-

86  "Supreme Court Says Guantanamo Bay Military Commissions are Unconstitutional; ACLU Calls Decision a Victory for the 'Rule of Law'," (06/29/2006). http://www.aclu.org/scotus/2005/hamdanv. rumsfeld05184/26044prs20060629.html

87  http://thomas.loc.gov/cgi-bin/query/D?c109:1:./temp/~c109yjly92::

88  http://balkin.blogspot.com/PostHamdan.Bush.Draft.pdf.

jective as Senator Spencer's text, but had much broader implications. It gave to these military commissions the power to try American citizens accused of terrorism. The elimination of the term "alien" in the title and text of the bill indicates clearly the ambitions of the Administration to have the power to seize any American whom it considers a terrorist, detain that person at its discretion and, ultimately, try him or her outside of any Constitutional protections.

The latter objective was not achieved and "The Enemy Combatant Military Commissions Act" was transformed into "The Military Commissions Act." It assumed its final form on September 21, 2006 after the compromise between the Administration and Republican Senators McCain, Warner and Graham on the use of torture as a technique for interrogating prisoners. The Senate hurriedly passed the Military Commissions Act of 2006[89] on September 29. The House of Representatives had passed the bill the previous evening.

By adopting the Military Commissions Act, Congress permanently granted to the executive branch extraordinary judicial prerogatives that conflict with the Constitution. The law permits the indefinite detention of any person considered to be an "enemy combatant" by the executive authorities. This designation, recorded for the first time in the text of a law, is defined as "a person who has engaged in hostilities or who has purposefully and materially supported hostilities against the United states or its co-belligerents who is not a lawful enemy combatant (including a person who is part of the Taliban, al-Qaeda, or associated forces); or a person who, before, on, or after the date of the enactment of the Military Commissions Act of 2006, has been determined to be an unlawful enemy combatant by a Combatant Status Review Tribunal or another competent tribunal established under the authority of the President or the Secretary of Defense."[90] Here, for the first time, is a definition of the term "enemy combatant," concocted by the Bush Administration in 2001 to describe suspects arrested within the context of the war on terrorism. It now makes them into "unlawful enemy combatants," thereby bringing the formulation closer to the division between lawful com-

---

89   S.3930 Military Commissions Act of 2006, http://www.govtrack.us/data/us/bills.text/109/s/s3930.pdf.

90   Military Commissions Act of 2006, Sec 948 a-Definitions.

batants (armies) and unlawful ones recognized by international law. Anyone in the world can now be considered an enemy combatant by the Administration. Even American citizens can be designated as such.

The law authorizes the President to establish military commissions to try "enemy combatants" who are not American citizens. It authorizes the Secretary of Defense, in cooperation with the Attorney General, to lay down the rules and procedures organizing these tribunals. Thus, once detained, foreigners will no longer have normal legal recourse to appeal the validity of their detention, even if they are not charged.[91] On the other hand, American suspects will be able to resort to federal courts to put forward their Habeas Corpus petition.

*Legalization of Military Commissions*

The law sets up a barely watered down version of the military commissions authorized by the Executive Order of November 13, 2001. In fact, it legalizes the commissions established by this administrative act. This type of exceptional tribunal has a long history. Examples existed during the Civil War and above all during the Second World War. The Roosevelt Administration created a Military Commission to try a group of Nazi saboteurs who had landed on a Long Island beach, close to New York. These examples directly inspired George Bush's jurists.

These special jurisdictions are intended to try "alien unlawful enemy combatants engaged in hostilities against the United States for violations of the law of war and other offenses triable by military commission."[92] One measure in the law expands the notion of "enemy combatant" to include persons suspected of financing or supporting organizations considered to be terrorist.

Distinct from the military commissions operating under the Executive Order of 2001, the applicability of these tribunals is no longer solely limited to foreigners captured outside of US territory, but is expanded to include foreigners residing in the United States. The

---

91  Section 948 a-c.

92  Section 948b.

Military Commissions Act increases the prerogatives of the military commissions that function under the 2001 Executive Order. Henceforth, they can direct their attention to persons who are not implicated in acts linked to international terrorism. Such persons include those accused of joining or associating with terrorist groups engaged in anti-American hostilities or who commit or assist in the hostile acts carried out by these groups.[93]

The law establishes the crimes that can be tried by the military commissions. Among them are definitions of acts that directly refer to social movements, such as the idea of an attack on protected property or the definition of pillaging that transforms any illegal seizure of protected property into terrorism. Thus "any person subject to this chapter who intentionally engages in an attack upon protected property shall be punished as a military commission under this chapter may direct."[94] The term protected property "means property specifically protected by the law of war (such as buildings dedicated to religion, education, art, science or charitable purposes, historic monuments, hospitals or places where the sick and wounded are collected), … ".[95] Pillaging is defined as "any person subject to this chapter who intentionally and in the absence of military necessity appropriates or seizes property for private or personal use, without the consent of a person with authority to permit such appropriation of seizure."[96] As for "conspiracy,"[97] the law creates a crime of intention and detaches the offense from any material element.

These commissions are closely dependent on the executive branch of the government, which establishes their operating rules and appoints their members. The right to appeal to a higher jurisdiction is considerably restricted. The Court of Appeals for the District of Columbia is the only higher jurisdiction with the competence to be cognizant of the cases tried by the military commissions. Also, it

---

93   Jeffrey Smith, "White House Proposal Would Expand Authority of Military Courts," *Washington Post*, August 2, 2006, Page A04.

94   Section 950v. (b) 4.

95   Section 950v. (a) 3.

96   Section 950v. (b) 5.

97   Section 950v. (b) 28.

alone is authorized to validate that the decision was carried out in conformity with the procedures established by these commissions, even though it is precisely these procedures that pose the problem. There is no investigation into the veracity of the allegations contained in the indictment. There is a right to appeal against the norms and procedures of the commissions, but only "insofar as the Constitution and the laws of the United States are applicable." This right is purely formal since the objective of this law is to make constitutional protections inapplicable for foreigners suspected of terrorism.

The law rejects the right of a prisoner to a speedy trial (thereby authorizing unlimited detention without trial) and the right to represent him or herself. US military attorneys are assigned to carry out the defense of the accused. Contrary to the military commissions operating under the authority of the Executive Order of 2001, the accused can request to be defended by a civilian attorney. This right, however, is strictly limited since the civilian defense attorney must be a US citizen and must submit to a security clearance. This attorney is not guaranteed access to information classified as secret and cannot attend closed-door sessions of the commission. Beyond that, the US government is not responsible for covering the costs associated with defense by a civilian attorney.[98]

Under the Military Commissions Act, the military attorney appointed by the Administration has access to the entire file and can participate in all phases of the trial. As for the accused, he or she cannot have access to any evidence that is classified as secret and thus has no possibility to refute it. The accused can also be excluded "for security reasons" from specific phases of the trial. Under the new procedures, the trials are supposed to be open to the public, but closed sessions can be held in order to protect individuals or for reasons of national security.

Military prosecutors will have the right to use evidence obtained by hearsay in these tribunals. The use of hearsay evidence as the basis for making decisions is not a pure possibility or pure conjecture, but is already a reality. Administrative procedures, such as those of the Combatant Status review Tribunals under which the Guantanamo

---

98  http://web.amnesty.org/library/index/ENGAMR511542006.

detainees are supposed to be tried, already function on the basis of such evidence. Commander James Crisfield, Navy judge advocate general who has acted as legal adviser to these commissions, has revealed the level of confidence given to hearsay evidence: "the evidence considered persuasive by the tribunal is made up almost entirely of hearsay evidence recorded by unidentified individuals with no firsthand knowledge of the events they describe."[99]

## Legalization of Ill Treatment

The law from now on prohibits "cruel or inhuman treatment," defined as "torture," and techniques inflicting "serious bodily or mental harm." But the President is authorized to interpret the "meaning and application" of the Geneva Conventions and to promulgate standards for violations of the Conventions that are not considered grave breaches, i.e., those falling between "cruel" and "minor abuses." Bush is thus conferred with the power to determine, within certain limits, the degree of ill treatment that could be inflicted on terrorist suspects. This clause is particularly indicative of the nature of the new legal order set up under cover of the war on terrorism: a law that is purely subjective and circumstantial, which entirely subordinates the objectivity of the text to a particular reading of it by the executive authorities.

In practice, declarations made under torture could no longer be used as evidence, but information obtained by using harsh methods of interrogation, which is likened to "cruel, inhuman or degrading treatment," could be taken into consideration if a judge finds them "reliable" and useful for the "interests of justice." Thus article 948r stipulates: "A statement ... in which the degree of coercion is disputed may be admitted only if the military judge finds that the totality of the circumstances renders the statement reliable and possessing sufficient probative value and the interests of justice would best be served by admission of the statement into evidence." The degree of coercion accepted by a tribunal will thus itself be variable, dependent

---

99 Joanne Mariner, "Military Commissions Redux," *Findlay*, le 2 Août 2006, http://writ.news.findlaw. com/mariner/20060802.html.

upon a Presidential interpretation of the Geneva Conventions, now and in the future.

At the same time, the law prohibits any prosecution of American agents for acts of torture or ill treatment of prisoners captured by the Army or the CIA prior to the end of 2005. This allows President Bush to declare that, upon his signature, the law authorizes the CIA to continue its program of detaining and interrogating persons suspected of terrorism in secret prisons located outside the United States.[100]

*Legalization of Combatant Status Review Tribunals*

The Military Commissions Act also legalizes the Combatant Status Review Tribunals (CSRT). The Defense Department created these tribunals nine days after the Supreme Court's decision in the Rasul case. Their function is to decide if a prisoner held at Guantanamo is indeed an enemy combatant.

The CSRT, however, expands the concept of enemy combatant. The Supreme Court decision in Hamdi v. Rumsfeld concerned persons engaged in combat against the United States and its allies in Afghanistan. The CSRT expands this restrictive definition by including anyone who belongs to al-Qaeda and associated groups. What is more, it expands its applicability to the entire world. Recall that the Military Commissions Act again widens the concept of enemy combatant even further to include anyone, regardless of nationality, who is engaged in hostilities against the United States.

The Military Commissions Act temporarily foils judicial decisions that have called into question the procedures of the Combatant Status Review Tribunals by relying on the particularly vague and really arbitrary character of the idea of enemy combatant. Thus, in January 2005, Judge Joyce Hens Green of the Federal District Court in Washington had already ruled that the Combatant Status Review Tribunals violated two clauses of the Fifth Amendment by allowing the use of secret evidence obtained under torture, denying access to

---

100 William Branigin, "Bush Signs Bill Authorizing Detainee Interrogations, Military Commissions, *Washington Post,* October 17, 2006.

a civilian attorney and by using a vague definition of enemy combatant. Such a vague definition makes it possible to incriminate anyone who is in contact with a person or organization considered to be terrorist. In reference to this definition, the judge posed a series of questions to determine who can be detained as enemy combatant: what about "a little old lady in Switzerland who writes checks to what she thinks is a charitable organization that helps orphans in Afghanistan but really is a front to finance al-Qaeda activities?" she asked. And what about a resident of Dublin "who teaches English to the son of a person the CIA knows to be a member of al-Qaeda?"[101]

*State of Exception or Dictatorship*

The Military Commissions Act of 2006 incorporates into the law the fact that anyone, even if he or she is an American citizen, can be named an enemy combatant by the Administration. The use of such a label has a directly political character. It goes beyond the context of the fight against international terrorism. It can be applied to persons engaged in acts that the Administration can interpret as hostilities towards the United States. The vague character of the crime means that it can be applied to acts opposing government policies or to demonstrations supporting such acts.

Thus the Military Commissions Act directly affects American citizens, even if they can appeal to a civilian jurisdiction to contest a possible decision of the Administration to seize and detain them indefinitely.[102] Moreover, the structure of the text of the Military Commissions Act reveals that the law had the original objective of codifying the power to seize anyone, whether an American citizen or not, in order to incarcerate that person for an indefinite period of time without trial or to try that person before a military commission. Some parts of the law clearly indicate that it was written in order to prosecute Americans. Thus, the law stipulates that "Any person subject to this chapter who, in breach of an allegiance or duty to the United States, knowingly and intentionally aids an enemy of

---

101 http://randomselections.blogspot.com/2005_11_01_randomselections_archive.html.

102 http://balkin.blogspot.com/2006/09/does-military-commissions-act-apply-to.html.

the United States, or one of the co-belligerents of the enemy, shall be punished as a military commission under this chapter may direct."[103] Only a citizen of the United States can be held accountable to an allegiance or duty to the American government.[104]

In the law as initially proposed, the word "alien" had been removed from the term enemy combatant.[105] After resistance from Republican Senators, the word "alien" was reintroduced to specify those enemy combatants who could be tried by the military commissions. The final version of the Military Commissions Act is thus a setback in relation to the initial version. A double legal system is established, a restricted rule of law for citizens and pure violence for foreigners. However, this is really just a transition period. The Military Commissions Act still maintains constitutional guarantees for citizens, but as Republican Senator Lindsey Graham said, "it is a good beginning."[106] The government's objective is indeed to have the power to seize anyone, American or foreigner, and deal with that person as it sees fit.

The rulings of the Supreme Court, whether it be in the Rasul v. Bush and Hamdi v. Rumsfeld decisions of June 2004 or the Hamdan v. Rumsfeld decision of June 29, 2006, do not reinstate the rule of law but inject pure violence into it. They provide confirmation of the interpretation of the legal theoretician, Carl Schmitt,[107] for whom the exception serves as the basis of a new legal regime. The executive can thus grant itself legislative and judicial privileges that weaken the formal separation of powers. The Supreme Court's decisions strengthen the President's self-appointed role as judge and jury.

In the state of emergency, the extent of the powers magistrates have at their disposal is a direct result of the suspension of laws limit-

---

103 Article 950v. (b) 26.

104 Joseph Watson et Alex Jones, "Torture Bill States Non-Allegiance to Bush Is Terrorism," *Prison Planet.com* htp://www.prisonplanet.com/articles/september2006/290906torturebill.htm.

105 "Can this possibly be right?," *The Next Hurrah,* July 29, 2006. http://thenexthurrah.typepad.com/ the_next_hurrah/2006/07/can_this_possib.html.

106 Patrick Martin, "Bush veut étendre aux citoyens américains les procédures de Guantanamo," WSWS.org, le 2 août 2006.

107 Carl Schmitt, *La Dictature* (Paris: Seuil, 2000).

ing their privileges. The extraordinary powers of both the executive and police stem from weakening the mechanisms that protect fundamental freedoms. The state of exception is a state without law.

Historically, this form of government tends to suspend public and private freedoms when threatened. The procedure is not associated with any specific circumstances, nor is it timebound. It is instituted for the duration, but its role is to become the rule. The state of emergency becomes a permanent fixture.

The concept of a generalized state of exception is in itself a contradiction. The generalized state of exception —as Agamben conceives it—[108] is not stable. In the war against terrorism the suspension of the rule of law is not an end in itself.

A state of emergency that takes indefinite hold, and a state of exception that affects all public and private spheres, bring about a political sea change. It marks an end to the formal separation of powers, and gives the executive the kind of authority allotted to judges: the authority to state and interpret the law, the authoritarian power of dictatorship.

108 Giorgio Agamben, "L'état d'exception," Le Monde, 12 September 2002.

# 2

## IN THE UNITED KINGDOM

The Framework Decision of the European Union is strongly influenced by the English law, the Terrorism Act 2000, which came into force in February 2001. This law defines terrorism as an action or a threat of action that "aims to influence the government or intimidate all or a part of the population" or as "the action or threat of action that aims to promote a political, religious or ideological cause."[1] This subjective element stipulates that the offense is terrorist when it includes "serious violence against a person" or "puts a person's life in danger" or includes "serious damage against property" or "entails a serious risk for the health or security of all or part of the population" or "seriously interferes with or disrupts an electronic system."

It is the desired goal that defines the act as terrorist. The subjective character of this criminalization also appears in the characterization of the acts. The term "serious" permits an indeterminate margin of interpretation. It is the ruling authorities who will decide whether or not the acts in question constitute a terrorist threat.

In relation to prior antiterrorist laws, eight between 1973 and 1996, the Terrorism Act 2000 is firmly modern. It breaks new ground in several areas: the subjective character of the offenses, the general scope of the law as well as its use in monitoring the Net. This law must then be read parallel to the "Regulation of Investigatory Powers Bill" (RIP Act). The latter, adopted in July 2000, makes the simple intrusion into a computer system a terrorist act.

The Framework Decision of the European Union enhances its Anglo-Saxon model by criminalizing acts that have the potential of being carried out during collective protest movements.

---

1    Terrorism Act 2000, http://www.uk-legislation.hmso.gov.uk/acts/acts2000/20000011.htm.

The attacks of September 11 allowed the British government to force the urgent adoption of a new antiterrorist law, The Antiterrorism, Crime and Security Act, which was enacted on December 14, 2001. In comparison with the Terrorism Act 2000, which is still in force, the 2001 legislation authorizes the indefinite detention, without an indictment, of a foreigner suspected of terrorist activities, just as in the United States. Article 21 allows indefinite incarceration based on a certificate issued by the Secretary of State for Home Affairs. "The Secretary of State may issue a certificate under this section in respect of a person if the Secretary of State reasonably believes that (a) the person present in the United Kingdom is a risk to national security, and (b) suspects that the person is a terrorist."[2] No objective fact is necessary to justify the decision. The time limit for "conviction" is entirely subjective.

A terrorist is "a person who is involved in committing, preparing or studying acts of international terrorism" or "who is a member of an international terrorist group" or who "has links with such a group." The concept of "link" is not at all defined. It is even more indefinite and extensible that the approach developed by the Terrorism Act 2000, which stipulated that any person who "supports or assists" such a group would be prosecuted. This change allows an uncontrollable expansion of the possibilities of prosecution that could, for example, involve a committee for the defense of persons incarcerated as a result of this law.

The certificate issued by the Home Secretary permits the detention of the accused person within the terms of the Immigration Act of 1971, i.e., for the purpose of either expulsion or return to their country of origin. The possibility of detention for an indefinite period is necessary when expulsion is prevented by an international agreement or another reason. In this case, the person has the choice between remaining in indefinite detention in the United Kingdom or returning to his or her country of origin and being subjected there to a whole set of proceedings that are exceptional under the terms of

---

2   Anti-Terrorism, Crime and Security Act 2001, http://www.opsi.gov.uk/acts/acts2001/2001004/htm.

international law. Most often, the countries of origin of the incarcerated persons are well known for their systematic violations of human rights. It is in these terms, moreover, that the debate was presented to Parliament.[3] The foreigner suspected of terrorism by the English government thus enters into a global system of non-law in which every option is closed to him or her.

## A Suspension of the Law

By permitting potentially unlimited detention, this act effectively suspends the law for all persons not having British citizenship or a right of residence or a right of protection as refugees. Thus, the suspension of habeas corpus is less extensive than in the United States, where all foreigners are affected.

In order to pass this law, the British government instituted an exception to the European Convention on Human Rights. This exception is based on the concept of a state of emergency and is thus an exception to Article 5, Paragraph 1 of this Convention, which guarantees the liberty of persons. According to Article 15 of the Convention, exceptional measures must be limited strictly to the minimum necessary as required by the situation. As judged by the Special Immigration Appeals Commission (SIAC), this is not true of unlimited detention. The SIAC was created in order to assure some control over detentions. The law does not allow appeals to be made before this commission. That has not prevented the latter from ordering the release of nine out of the eleven detained under this law, the other two having chosen expulsion. The government reacted to the judgment by announcing its intention to resort to other procedures that would allow it to pursue incarceration. It has thus clearly announced that it does not intend to respect the judgment of a Special Commission that it established. The government appealed and the higher court fundamentally found in its favor on the question of discrimination between foreign nationals and British citizens.[4]

---

3  Home Affairs Select Committee, "The Anti-terrorism, Crime and Security Bill," HC(2001-O2) 351,10/11/2001, First Report.

4  Elspeth Guild, "Facettes de l'insécurité. Agamben face aux juges. Souveraineté, exception et antiterrorisme," *Cultures et Conflits*, no. 51.

*Suspension of the Law Questioned by the Law Lords*

On December 22, 2004, the Secretary-General of the Council of Europe demanded the immediate abrogation of the Terrorism Act 2001: "Antiterrorist legislation in the United Kingdom must be changed immediately. We will not win the war on terrorism if we undermine the foundation of our democratic societies."[5] This position follows a decision reached by the Appeals Court of the House of Lords, the highest judicial body in Great Britain, on December 16, 2004 that considers the unlimited detention, without indictment and trial, of foreigners suspected of terrorist activities as illegal and contrary to the European Convention on Human Rights.[6]

The judgment resulted from a challenge made by nine detainees, the same ones who had earlier, in July 2002, obtained a victory before the Special Immigration Appeals Commission (SIAC). However, they had seen their demand for release rejected once again in August 2004 by the Appeals Court in London.

None of the applicants is the subject of legal proceedings nor have any charges been filed. The appellants contest the legality of their detention, asserting that it is contrary to the obligations assumed by the United Kingdom with regard to the European Convention on Human Rights and thus with the Human Rights Act 1998, which integrates this Convention into British law.

In its opinion, the Appeals Court of the House of Lords found in favor of the applicants. The judgment indeed recognizes that the Immigration Act 1971 provides the possibility of detaining an individual who is not a British citizen with the intention of proceeding with that individual's extradition, but specifies that this law does not grant any mandate permitting a long or indefinite detention.

---

5   Statewatch News Online, 22 décembre 2004, http://www.statewatch.org/news/archive2004.htm.

6   Opinions of the Lords of Appeal for judgement in the cause : A(FC) and others(FC) (appellants) v. Secretary of State for the Home department (Respondent), House of Lords, session 2004-05, (2004) UKHL 56, 16 December 2004. http://www.statewatch.org/news/2004/dec/belmarsh-appeal.pdf.

The grounds for the decision clarify the opposition between the classic definition of the state of emergency, limited in time and objectively defined, defended by the Law Lords and the position of the government, which wants to implement an indefinite and unverifiable suspension of constitutional liberties. The decision stipulates that the indefinite incarceration authorized by the Terrorism Act 2001, which would not be, moreover, the result of any judicial verdict, is indeed contrary to Article 5 of the European Convention on Human Rights, which guarantees the liberty of persons. At the same time, the decision invalidates the exception to this article instituted by the government. This exception refers to Article 15 of the Convention that stipulates: "In time of war or other public emergency threatening the life of the nation, any High Contracting Party may take measures derogating from its obligations under this Convention to the extent strictly required by the exigencies of the situation...."

The Court agreed with the argument presented by the applicants that the exceptions to Article 5, which are strictly limited to situations of war or emergency in which the life of the nation is threatened, are not applicable in the present situation. For the Court, the state of emergency is limited in time. There must be an imminent danger or exceptional circumstances that must be objectively determined. Article 15 does not refer to the specific nature of the danger, but this question was treated by the European Court as a necessary condition of the suspension of Article 5. The Court quoted from the Siracusa Principles in this context: "The principle of strict necessity shall be applied in an objective manner. Each measure shall be directed to an actual, clear, present, or imminent danger and may not be imposed merely because of an apprehension of potential danger."[7]

By returning to these basic principles, the Law Lords opposed the argument presented by the Attorney General, for whom a situation of emergency is not necessarily temporary and can cover a considerable number of years. For him, it falls within the competence of the executive power to protect the population. He did "resist the imposi-

---

7   Opinions of the Lords of Appeal, *Op.cit.*, p. 13.

78

tion of any artificial temporal limit to an emergency of the present kind..."[8] For the executive power, the question of the suspension of liberties is a purely political matter, in the narrow sense of the term. It is a matter for its own initiative and under the control of Parliament. As "it is the function of political and not judicial bodies to resolve political questions[9] the question of the exception to the law must be outside the jurisdiction of various judicial authorities. The Law Lords opposed to this position the idea that the role of the courts consists of verifying the legality of the acts of various authorities. By doing this, the highest British judicial authority evoked the principle of separation of powers and did "not accept the full breadth of the Attorney General's argument on what is generally called the deference owed by the courts to the political authorities."[10]

## THE PREVENTION OF TERRORISM BILL

The British Parliament adopted a new antiterrorist law, The Prevention of Terrorism Act, on March 11, 2005. By doing so, Parliament made it possible for the government to carry out the long-standing project of expanding the emergency provisions, to which foreigners are subjected within the context of the war on terrorism, to cover the whole population, including citizens. This change is important because it calls into question the concept of habeas corpus. The law attacks the formal separation of powers by giving to the Secretary of State for Home Affairs judicial prerogatives. Further, it reduces the rights of the defense practically to nothing. It also establishes the primacy of suspicion over fact, since measures restricting liberties, potentially leading to house arrest, could be imposed on individuals not for what they have done, but according to what the Home Secretary thinks they could have done or could do. Thus, this law deliberately turns its back on the rule of law and establishes a new form of political regime.

---

8   Opinions of the Lords of Appeal, *Op.cit.*, p.15.

9   *Op. cit.*, p. 17.

10   *Op. cit.*, p. 17.

The Prevention of Terrorism Act is a modification of Part Four of the Antiterrorism Crime and Security Act 2001, whose specific provisions concerning detention of foreigners accused of terrorism expired on March 14, 2005.

## A Generalized State of Exception

The decision of the Lords of Appeal is a simple opinion without constraining force. The government can choose not to take it into account. But in the end, the government concluded that taking the decision into consideration was a good occasion to legitimize the generalization of the emergency provisions to the whole population. The highest British court considered that the indefinite detention, without indictment or trial, of foreigners suspected of terrorist activities is illegal and contrary to the European Convention on Human Rights.[11] It also considered the distinction between foreigners and citizens as discriminatory.

The Prevention of Terrorism Act 2005 appears to be non-discriminatory since it concerns British citizens as much as foreigners. By pushing the enactment of a modification to Part 4 of the Terrorism Act 2001, which allows the indefinite detention of foreigners without evidence or trial, the English Prime Minister succeeded in extending to British citizens a whole series of exceptional procedures that call into question the individual liberties of all Britons. Tony Blair appealed to fear in order to justify his project. He claimed: "The present law is called for by the police and security services. Voting it down would mean jeopardising the country's security."[12]

Tony Blair has been able to impose on the United Kingdom what George W. Bush has not yet succeeded in imposing on the United States, i.e., the possibility for the government to take measures that call into question the right of citizens to self-determination within the context of the war on terrorism. In the United States, the procedures that would extend to citizens the provisions of the Patriot Act authorizing imprisonment of indefinite duration, without charges

---

11  Opinions of the Lords of Appeal, *Op.cit.*

12  Jerôme Rassetti, "Blair revoit sa copie antiterroriste," *Le Soir* du 9 mars 20.

or indictment, of any foreigner suspected of terrorism have not been adopted. The Bush administration has been unable to put the bill, known as Patriot II,[13] on the Congressional agenda.

The Prevention of Terrorism Act 2005,[14] passed on March 11 of 2005, authorizes the Home Secretary to initiate control orders over a person, potentially leading to house arrest, when he has reasons to suspect that an individual is or was implicated in an action linked to terrorism. He would also be able to prohibit the use of a mobile telephone, limit access to the internet, prevent that person from having contacts with certain persons, oblige him or her to be at home at certain times, and authorize the police and special services to have access to his or her home at all hours. He also has the possibility of limiting access to employment or to an occupation. The list of 15 control orders provided for by the law is not exhaustive and is only provided as a list of examples. The government has the possibility of indefinitely introducing new provisions that limit the freedom of movement of the persons concerned. If the latter do not respect these orders, they are liable for imprisonment. These provisions could be taken when the Home Secretary considers that the individual in question presents a danger for national security, but that the facts in his possession do not allow him to take the case before a court. Home Secretary Charles Clarke declared before Parliament that control orders could be taken "on the basis of an intelligence assessement provided by the Security Service (where) there are reasonable grounds for suspecting that an individual is, or has been, concerned with terrorism.[15]

### A Subjective Law

The justification for the decision to place a person under supervision is not found in objective facts, but in the suspicion that falls on that person or in the intention that is attributed to that person. Terrorist activity is defined as: "(a) the commission, preparation or instigation

---

13  Domestic Security Enhancement Act of 2003, http://www.publicintegrity.org/docs/PatriotAct/ Story_01_020703_doc_1.pdf.

14  Prevention of Terrorism Bill," http://www.homeoffice.gov.uk/docs4/terrorism_bill.pdf.

15  Statewatch report, "The exceptional and draconian become the norm," p. 9, http://www. statewatch.org/news/2005/mar/exceptional-and-draconian.pdf.

of acts of terrorism; (b) conduct which facilitates the commission, preparation or instigation of such acts, or which is intended to do so; (c) conduct which gives encouragement to the commission, preparation or instigation of such acts, or which is intended to do so; (d) conduct which gives support or assistance to individuals who are known or believed to be involved in terrorism-related activity."[16] Thus the law does not concern definite acts, but punishes assistance to persons who are simply suspected of activities or intentions linked to terrorism. This concept is particularly indeterminate and subjective. Its area of application is very large, nearly unlimited, and totally unverifiable. What is an activity linked to terrorism? Is it, for example, to have accommodated persons who later were suspected of participating or of having had the intention of participating in actions designated as terrorist? Does it include belonging to a support group for political prisoners?

The reaction of the House of Lords was problematic for the government. Initially, the Lords rejected the project, considering the text as an attack on liberties. It ended up accepting it after thirty hours of debate and after having gotten agreement that control orders would be taken with the consent of a court. In accordance with the new text, the Home Secretary must apply to a judge before carrying out a house arrest, but, in cases of emergency, he could immediately order minimal measures and ask for a court's concurrence within seven days. Above all, the upper house laid down the condition that passage of the law must be accompanied by a sunset clause effective in one year. Thus the law would have to be submitted to debate again in July 2006. The work of an independent commission, charged with following the application of the law, must serve as the basis for future parliamentary work.

Even if the Home Secretary makes a decision with the consent of a court, this judicial guarantee obtained by the House of Lords has nothing in common with the classic judicial procedure that guarantees the rights of the defense. Under the provisions of this law, the defense has no access to the file containing the alleged facts and no possibility of contesting them. The only ones with access to these facts

16   Prevention of terrorism Act 2005, article 1(9), http://www.opsi.gov.uk/acts/acts2005/20050002.htm.

are the judge and "special attorneys" selected by the Home Secretary. The latter are responsible for representing the point of view of the defense, without providing the latter with the "proof" held against it and without giving it the possibility of refuting that proof. The decision is made in the absence of the incriminated person.

Contrary to what the Home Secretary claims, this exceptional procedure has nothing in common with long-term preventive detention as applied in matters of terrorism by countries such as Spain or Germany. In those countries, the detention is exclusively ordered by a judge, the incriminated person knows the charges that are held against him or her and the defense has the possibility of contesting the evidence or the reasons for the detention. This new procedure results in the abolition of the presumption of innocence that is normally granted to persons prosecuted within a judicial context.

*An Evaluation by Secret Services*

Control orders can be made based on information provided by a security service. This source can be from outside the United Kingdom and come from the United States, for example. During the debates in the House of Lords, the government had conceded that the prosecution could not use evidence obtained through torture. However, the government does not appear to have renounced using such information. The Independent related the statements of the Foreign Secretary who claimed that "while torture is of course thoroughly unacceptable, our country cannot dismiss intelligence that has been gained in this way by the US, especially when the lives of 3,000 people are at stake."[17]

The assessment made by the security services can rely on a great diversity of sources, many of which could not serve as proof in judicial proceedings. It is not only a question of intercepting telephone calls or emails, but all of the intrusive acts implemented by a secret service, such as video surveillance, infiltration, information obtained by undercover agents, etc. The information contained in the reports or statements made by such agents or informers are evaluated according to a scale of plausibility dependent on "various degrees of

---

17   Colin Brown, "Straw : Britain cannot evidence obtained by torture," *The Independent*, 11/3/2005.

truthfulness and accuracy." The evaluation made by the intelligence services on the danger to national security presented by an individual is separate from the observation of a specific act. An individual can be considered dangerous and subjected to control orders if he or she is suspected of being "a member of or associated with suspect organizations." It is not necessary that the "proofs" established on the basis of information supplied by the secret services be objective. They can amount to the subjective evaluation of a potential danger to which a determinate level of dangerousness is attributed. The law's explanatory notes insist on the preventive character of the surveillance provisions, since these measures are designed to prevent terrorist attacks on Great Britain.

The fate reserved by the government for English citizens imprisoned at Guantanamo is a good example of the anticipated implementation of this law. Four Britons, detained at Guantanamo for more than three years, were freed in January 2005. After having been interrogated by the English antiterrorist police, they were freed one day later. No charge was filed against them. This fact did not prevent the Home Secretary from considering them a terrorist danger for Great Britain. He initiated control orders on them, such as prohibiting travel to foreign countries and making it impossible to obtain a passport. He justified these measures on the basis of information obtained from interrogations at Guantanamo.[18] Thus, on the basis of "intelligence" given by the United States, obtained in conditions of torture or mistreatment, and without possibility of verification or contestation, the prisoners freed from Guantanamo remain in an international system of non-law.

THE END OF HABEAS CORPUS

The most significant part of the Prevention of Terrorism Bill is the fact that it expands the suspension of law to include citizens. It puts an end to a double judicial system: rule of law for citizens and pure violence for foreigners. The suppression of habeas corpus is extended to the whole population. It is now a generalized state of exception. This law,

---

18   Statewatch report, "The exceptional and draconian become the norm," *Op. Cit*, p. 8.

like the American Patriot II project, should be envisaged as the first step in a process that aims at extending measures that suspend the law to the entire population, including citizens, within the context of the war on terrorism. The Home Secretary already revealed this project. He also spoke of the possibility of trying suspects in special courts of law. The accused would not have the choice of his or her attorney. The latter would be selected by the executive power, on the basis of a list approved by the secret services.

The "USA Patriot Act" and the English "Antiterrorism, Crime and Security Act 2001" are still based on the existence of a double judicial system: on the one hand, protection of the law for citizens, even if it is increasingly restricted, and, on the other hand, suspension of the law for foreigners. It is this double legal order that begins to disappear with the Patriot II project as well as the Prevention of Terrorism Bill. The war on terrorism thus marks a rupture in the western mode of political organization, founded traditionally on a double system that takes the form of the rule of law inside a society and the use of "pure violence" outside of it. The exception becomes the rule. The rule, which inscribes the exception in the law, is constructed as a function of the exception. This is exactly the process that is unfolding before our eyes.

### State of Emergency or Dictatorship

By imposing a review clause (sunset provision) on the Prevention of Terrorism Act 2005 that authorizes evaluation of the law after one year, the House of Lords kept that law within the formal context of a state of emergency, since these measures could be abrogated after one year. The government did not want to set any temporal limit, the antiterrorist struggle being viewed as a struggle of long duration against a multiform enemy. It has not, however, renounced its project and wishes to profit from the review procedure by pushing for the adoption of control orders freed from their temporal constraints.

However, this law is no more than formally part of a state of emergency. It gives judicial prerogatives to the Home Secretary. A person is designated as terrorist not by the decision of a court, but by a certificate issued by a representative of the executive power. At no point does the latter have to justify a decision that is applied to a mere suspect. Objective facts, which should be used as the basis of these suspicions, are not even necessary since they remain secret. It suffices that the administrative authority assert that it is detaining the suspects and that this declaration be corroborated by a court. What is the value of judicial supervision that is exercised without the possibility for the defendant to assert his or her rights, even to know what he or she is being charged with? What independence can the judicial power assert in a decision-making process in which it does not have the means either to verify the information that is given to it or the means of proof?

This law represents one step forward in the dismantling of the rule of law. It is an example of a purely subjective law, allowing a maximum of interpretation. It is a law that assures the primacy of firm belief over facts. The executive power concentrates in its hands all the power, including judicial prerogatives. With this legislation, the United Kingdom moves into a new type of political regime called by the theory of law a dictatorship.

*A Change in the System*

The Anti-Terrorism, Crime and security Act 2001 as well as the Prevention of Terrorism Act 2005 represent additional steps in the dismantling of the rule of law. These laws give to the Home Secretary the powers of a judge. A person is designated a terrorist, not as a result of a legal verdict, but through a certificate drawn up by a representative of the Executive. The latter does not, at any moment, have to justify a decision that is applied to suspects. "Firm belief" suffices. What is more, this measure establishes an explicit link between the methods of managing immigration and the organization of the war against terrorism. It makes the latter a tool of the former.

These laws should be seen as the first step in a process aimed at extending measures that suspend the law to the whole population, including citizens. This objective was clearly revealed by the Home Secretary. He also spoke of the possibility of trying ordinary suspects secretly in special courts of law. The accused would not have the choice of his/her own lawyer. The Executive would select a lawyer from a list authorized by the secret services.

There exists a qualitative change between the Terrorism Act 2000 and these new laws. The former represents the ultimate point in a change that is internal to criminal law. The latter is reorganized around the procedure of exception. This is a dismantling of the rule of law carried out within the framework of the law itself. In the Anti-Terrorism, Crime and Security Act, the exception offers to the Executive the possibility of seizing any foreign person, without legal constraint, while in the Prevention of Terrorism 2005, it extends that possibility to any person suspected of terrorism. This exception is the first constitutive element in a change in the political system itself, a change that affects the whole population. This change inserts the population into a generalized state of exception and into a state of emergency that is established for the long run. Here, the derogation turns out to be an act of pure violence, outside of the established legal system. It is the principle from which a new form of government is constructed, one that puts an end to the formal separation of powers.

As the Home Secretary, David Blunkett, indicated, the government aims to extend the possibility of seizing British citizens accused of terrorism and imprisoning them without trial for an indefinite period. Thus, the exception is not only the transformative principle of the legal order, but the basis on which a new political order is constructed, nationally and globally.

The government, moreover, points to international necessities as justification for this measure. The Home Secretary "considered that the continuous and free presence in the United Kingdom of persons suspected of terrorism, who could not be transferred to a third country, had harmful effects on the country in the current emergency situation. Government at the highest level has concluded that this situation would have a negative impact on the ability of the United

Kingdom to build and protect an effective international coalition in the fight against terrorism."[19]

As in the United States, the exception is the principle from which a new legal and political order is built at the international level. This measure should be considered in relation to the role that Great Britain plays in organizing an imperial structure under American direction.

The Anti-Terrorism, Crime and Security Act 2001 and its updated form, the Prevention of Terrorism Act 2005, could possibly have a double effect on the legislation of other Member States of the European Union. The Terrorism Act 2000, as well as various laws that provided for surveillance of the Internet, provided a model that was gradually adopted by other countries. The Anti-Terrorism, Crime and Security Act plays the same role with regard to the recourse to a right of exception for foreigners accused of terrorism. Thus, this law has a direct effect on the international level. It serves to mobilize various governments in the periphery in the antiterrorist struggle. It is a key element in the implementation of imperial politics, in the formation of the "camp of good versus the camp of evil."

## THE LEGALIZATION OF TORTURE

The Home Secretary and the Prime Minister, Tony Blair, want to remove any obstacle to the new laws. The latter declared during the presentation of the government's plan for the fight against terrorism "Should legal obstacles arise ... we will legislate further, including, if necessary amending the Human Rights Act in respect of the interpretation of the European convention on human rights."[20] Michael Howard also promised a revision of this act by a future Conservative government. The Human Rights Act, which became law in 2000, obliges judges to take into account the jurisprudence of the European Court on Human Rights in their decisions.

Charles Clarke challenged the legal decisions of this Court on the protection of refugees. These decisions prohibit torture and inhu-

---

19  A, X, and Y and others v. Secretary of State for the Home Department (2002), EWCA Civ 1502, paragraph 110.

20  Marcel Berlins, "Human rights in peril," *The Guardian,* October 31, 2005.

man and degrading treatment. They oppose the return of refugees when they are threatened with such treatment. The Court's decisions are thus an obstacle to the government's plan, which wants to return foreigners accused of defending or supporting terrorism to their country of origin or deport them to third countries, even if they risk torture.

Despite the integration of the Convention on Human Rights into British law, London has already been involved in negotiations with Libya, Algeria and Lebanon to return these "undesirables." London signed an agreement with Libya on October 18, 2005 to transfer to the latter Libyan citizens considered to be "a threat to national security." Great Britain is satisfied with the commitment of this country not to mistreat these prisoners upon their return. An initial agreement has already been signed with Jordan and another is in preparation with Algeria.[21]

The government position was strengthened by a decision of the Appeal Court of England and Wales in August of 2004 which had ruled that "evidence" obtained under torture in third countries was admissible within the context of the proceedings of the Special Immigration Appeals Commission (SIAC), providing the torture was not committed by or done with the secret cooperation of British agents. Torture still remains absolutely prohibited in the United Kingdom.[22] The Appeal Court justified its decision by the fact that the European Convention on Human Rights is not part of British law. Thus the courts cannot exclude such evidence.[23] By a two to one majority, the Appeal Court ruled that if the evidence is obtained by an agent of a foreign country, without the involvement of Great Britain, there is no good reason to inquire into the origin of such evidence.[24]

On December 8, 2005, the Court of Appeal of the House of Lords, the Law Lords, in a unanimous judgment, challenged the decision

---

21 Armelle Thoraval, "Accord d'extradition entre Londres et Tripoli," *Le Monde*, le 20 octobre 2005.

22 "United Kingdom: to use 'torture evidence' in courts is to accept the unacceptable," *Amnesty International*, AI Index: EUR 45/044/2005 (Public), October 17, 2005. http://web.amnesty.org/library/index/engEUR450442005.

23 Clare Dyer, "Lords to rule on evidence from torture," *The Guardian*, October 17, 2005.

24 Clare Dyer, "UK wins allies in challenge to torture ruling," *The Guardian*, October 18, 2005.

of the Appeal Court. The Law Lords ruled that evidence obtained under torture is not admissible by English courts and particularly by the Special Immigration Appeals Commission (SIAC). This decision has several implications concerning government action. The government must review all cases where such evidence was used. In particular, it must refrain from deporting individuals to countries that practice torture. The government must indicate from where evidence was obtained. If it cannot reveal its sources for security reasons, it must present other evidence. The decision obliges the Home Secretary to review all cases where evidence used to convict terror suspects was obtained from sources kept secret.[25] The ruling is the result of a case brought on behalf of ten prisoners, eight of whom have been detained without charge since December 2001, the other two since February and April of 2002.[26]

The ruling of the Law Lords requires the Special Immigration Appeals Commission (SIAC) to investigate whether or not there are reasonable grounds to believe that the evidence presented before it was obtained under torture. If three judges conclude that there is some doubt on whether or not torture has been or could have been used, then the evidence cannot be admitted.[27] The court's ruling implies that, rather than the government having to demonstrate that there was no active participation on the part of British agents in using torture to obtain evidence, the prosecutor must show that such improper methods were not used at any point to obtain such evidence. This ruling also has an impact on government intentions to deport "undesirable" foreigner to countries that practice torture.

---

25  D. Wes Rist, "UK law lords rule against use of violence," *Jurist*, December 8, 2005, http://jurist.law. pitt.edu/paperchase/2005_12_08_indexarch.php#113404465219984764.

26  "House of Lords rule that torture evidence is not admissible in UK courts," *Liberty*, December 8, 2005, http://www.liberty-human-rights.org.uk/press/2005/lords-rule-torture-inadmissible.shtml.

27  "Opinions of the Lords of Appeal for judgement in the cause A(FC) and others (FC) (Appelants) v, Secretary of State for the Home Department (Respondent) (2004), House of Lords, Session 2005-06 {2005} UKHL 71, http://www.publications.parliament.uk/pa/ld200506/ldjudgmt/jd051208/aand.pdf.

On March 22, 2006, the House of Lords approved the proposed antiterrorist law[28] introduced by the government after the attacks of July 2005. This law represents a new step forward in the ability of the British government to criminalize any political action as well as any support for such action or even any radical opposition in words. Not only is the materiality of the acts in question no longer necessary to prosecute such behaviors, neither is the intention attributed to the accused individuals. The specific contribution of this law is this: it suffices that a person, no matter who, states that he or she felt encouraged to commit terrorist acts by words uttered by another individual. It then becomes possible to prosecute the speaker of those words. The person who speaks is thus responsible for the manner in which his or her speech may be received, regardless of his or her intention. It is no longer necessary that there be a material link between the content of the speech, for example words of support for the Palestinian resistance, and the acts that they "incited," for example the placing of bombs in the London metro. Prosecution may proceed solely on the basis that a court concludes that these words created a "climate" favorable to terrorism.

This law also gives universal competence to British courts to label any political action anywhere in the world as terrorist and thus to criminalize any support, whether actual or in words only, of these acts.

The law introduces new crimes. It aims at dealing with "acts preparatory to terrorism," "training for terrorism" as well as "encouraging terrorism."

The reasons for creating the new crime concerning acts preparatory to terrorism are not obvious. The Terrorism Act 2000 already considered as a serious crime the fact of "collecting information" or "possessing documents" that could be used for terrorism.[29] That law also provides for possible imprisonment up to ten years for any person in possession of an article "in circumstances which give rise to a reason-

---

28  Jeannie Shawl, "UK anti-terror bill becames law, *Jurist,* March 30, 2006 , http://jurist.law.pitt.edu/paperchase/2006/03/uk-anti-terror-bill-becames-law.php.

29  Terrorism Act 2000, Section 58., http://www.opsi.gov.uk/acts/acts2000/20000011.htm#aofs.

able suspicion that his possession is for a purpose connected with the commission, preparation or instigation of an act of terrorism."[30]

This law truly introduces something new with the idea of encouraging terrorism, which "applies to a statement that is likely to be understood by members of the public to whom it is published as a direct or indirect encouragement or other inducement to them to the commisson, preparation or instigation of acts of terrorism or Convention offenses"[31] The offense exists not only when the person intended to incite terrorism or knew that terrorism was likely to be incited by his or her actions but took the actions anyway, but also wherever a reasonable person would conclude that the statement was likely to incite terrorism, regardless of what the speaker intended.

Indirect encouragement of terrorism is defined as a statement praising the committing of acts of terrorism, a statement from which people can "reasonably" conclude that they were encouraged to commit such acts.

Thus the law includes a crime of direct incitement, when the person directly defends violence, and indirect incitement, when the person does not directly defend violence, but makes a statement that can be understood as something likely to incite violence.

## A Crime of "Recklessness"

The crimes of encouraging terrorism and indirect incitement do not require that there be any intention of urging other persons to commit criminal acts. A person can commit the act of encouraging terrorism without realizing it. The crime of indirect incitement exists if a person who publishes a statement is simply "reckless" as to the probability that his or her discourse may or may not be understood as encouraging terrorism. This is how the law defines "reckless": "the cases in which a person is to be taken as reckless ... include any case in which he could not reasonably have failed to be aware of that likelihood."[32] The use of the term "include" suggests that this

---

30   Terrorism Act 2000, Section 57.

31   Terrorism Act 2006, clause 1(1). http://www.opsi.gov/uk/acts/acts2006/ukga_2006011_en_pdf.

32   Terrorism Bill, clause 1(3).

article applies to the case where the person who speaks is unaware of the effects that his or her words may have.

The novelty of this crime of encouraging terrorism is that the crime exists without any intentionality on the part of the person who has allegedly committed the crime. This change in the concept of incitement is in opposition to the tradition of common law. Incitement in criminal law has always included an intentional component. The alleged criminal must know that his or her words or acts can have the consequence of urging another to commit a crime.

The government justifies introducing the crime of "indirect incitement to terrorism" by arguing that it is a question of ratifying the Council of Europe Convention on the Prevention of Terrorism,[33] signed in April 2005. Article 5 of the Convention defines "public provocation" as "the distribution, or otherwise making available, of a message to the public, with the intention to incite the commission of a terrorist offense, where such conduct, whether or not directly advocating terrorist offenses, causes a danger that one or more such offences may be committed."[34]

The Convention requires that States "adopt such measures as may be necessary to establish public provocation to commit a terrorist offense ... when committed unlawfully and intentionally, as a criminal offense under its domestic law."[35]

This Convention indeed introduces ideas such as direct or indirect incitement to terrorism. However, the crime is committed when a public statement, "with the intent to incite the commission of a terrorist act," "causes a danger" such that a crime can be committed. One must be able to establish a link between the affirmation that is considered provocative and the act that is to be prevented.[36] The British law, while it generally follows in the footsteps of the Conven-

---

33  Council of Europe Convention on the Prevention of Terrorism, May 2005, http://conventions.coe.int/Treaty/EN/Treaties/Html/196.htm

34  http://conventions.coe.int/Treaty/Commun/QueVoulezVous.asp?NT=196&CM=8&DF=19/07/2005&CL=ENG

35  *Ibid.*, Article 5(2).

36  "Briefing on the Terrorism Bill 2005," *Human Rights Watch*, November 2005, http://hrw.org/backgrounder/eca/uk1105/uk1105.pdf.

tion of the Council of Europe, clearly goes much further since, in order for a crime to have been committed, neither an element of intentionality nor the existence of a concrete crime incited by a statement is necessary.

The new British law openly violates the principle of legality, according to which crimes must be precisely defined in order to avoid any possible arbitrariness at the level of interpretation. Alvaro Gil-Robles, Council of Europe Commissioner for Human Rights, in his commentary on Article 5 of the Convention, which includes the idea of indirect incitement, asserts that "...it would be particularly difficult to predict the circumstances in which a message would be considered as public provocation to commit an act of terrorism and those in which it would represent the legitimate exercise of the right to express an idea or voice criticism freely."[37] This observation is even more pertinent if one were to apply it to the British law, since in the latter the intention to commit a crime, the presence of a danger and the existence of a material crime are not necessary to criminalize the statement.

*Criminalizing a "Climate" Favorable to Terrorism*

Members of the House of Commons reintroduced a measure that had been removed by the House of Lords in January concerning the new crime of "glorifying terrorism." The Lords had concluded that this proposed crime constituted a danger for freedom of expression. In order to circumvent this vote, the government had reintroduced the idea of glorification, by making it a crime of "indirect incitement of terrorism." Making the glorification of terrorism a specific offense has always been an open objective of the political authorities, however, even so far as including it as a point in the electoral program of the Labour Party.

The determination of the government to reintroduce this idea at any price cannot easily be understood. The crime of "indirect incite-

---

37  Opinion of the Commissionner for Human Rigths, Alvaro Gil-Robles, on the draft Convention on the Prevention of Terrorism, Strasbourg, February 2, 2005, BCommH(2005)1, p. 28, http://www.coe.int/T/E/Legal_affairs/Legal_co-operation/Fight_against_terrorism/3_CODEXTER/Working_Documents/BCommDH_2005_1_E Final - Opinion on the draft conv.pdf.

ment" already allows a degree of arbitrariness, of which glorification, following the vote in the House of Lords, had become a secondary constitutive element.

According to the government, this new crime aims to punish those who "praise" or "celebrate" acts of terrorism. The government claims that it wants, above all, to penalize radical imams, who are presented as "preachers of hate." The Conservative and Liberal parties defended the position that criminalizing indirect incitement of terrorism was more than enough. For Charles Clarke, that definition of a crime would be too narrow because it would not cover writings or Internet sites.

The term "glorification" is not defined. In response to this observation, the Home Secretary stated that it would not be necessary to be more specific because "those who seek to recruit terrorism know what it means."[38]

The government's interest in introducing this new crime can be understood, however, if it is observed that MPs also adopted an amendment that specifies that the police do not need to request a warrant from a judge to force an Internet access provider to remove material deemed to glorify terrorism from web sites. The vague character of the new law makes it possible to separate the crime of preparing terrorist acts from any material basis. It is thus possible to criminalize the fact of visiting a "jihadist" web site. Such a crime can be described as "inappropriate use of the Internet."[39]

The use of such a vague notion of criminal activity authorizes all interpretations. An individual could be charged with glorifying terrorism if "the circumstances and manner of the statement's publication (taken together with its contents) were such that it would be reasonable for members of the public to whom it was published to

---

38  Alan Travis and Patrick Winters, "Extremist Muslim Groups to be Banned," *The Guardian*, February 16, 2006.

39  "A briefing document on the government's anti-terrorism proposals," *Protect Our Rights*, p. 4, http://www.blink.org.uk/docs/protectourrightsbriefing.pdf.

assume that the statement expressed the views of that person or had his endorsement."[40]

According to the Home Secretary, Charles Clarke, this crime is necessary in order to take action against organizations "which tried to promote terrorism and created an atmosphere where impressionable young men thought suicide bombings were a noble and holy activity."[41] In the same vein, Clarke also stated that this crime is justified because "people who glorify terrorism help to create a climate in which terrorism is regarded as in some way acceptable."[42]

A statement considered to be glorifying terrorism can be made about particular past events, possible future events or simply be a general statement. The crime of glorifying terrorism can thus be applied to past events, without any concrete relation to the attributed consequence: the current terrorist "climate" or "atmosphere." The offense would apply to anything occurring within 20 years of the publication of the statement to which the offense is related, "unless the Secretary of State had made an order specifying conduct or events which occurred outside this period."[43] Thus the actual period of time involved is somewhat indeterminate.

### Political Crimes

The Prime Minister stated that the "glorification" or "justification" of terrorism is behavior that can lead to expulsion from the country, closing of mosques or use of "control orders." The British government has defined "unacceptable behaviors" which could possibly lead to deportation of the incriminated foreigner. These include, notably, "fomenting, justifying or glorifying terrorist violence," "seeking to provoke terrorist acts," or "fomenting hate possibly leading to violence among various communities in the United Kingdom." Thus the

---

40  "The Terrorism Bill," House of Lords, Research Paper 05/66, October 20, 2005, p. 15. http://parliament.uk/commons/lib/research//rp2005/rp05-066pdf.

41  MPs back ban on glorifying terror," *BBC News*, http://news.bbc.co.uk/1/hi/uk_politics/4714578.stm.

42  Beth Gardiner, "Britain's House of Commons votes to outlaw the glorification of terrorism," http://cnews.canoe.ca/CNEWS/World/WarOnTerrorism/2006/02/15/1444273-ap.html.

43  *Ibid.*

new law provides a legal basis for the administrative decision to ban groups that are considered to be glorifying terrorism.

Ken Livingstone, mayor of London, like civil liberties organizations, is not convinced by the statements of minister Charles Clarke claiming that the intentions of the government are not "to stifle freedom of expression or legitimate debate on religions or other themes."[44] He claimed that these new measures do not stand up to the "Nelson Mandela test." "If the law had been in existence twenty-five years ago in Great Britain, the partisans of Nelson Mandela would have been expelled from our country because they supported the campaign of bomb attacks against the racist apartheid regime in South Africa," he stated. "If yes, then Parliament should rise up against this measure," he added.[45]

For him, these measures should not be allowed to prohibit someone like Youssef al-Qardaoui, an influential Qatari religious figure, from entering British territory. The latter has been prohibited from staying in the United States because of his statements justifying the suicide attacks in Israel. If this prohibition should be confirmed "there would be very few imams or militants accepted into British territory because the vast majority of them identify with the struggle of the Palestinian people."[46]

In fact, the new English law gives the government the possibility to proscribe any political organization and imprison or deport any person who expresses, has expressed or will express a political opinion different from the government's position concerning a violent conflict anywhere in the world. For example, the statement of the journalist John Pilger during an interview on Australian television,[47] in which he stated that the resistance against American forces in Iraq

---

44 "Terrorisme : Londres publie une liste des comportements qui justifient une expulsion," *Le Monde avec AFP et Reuters,* 24/8/2005.

45 *Ibid.*

46 *Ibid.*

47 ABC News (Australia), Interview transcript: "Pilger on the US and terrorism," March 10, 2004(online), http://www.abc.net.au/lateline/content/2004/s1063309.htm (retrieved November 15, 2005).

is legitimate and desirable, would fall under the field of application of Article 1 of this law.

In order to understand the full significance of these new crimes of indirect incitement and glorification of terrorism, one should connect them to Terrorism Act 2000 which defines a terrorist act as one that entails "serious damage of property," is "designed to influence the government or to intimidate the public or a section of the public" and is "made for the purpose of advancing a political, religious or ideological cause."[48]

As we have already noted, such a definition of terrorism makes it possible to criminalize not only actions with religious references, but also social movements for the defense of political and economic rights. It is immediately clear what use the government can make of these new crimes to attack non-violent actions, statements of solidarity for individuals who have committed acts considered to be terrorist or simply statements and/or policies that are hostile to the political, economic or social actions of the government or an international organization.

Compared to the Terrorism Act 2000, the Terrorism Act 2006 is a new step in the erosion of civil liberties. The Terrorism Act 2000, like the antiterrorist laws adopted at the European Union level, allows for the prosecution of any political activity that the government considers to be unwarranted. It criminalizes the objective of a crime's perpetrator, specifically the aim of putting pressure on a government or an international organization. It establishes a crime of intention.

The Terrorism Act 2006 calls into question the very possibility of expressing a political opinion that the government considers unacceptable, whether this concern internal affairs or foreign policy. Its provisions are even less concerned with material acts than the earlier law and focus completely on the realm of mere possibility. The intention of a person to achieve a specific result from his or her statements is no longer a necessary consideration for prosecution. The only thing that matters is the way in which those statements may be interpreted,

---

48  Terrorism Act 2000, Section 1.

without there necessarily being any objective relationship between such statements and the criminal acts in question.

## Deterritorialization of Criminal Law

The Terrorism Bill 2006 represents an important step in relation to the Terrorism Act 2000 in its capacity to criminalize increasingly larger sections of the population. Clause 21 of the new law makes it possible to extend the reasons that authorize placing stigmatized persons outside the law. Terrorism Act 2000 allows prosecution of violent individuals and organizations. To be a member of such an organization is a crime[49] which can lead to a sentence of ten years in prison. Support for such organizations is also prosecuted.[50] The notion of support is not limited to financial or material aspects. It is sufficient "to support or further the activities of an organization by literally any method." To wear a distinctive sign or clothing "or to wear or display any article which can give rise to reasonable suspicion of membership or support of a proscribed group" can be prosecuted.[51] The new law makes it possible, by means of the concept of glorification, to attack non-violent groups and to criminalize individuals who support violent groups even if only by speech or writings. It attacks what it calls "unlawful" glorification.[52]

Article 17 of the Terrorism Bill provides for an extra-territorial extension of the competence of British courts concerning the new crimes: the encouragement of terrorism, distribution of publications, and preparation and training for acts of terrorism. This extension also applies to the offenses covered in the Terrorism Act 2000: belonging to a prohibited organization and the conspiracy, attempt, assistance and encouragement to commit terrorist acts. A British court can prosecute anyone who commits one of these acts anywhere outside of the United Kingdom. This measure does not ap-

---

49   *Ibid.*, Section 11(1).

50   *Ibid.*, Section 12.

51   *Ibid.*, Section 13.

52   "Terrorism bill, Liberty briefing for Second Reading in the House of Lords," *Liberty* ,November 2005, http://www.liberty-human-rights.org.uk/resources/policy-papers/2005/terrorism-bill-2nd-reading-lords.PDF.

ply only to citizens, but to any person involved, whatever his/her nationality may be.

The concepts of indirect incitement and glorification of terrorism formulated in the Terrorism Bill give to the executive authorities and British courts the power, not only to criminalize any form of support for a social movement or any action designed to put pressure on the English government, but also to determine what is good and what is bad anywhere in the world. This law denies the very essence of politics. There are no longer conflicts of interest, but simply a fight of good against evil.

It also establishes solidarity among constituted authorities in relation to their political opposition by criminalizing any act of armed resistance as well as any act of material solidarity or verbal or written support for groups or persons who defend, or who defended in the past, such resistance. In fact, to take a political position can become a crime.

The Terrorism Bill represents the most advanced point in setting up a new legal order. The law is no longer what delimits the prerogatives of the government, but, on the contrary, what eliminates any barrier to its activity. The legal order becomes the symbolization of non-law. Any delimitation between the materiality of an act and its mere possibility is increasingly blurred. The crime exists because the government has proclaimed its possibility.

# 3

## THE FIGHT AGAINST TERRORISM IN
## THE EUROPEAN UNION

In July 2001, the European Parliament approved a report by Deputy Marco Cappato, rapporteur of the Committee on Civil Liberties, Justice and Home Affairs, favoring the strict control over access by the police to data collected by Internet access providers.

The report of the Council of Europe's Legal Service, made public on October 12, 2001, also explained that the government of the Union already had all the powers necessary to intercept communications in order to combat terrorism. Agreeing with the position of the Parliament, this report opposed extending prerogatives appropriate to antiterrorist activities to investigations concerned with other sorts of crimes.

The Parliament also opposed the insistent demands of President Bush to remove from the European Directive on the Protection of Personal Data the principle of automatically erasing connection data. On May 30, 2002, following pressure from the Council and from different governments, the Parliament went back on its preceding position and passed the proposed Directive from the Council that authorized the preventive retention of connection data. It thus authorized setting up a general and exploratory surveillance of Internet users.

The European Parliament thus conformed to demands by different European police forces and the Americans expressed through the working group of the Council ENFOPOL. The antiterrorist campaigns developed after the attacks had thus made it possible to modify certain relations of forces at the level of European institutions. The fight of the European Parliament already appeared as a rear-guard action, the last institutional center of resistance in the face of a general political desire to reduce public and private liberties. The European Union was behind compared to a number of Member States that had already set up the legal apparatus to authorize the retention of computer data, as in Belgium,[1] or in France,[2] or, in the English case,[3] to permit the police to read email in real time.

## THE JOINT CRIMINALIZATION OF TERRORISM

As a result of an agreement on a proposal presented by the Commission, European Ministers of Justice and Home Affairs adopted the European Union Framework Decision on Combating Terrorism on December 6, 2001.[4] This measure was introduced as a response to the September 11 attacks. However, the speed with which the text of the proposal was introduced confirms the fact that the proposal was already devised earlier and brought out of storage following the attacks. A preliminary version of the proposed European Union Framework Decision on Combating Terrorism had been introduced on September 19.[5] Its declared objective was to reconcile the laws of Member States concerning terrorism.

The integration of a common European criminalization of terrorism will lead to significant changes in national laws of Member States. Relative to the high stakes involved, the debates were limited. The process can even be characterized as a technocratic decision that avoids all political debate and gives far more weight to the work of experts than it is due. The essentials of the draft were provided by the Committee of Permanent Representatives (COROPER), a perma-

---

1   The law of November 22, 2000 criminalizes the unauthorized intrusion into a computer system and orders the retention of computer data for a period of at least 12 months. *Moniteur belge*, 3 février 2001.

2   The "Bloche" law, adopted in 2000, already required Internet users to identify themselves prior to bringing a site online and ordered web site hosts to keep a current file containing the identity of internet users opening a site as well as a complete listing of the names and addresses of users. The law on everyday security, adopted on October 31, 2001, introduces supplementary measures that order the retention of computer data for a period of 12 months.

3   The Terrorism Act 2000, which came into force in February 2000, puts hacking into the same category as terrorism. The Regulation of Investigatory Power Bill already provided for the possibility of unscrambled reading of email by the police thanks to the installation of black boxes at Internet access providers.

4   Council Framework Decision of 13 June 2002 on Combating Terrorism, *Official Journal of the European*, 22.6.2002, L 164.

5   Proposal for a Council Framework Decision on Combating Terrorism, COM(2001)521 final, 2001/0217(CNS), Brussels, 19.9.2001.

nent committee of functionaries attached to the European Council, as well as by the "Article 36 Committee," a working group of this committee.

Paradoxically, the proposal's preamble justifies the creation of a common definition of terrorism because the requirement for double incrimination raises obstacles that must be overcome for certain forms of legal cooperation to occur.[6] The introduction of this proposal, relative to the fight against terrorism, was made at the same time as the introduction of the proposed Framework Decision creating a European arrest warrant that, precisely, removes the double incrimination requirement for a set of offenses, including terrorism. The discussions concerning these two proposals were, moreover, carried out at the same time. Thus one can assume that the objective of coming up with a common definition of terrorism is quite different than the one offered by the Commission.

### Definition of a Terrorist Organization

The purpose of the law is to define a terrorist act, but also to clarify the concept of a terrorist organization. The stakes in this latter definition are significant since, in the absence of an offense, certain organizations, if they are designated as terrorist, could be subjected to particular measures of surveillance or constraint, such as having their assets frozen.

In order to define this type of organization, explicit reference is made to the Joint Action of December 21, 1998 relative to participation in a criminal organization.[7] The Framework Decision understands by a terrorist group "a structured association established over a period of time, of more than two people, acting in concert to commit terrorist offenses."

The term "structured association" refers to an organization that is not formed by chance to commit an offense straight away and "that

---

6    Proposal for a Council Framework, p. 8.

7    Joint Action of 21 December 1998 adopted by the Council on the basis of article K.3 of the Treaty on European Union, on making it a criminal offence to participate in a criminal organisation in the Member States of the European Union. *Official Journal of the European Communities*, 29.12.1998, L351, p.1.

does not necessarily have formally defined roles for its members, continuity in its composition or a developed structure."

This definition is particularly elastic. What would a structured association be without a developed structure, without continuity in its composition and without defined roles for its members? In fact, any organization can be made to fit this definition, for example, an informal gathering in a demonstration or a short-lived organization to assist political prisoners.

The definition of a terrorist organization is immediately at issue in the preparation of lists of organizations designated as terrorist, either by the European Council or police institutions. There are public lists and others that are closely guarded secrets. For the latter, of course, there are no problems of definition.

The political branch of Hamas became a terrorist organization, included in a European Union list, as a result of a political decision taken following American political pressure. The purpose of the public lists is to confiscate or freeze the assets of the listed organizations.[8] The purpose of the secret lists, such as the Europol list, is to coordinate intelligence work and justify the use of special investigation techniques.

*Definition of a Terrorist Act*

The Framework Decision contains a list of crimes that are already considered common law offenses in the criminal codes of Member States. These include, among others, murder, bodily injuries, kidnapping, hostage taking, extortion, fabrication or possession of explosives, and the unlawful seizure of or damage to State or government facilities, means of public transport, infrastructure facilities, places of public use and property. Offenses related to releasing contaminating substances, or causing fires, explosions or floods, interfering with or disrupting the supply of water, power or other fundamental resource and attacks through interference with an information system are also covered in the same paragraph.

---

8   Council Decision of 17 June 2002 implementing article 2(3) of Regulation (EC) No 2580/2001 on specific restrictive measures directed against certain persons and entities with a view to combating terrorism and repealing Decision 2002/334/EC. *Official Journal of the European Communities*, 18.6.2002, L160/26.

The argument advanced to justify setting up a specific category of terrorist offenses is that they differ from the same common law crimes, even if they can generally be assimilated to the latter, because of their concrete effect. The difference results from the fact that terrorist offenses undermine the structures of society and the State. They are defined "as offenses intentionally committed by an individual or a group against one or more countries, their institutions or people, with the aim of intimidating them and seriously altering or destroying the political, economic or social structures of a country."[9] Thus the accusation of terrorism rests on the idea that the motivation of the perpetrator of the offense is different, even if the acts themselves are similar to common offenses. The definition of a terrorist offense includes an objective element, the enumerated crimes, and a subjective element, the perpetrator's intention.

Among the stated "crimes," which are added to existing national laws, such as occupying and seizing means of public transport or interfering with or disrupting the supply of water or electricity (the preparatory texts also referred to the seizure of infrastructure facilities and places of public use), are means used by the antiglobalization struggle, civil disobedience movements and union struggles. These additions are essential in order to understand the specificity of the Framework Decision and the most recent legislation. They indicate what groups are aimed at in this criminalization.

While these different acts are considered terrorist in so far as they result in putting human life into danger, this restrictive condition leaves considerable room for judgment on the part of judges in that the criminalization of terrorism also punishes the threat of committing the listed offenses.

*A Crime of Intention*

Although admitting that certain acts such as aggravated theft, drawing up false administrative documents or blackmail cannot be considered in themselves terrorist behaviors, the Council considers them, however, as offenses linked to such activities if their "aim can be, in

---

9   Proposal for a Council Framework, p. 8.

the end, to make possible a terrorist act not yet determined or known by the perpetrators at the moment they commit the act."[10]

In this case, the qualification of a crime as terrorist does not depend on the act itself but on the fact that it could be linked to an action recognized as terrorist or to the fact of attributing to the perpetrators the abstract intention of intimidating the population or the authorities, even if the concrete aim, "the carrying out of a terrorist offense, is not yet determined or known to the perpetrator of the criminal act." Here terrorist criminality is increasingly separated from any concrete basis in facts. Instead, it is the result of a speculative construction in which the acts committed and their link can be interpreted à posteriori.

Each Member State should also take necessary measures to make punishable the act of leading a terrorist group as well as participating in the activities of such a group "by supplying information or material resources or by financing such activities and by having knowledge that this participation will contribute to the criminal activities of the group."

Inciting, complicity in and attempting a crime can also be prosecuted. The criminality of participating, even indirectly, in the activities and not just the offenses of a group constitutes a significant change in criminality. This change is part of the trend begun with the legal definition of a criminal organization. Traditionally, criminal law punished just the attempt alone, prior to the crime. This idea implies the existence of a material fact, of definite acts considered criminal. If the offense could not be committed, that results from factors that elude the will of the perpetrator of the acts. Prosecution is a reaction; it takes place after the acts have occurred even if they were unsuccessful.

The approach taken in this Framework Decision is, on the contrary, preventative. It permits prosecution before the criminal acts have taken place on the simple presumption that they could have occurred. Such an intention is attributed to the prosecuted persons.

---

10　Emmanuel Barbe, «Une triple étape pour le troisième pilier de l'Union européenne, mandat d'arrêt européen, terrorisme et Eurojust», *Revue du Marché commun et de l'Union européenne*, no. 454, janvier 2002, p. 9.

## A Subjective Definition

A terrorist offense is not stipulated objectively by a list of material acts (murders, kidnappings, attempted assassination and the like), but by the intention of the perpetrator of these crimes. This subjective element consists in the aim "of seriously intimidating a population, destabilizing the fundamental structures of a country or compelling public authorities to carry out or not carry out some act or other." It is the subjective element, the objective pursued, that is determinant for characterizing the crime as terrorist. Concrete offenses only form the context in which this definition can take place.

The concept of destabilization is already, in itself, eminently subjective. It is all the more so because it does not concern a result but an intention and the qualification "seriously" does not provide any precision. In fact, the definition of the concept of a terrorist act, be it in its subjective or objective aspect, strictly depends on the policies of the antiterrorist struggle. It results from the subjectivity of the ruling authorities, their interpretation of social reality, their definition of the sphere of politics, and their ability to impose the government's point of view.

Thus, if the definition establishes a list of acts, the latter are not defined in a clear and univocal manner. This shortcoming is compensated for by the introduction of a subjective element, the intention of the perpetrator, which defines these offenses as terrorist.

The move from the precise description of an act to a determination of the nature of the latter based on its aim implies a radical change in criminal doctrine. While classical criminal law does not view the motive as a constitutive element of an offense, here it is the intention that is determinant. It is no longer the act that is criminalized and punished, but the criminal potential of a person or organization. Thus, such a person or organization will be subjected to a whole series of measures of surveillance and repression. This approach is particularly clear in the formation of lists of organizations designated as criminal by European institutions. At no moment do these different levels of authority have to justify the measures taken.

*A Political Criminality*

The directly political character of the criminality results from the intention of the perpetrator. The offense is considered terrorist, not only when its "aim is to destroy the political, economic and social structures of a country," but also when its "aim is seriously to destabilize."

The concepts of destabilization and destruction of economic or political structures of a country make possible a frontal attack on social movements. Margaret Thatcher attempted to apply an antiterrorist law to the miners strike at the beginning of the 1980's using these arguments.

An offense is also defined as terrorist when its "aim is unduly to compel public authorities or an international organization to carry out or not carry out some act or other." This definition is vague and allows for a very wide interpretation. Any social movement has the effect of intimidating a more or less significant part of the population and aims at compelling the government to initiate certain acts or not. The terms "serious" or "unduly" do not provide any objective precision for describing the act. It is the government itself that will determine if the pressure it is under is normal or undue.

As a whole, the category of terrorism is constructed in such a way that "it is governments that decide who is a terrorist and who is not."[11] "The term terrorism fluctuates according to ethical and political opposition. It is an administrative label filled with legal weight when it appears in different penal codes. But for all that it is not an effective conceptualization to account for the violence of clandestine organizations against States."[12] The war against terrorism is more a means of criminalizing those who oppose a particular conception of political policy than a means of countering attacks.

The freedom-killing character of the Framework Decision is so apparent that, in the preamble, it is stipulated that "nothing in this Framework Decision may be interpreted as being intended to reduce or restrict fundamental rights or freedoms such as the right to strike, freedom of assembly, of association or of expression, including the

---

11  Daniel Herman and Didier Bigo, "Les politiques de lutte contre le terrorisme," p. 74.

12  *Ibid.*, p. 75.

right of everyone to form and to join trade unions with others for the protection of his or her interests and the related right to demonstrate."[13] But this is a commitment without any legal force that leaves each Member State free to pursue policies of its own choice in this matter,

## The Idea of Seizure

The directly political character of the criminalization of terrorism does not result only from its subjective element. The list of crimes that constitute the objective element also includes ideas that display a strong political connotation. The concept of "seizure" is representative in this respect.

The initial text presented by the Commission was even more explicit and redundant in its formulation. It spoke of "unlawful seizure" of infrastructure facilities, of public places, and of both private and public property. The preamble specifies that this last offense "could include, for instance, acts of urban violence."[14]

This concept is particularly illuminating on the objective of this reform. Seizure is the act of seizing something or someone by force. Seizure of a public or private facility by a social movement always has an illegal character. The seizure of facilities is in conflict with the right to property or to use such facilities. It was thus paradoxical to imply in a text that was supposed to be introduced into criminal codes that some seizures could be legal.[15] The government itself would apply the qualification, illegal or legal, according to the stakes involved and the relation of forces at the time. It is the result of a political decision.

In the final version of the text, the simple idea of seizing the means of public transport was retained, the qualification "illegal" having been abandoned. Any seizure, any process of collective reappropriation could all the same be criminalized. The significance of such leg-

---

13  Council Framework Decision of 13 June 2002 on Combating Terrorism, 2002/475/JHA, p. 2.

14  Proposal for a Council Framework, p. 9.

15  John Brown, "Analyse des propositions antiterroristes de l'Union européene," November 20, 2001, text available by request from the author at johannesbrown@hotmail.com.

islation in the context of the privatization of public services can be seen. Any collective seizure that aims at preventing a private seizure, a privatization, could be criminalized.[16]

## LISTS OF TERRORIST ORGANIZATIONS

The Council of the European Union is not content with intervening into the criminal codes of Member States by imposing a specific criminalization of terrorism; it has also issued a list of organizations and persons named as terrorist.[17] These lists are not aimed only at persons or organizations that commit or participate in terrorist acts but persons or entities that "facilitate" such acts. The concept of "facilitate" is not defined, which allows very broad interpretations.

The first lists issued by the Council contained the names of organizations and persons linked to the Middle East conflict (Hezbollah, Jihad, Hamas) as well as Basque and Irish movements.[18] Then national liberation movements conducting an armed struggle in their countries were included, such as the Popular Front for the Liberation of Palestine (PFLP), the Workers Party of Kurdistan (PKK) or the Martyrs Brigade of Al-Aqsa, linked to Fatah. Although these organizations have not carried out violent acts in Europe, their activities are disrupted or prohibited on the territory of the Union. Also criminalized are organizations that use armed struggle as a means of political emancipation. Gradually, any military opposition to a constituted power is stigmatized as terrorist.

---

16 It is, moreover, interesting to note that, within the context of the negotiations on the General Agreement on Trade in Services, the lobbies that put pressure on the WTO did not hesitate to speak of seizing these services when stating their demands. See Coordination pour le Contrôle Citoyen de l'OMC, "Alerte generale à la capture des services publics," avril 2000, p. 8.

17 Council Regulation (EC) No 2580/2001 of 27 December 2001 on specific restrictive measures directed against certain persons and entities with a view to combating terrorism, *Official Journal of the European Communities*, 28.12.2001, L344, p. 70-75; Council Decision of 12 December 2002 implementing Article 2(3) of Regulation (EC) No 2580/2001 on specific restrictive measures directed against certain persons and entities with a view to combating terrorism and repealing Decision 2002/848/EC, *Official Journal of the European Communities*, 13.12.2002, L337, p. 85-86; Council Decision of 2 April 2004 implementing Article 2(3) of Regulation (EC) No 2580/2001 on specific restrictive measures directed against certain persons and entities with a view to combating terrorism and repealing Decision 2003/902/EC, *Official Journal of the European Communities*, 3 April 2004, L99, p. 28-29.

18 Council Common Position of 27 December 2001 on the application of specific measures to combat terrorism (2001/931/CFSP), *Official Journal of the European Communities*, 28 December 2001, p. 93-96.

The inclusion of a group on the list is not the result of a judicial act but a desire of national executives, which do not have to justify their decisions or prove their allegations. Regulation number (CE) 2580/2001 makes it possible, in fact, to adopt specific restrictive measures against persons or entities within the context of the antiterrorist struggle. For the organization or person concerned, this results in the freezing of their financial assets and economic resources. This regulation is the European version of a United Nations resolution.[19]

The decision-making process prevents any debate. These lists are the result of a "written procedure." The proposals are adopted if no explicit objections are raised. These exceptional procedures are, of course, unverifiable and no recourse is possible. An act of the Executive becomes the truth of the thing judged. There is no more formal separation of powers; the Executive and its autonomous agencies assume the role of a judge.

Following the attacks of March 11, 2004 in Spain, it was proposed, among measures designed to strengthen antiterrorist cooperation, that new organizations would be added to the lists on the basis of a vote of the qualified majority, instead of the usual procedure of unanimous decision-making. This new arrangement can only reinforce the arbitrary character of the procedure. A person is designated as a terrorist, not because of having committed a crime, but because of being a member of or participating in the activities, even legal ones, of an organization designated by the majority as being terrorist. The procedure, the ritual of political decision-making, is substituted for legal truth.

The European Police Office (Europol) also has a secret list. Any person suspected of being a member of or participating in the activities, even legal ones (for example, a defense committee for political prisoners), of an organization that is on the list, can legally be made the object of special surveillance and wiretapping measures.

The inclusion of a person on such a list entails not only the suspension of his/her public and private liberties but also his/her death in

---

19   United Nations Security Council Resolution 1373 (2001) of 28 September 2001 http://www.un.org/Docs/scres/2001/sc2001.htm.

civil terms. A concrete example[20] will help to understand this process. José Maria Sison, founder of the Communist Party of the Philippines, has lived in the Netherlands since 1988. Although the government had always refused to grant him the status of political refugee, he benefited from welfare as someone seeking asylum. Overnight, without prior notice, all his bank accounts (containing 200 Euros) were frozen, his social benefit was eliminated, although he has no permission to work, and he had to leave the house granted to him by the social service. These measures were justified by his inclusion on August 13, 2003 in the Dutch list of so-called terrorists. This decision was made following the inclusion of this person, on August 12, 2003, on the list from the American Office of Foreign Assets Control. Since then, José Maria Sison has been added to the list from the Council of the European Union. The Netherlands now justifies upholding the measures taken against him because of his appearance on this latter list.

There exists no possibility of recourse following the inclusion of a person or an organization on such a list. The file upon which such inclusion is based is secret. Any requests from the defense are met with the response that the information is secret and necessarily so for the protection of the intelligence services. This is an administrative procedure that flouts the rights of the defense and has more significant consequences for the life of affected persons than those engendered by a judicial decision, as the latter would be proportionate. Such inclusion entails not only a political death, but also a social one.

PRIOR METHODS OF CRIMINALIZING TERRORISM

The Framework Decision of the European Union relative to terrorism, ratified by national parliaments, brings substantial modifications into the criminal codes and procedures of Member States. The change is more important for States that do not have specific laws. A good way to evaluate these changes is to analyze the transformations that have taken place in countries that already had antiterrorist legislation.

---

20  Jan Fermon, communication to the colloquium "Législations antiterroristes européennes et protection des droits de l'homme," Progress Lawyers Network, Brussels, February 27, 2004.

A great diversity concerning the prosecution of terrorist offenses existed in the Member States. There were three methods of incrimination for terrorism.[21] The first consisted of using the classic concepts, such as murder, assassination, attacks on the physical integrity of people or goods or, more recently, airline hijacking and hostage taking, as the basis for indictments. What is more, the concepts of criminal conspiracy and criminal organization already allowed for the punishment of anyone participating in acts of terrorism as well as belonging to an organization designated as terrorist.

The second method resulted from the use of peripheral incriminations. These were generally adopted within the context of the fight against terrorism. However, there is no specific incrimination involved. The problem is approached under the procedural angle. This second method submits infractions that are already otherwise punishable to a particular system.[22] The objective of this process is to submit the prosecution of an offense, at the stage of the indictment, investigation or trial, to a particular procedural system rather than the usual system.

The third technique of prosecution was to prepare a definition of terrorism that adds an offense to the list of punishable crimes.

Six Member States already had specific legislation. Five Member States, the United Kingdom, Ireland, Germany, Italy and Spain had developed a specific definition of terrorism as a crime. As for France, it used a secondary incrimination method where the concept of terrorism was an aggravating circumstance in committed offenses.

All these penal approaches to the phenomenon of terrorism have a common element: they make the destabilization of political or economic power a defining element of a terrorist offense.

*Belgium: Standard Method of Incrimination*

In Belgium, beyond the standard crimes, such as murder, bomb attack or hijacking, recourse was also made to the idea of criminal con-

---

21  Adrien Masset, *La repression du terrorisme*, dissertation presented to obtain the degree of Doctor of Law, University of Liege, academic year 1993-1994.

22  Adrien Masset, *op. cit.*, p. 16.

spiracy, found in articles 322-325 of the criminal code that focuses on "conspiring to attack persons or property." Also, appeal was made to the law of July 29, 1934 prohibiting private militias. The latter was modified on August 5, 1992, by the law on the function of the police, which prohibits "all private militias or any other organization of private individuals the aim of which is to resort to force or to deputize for the army or police, interfere with their actions or act as substitutes for them."

The crime prosecuted under the concept of criminal conspiracy exists separately from any attacks against persons or property. These articles make it possible then to prosecute a simple crime of intention: the choice to belong to an organization. "Belonging to a gang must be conscious and deliberate, but this deliberate choice concerns only the existence of the conspiracy and its aim of attacking persons or property. It is not then necessary that the member seek to commit some offense or that he contemplate it, it is not even necessary that he be informed of all the current and future plans of the conspiracy, nor that he knows if any offense whatsoever will actually be committed. A certain doctrine considers that the moral element of the offense lies in the fact of consciously taking a risk by joining such a group and thus voluntarily submitting to a collective criminal will that leads to a group responsibility for any offenses."[23]

Jurisprudence and doctrine relative to the idea of criminal conspiracy indicate that "such a person can be prosecuted accordingly in the absence of the identification of other members of the conspiracy, that the requirements of what constitutes an organization are evaluated without appeal by the court, that even an ephemeral conspiracy can be punished, and that the absence of hierarchy or apparent structure is not an obstacle to incrimination, the deliberate choice of being a member of the conspiracy is identified with general fraud as the moral element of the offense."[24]

The crime of criminal conspiracy thus makes it possible to punish not only committing and participating in terrorist acts but also

---

23  J. Berkvens, "Criminele organisaties, een preadvies, Vereniging voor de vergelijkende studie van het recht van Belgïe en Nederland," Belgische sectie 1991,Doc. Parl., Sénat, 1- 326/9 p. 74.

24  Adrien Masset, *op. cit.*, p. 35.

simply belonging to the organization. While the jurisprudence associated with the concept of criminal conspiracy already creates a crime out of membership, the particular objective of the law on the definition of a criminal organization,[25] which explicitly includes the concept of a terrorist organization, is to create such a crime. This law can, of course, also be used within the context of the fight against terrorism.

### France: Peripheral Method of Incrimination

The French law of September 9, 1986 is a good example of the second procedure of criminalization. The crime possesses an objective element and a subjective one. The objective element of the terrorist offense consists of a list of 39 principal or closely related crimes.[26] The subjective element resides in the intention of the perpetrator of the offense.

A crime mentioned in the list falls under a special system of punishment when the incriminating facts "are part of an individual or collective undertaking that aims at seriously disturbing public order through intimidation or terror."

It is thus the intention that is the decisive element to qualify the act as terrorist. Since the objective is always considered to be political by the one who commits the act, "it is then the manner in which the government analyzes the intention of the perpetrator more than the perpetrator's intention itself that will count. Therefore, if he uses violence for political ends in France, he is a terrorist, since the violent form was already provided for as an offense."[27] This law does not create a new crime. The concept of terrorism is only introduced by means of criminal law procedure.

This technique is also found in the law of July 22, 1992,[28] that punishes acts of terrorism in accordance with a scale of specific penalties

---

25  "Loi relative aux organizatins criminelles," *Moniteur belge*, 26 février 1999.

26  Articles 706-716 of the old French penal code as revised by the laws of July 2, 1992 and March 1, 1994.

27  Daniel Herman et Didier Bigo, "Les politiques de lutte contre le terrorisme," *op.cit.*, p. 105.

28  Articles 421-1 to 421-5 of the penal code as inserted by law n° 92-686 of July 22, 1992.

that are, by implication, increased in comparison to penalties for the same offenses when they are not considered terrorist.

The French law of July 22, 1996 again enlarges the list of offenses that can be qualified as terrorist, adding crimes relating to criminal concealment, armed gangs and disbanded illegal organizations. (In fact, the French criminal code punishes attempts to reconstitute the latter.) This enlarged list poses a problem since the fact of accommodating in one's home anyone without identity papers could be considered an offense if it is proven, à posteriori, that that person committed or was an accomplice to terrorist acts on French territory.

This law could have gone even further if the Constitutional Council had not censured the proposed law for likening assistance to a foreign national whose papers are not in order to the presumption of assisting a terrorist undertaking.[29]

Law n° 2001-1062 of November 15, 2001 on everyday security introduced crimes regarding the management of funds or assets "knowing that they are meant to be used to commit an act of planned terrorism independently of the possible occurrence of such an act."

Across all the French laws targeting terrorism, the technique of incrimination is always the same. From the subjective element of the offense, which is constituted by the intentional character of acts "that aim at seriously disturbing public order through intimidation or terror," each new law adds to the objective element of the offense, the totality of crimes, the penalties for which will be adapted, that is, increased, if they can be interpreted in line with the intentional principle defined by the law.

The French criminal code also allowed punishment for participation in an organization devoted to perpetrating one of the mentioned acts. It was not a question of simply belonging to the organization, as in the Framework Decision of the European Union. It was necessary that there be actual participation in order to be prosecuted. It is at this level that the new French law integrating the European decision is actually to be distinguished from the former legislation. Now, any person can be prosecuted for simply belonging to a criminalized or-

---

29  Daniel Hermann et Didier Bigo "Les politiques de lutte contre le terrorisme," *op. cit.*, p.106.

ganization, without having committed criminal acts or having had the intention of doing so.

## Germany: Specific Mode of Incrimination[30]

While in the French case, terrorism is taken up only under the procedural angle, as an aggravating circumstance of already existing crimes, the German penal code recognizes in acts of terrorism a specific character and gives them autonomy in relation to other crimes.

In Germany, article 129a StGB of the penal code[31] introduces the idea of terrorism, which is set out solely on the basis of strictly enumerated offenses. The crimes mentioned are: assassination, murder or genocide, attacks on personal liberty, hostage taking, specific damages to police vehicles, arson, bomb attacks, causing floods, collective poisoning, dangerous actions against railroads, shipping or airlines, and disruption of public services, to the extent that the crime is the cause of a collective danger.

This article authorizes prosecution not only of the fact of having committed these offenses but also the fact of belonging to an organization recognized as terrorist. Recruitment of members is also punished. Any person who establishes or participates in the activities of an organization that has as its purpose to commit one of the listed crimes can be prosecuted.

Certain parallels with the definition offered in the Framework Decision of the European Union are immediately obvious. These parallels have to do with the type of offenses in question and the fact that some crimes are considered terrorist only insofar as they cause a collective danger. However, the definition in article 129a does not retain a particular moral element as the constitutive principle of the offense, such as the goal of seriously disrupting the activity or functioning of public or other institutions.

The adaptation of the Framework Decision to German law will thus undoubtedly have the consequence of extending the list of of-

---

30  Research on the German penal code was carried out by Jan Fermon.

31  Introduced by the law of August 18, 1976, modified by the law of December 19, 1986. http://www.iuscomp.org/gla/statutes/StGB.htm#129a.

fenses that can be considered as terrorist acts as well as the introduction of a new moral element.

Article 129a of the Penal Code, which criminalizes participation in and support for an organization considered to be terrorist, is supplemented by article 129b. Article 129a only allows the prosecution of persons belonging to organizations formed on the territory of the Federal Republic. Thus, based on judicial precedents, the German courts consider that Article 129a applies only to organizations having at least one branch in national territory.[32] The new Article 129b extends this criminality to persons participating in organizations considered to be terrorist formed outside the Federal Republic and having no local branches.

The Joint Action of the European Union of December 21, 1998 is invoked by the German government to justify an extension of the geographical space involved in applying the antiterrorist law to organizations with a branch or activities in the territory of one of the Member States. The attacks of September 11 are also explicitly invoked, in the preamble to the proposed law, to extend the field of application, by means of certain criteria, beyond the territory of the European Union.

Combined with the European Framework Decision and the consequences that it will have on national legislation, this extension of the field of application of Article 129 of the German penal code constitutes a new qualitative step. In fact, Germany establishes, by means of this modification, a sort of universal competence, justified by the defense of values considered to be fundamental. It is to be noted that it is not a universal competence covering just the direct participation in determinate acts but also for simply belonging to, and by implication supporting, an organization considered to be terrorist.

---

32  Bundesgerichtshof St.30, 328, 329.

Italy is conspicuous by the existence of a crime with an explicitly political motivation: the subversive association.[33] This crime is from the code "Rocco," named for Mussolini's Minister of Justice. This article has never been repealed. Italy thus combines in its laws measures coming from the fascist era with the most modern antiterrorist measures. The criminal code itself establishes the link between the measures adopted during the 1920's for the purpose of breaking up social movements and the fight against organizations designated as terrorist. This articulation forms a coherent whole aimed at criminalizing any radical opposition movement.

*The Concept of Subversive Association*

The Italian criminal code punishes anyone who undertakes to "promote" or "organize" a subversive association, an organization "aimed at violently establishing the dictatorship of one social class over others" or "overthrowing the economic or social organization established in the State through violence." The law also makes it possible to prosecute mere participation in such associations.

This law exhibits a directly political function: the defense of established economic and political power. The language in the criminal code speaks of overthrowing through violence. The acts are not defined. The term violence has a general bearing, as it focuses on any action that aims at overthrowing society, defined by the authors of the act as class society. Here also it is the intention of the perpetrator that is taken into account, which can include a forceful picket line just as well as a bomb attack.

Within the context of the antiterrorist fight at the end of the 1970's, Article 270 was reactivated in prosecuting subversive organizations.

---

33   Article 270 deals with "whoever, on the territory of the State, encourages, forms, organizes or directs associations aimed at instituting the dictatorship of one social class over others through violence, or violently eliminating a social class or again violently overturning the constituted economic and social order of the State, incurs imprisonment for 5 to 12 years. Whoever, on the territory of the State, encourages, forms, organizes, and directs associations whose aim is the violent elimination of all political and legal order in society is subject to the same penalty. Whoever participates in such associations incurs imprisonment for 1 to 3 years."

Through the decree of December 15, 1979, later becoming the "law Cossiga," Article 270 was transformed into Article 270b, which takes the whole text from the fascist code while increasing the penalties. Article 272 permits prosecution for "propaganda in favor of a subversive organization," the mere appeal to the "fight against class society."

It is on the basis of these laws that, after the Genoa summit of 2002, searches were undertaken into the local Indymedia Italia and documents and databases belonging to the organization were confiscated. Recall that the activity of Indymedia consists in distributing information over the Internet concerning social movements. An organization that is content to transmit information that evades State control and the private media groups associated with the State is in violation of this law. Here one can appreciate the broad applicability of the law as well as its actual purpose.

On November 15, 2002, the arrests of twenty militants of Rete Sud Ribelle were carried out by using these articles. The Public Prosecutor had already signed the requests in August, but the arrests were postponed until the end of the Social Forum in Florence.[34] This case, constructed on the basis of telephone wiretaps and the interception of email messages, is an outgrowth of the unity between an old fascist law and the most current freedom-killing measures, the unity of tradition and modernity, in a way. Despite this advantage, only the prosecutor's office in Cosenza found this case admissible.

The fact that the crime of being a subversive organization can be applied to persons who practice civil disobedience and non-violent activism clearly shows the subjective character of the concept of violence used in this article. Notice that, within the framework of the Italian criminal code, any action is violent if its objective is to oppose a society that the authors of the act define as a class society.

Undertaking action is not, moreover, necessary to be prosecuted, since Article 272, which deals with "propaganda" for the liquidation

---

34   Roberto Zanini, "La riposta," *Il Manifesto*, November 16, 2002.

of a class society, authorized the arrest of an official of the movement "Radio Gap."[35]

*An Almost Unlimited Margin of Interpretation*

In fact, Italy uses the three methods for criminalizing terrorism: classic criminalizations, peripheral criminalizations that elaborate upon aggravating circumstances linked to the intention of the perpetrator of the offense, when the latter pursues a "terrorist objective or the overthrow of the democratic order," and specific criminalizations concerning "an association having the goal of terrorism or overthrowing the democratic order."[36]

This last method comes from a framework law that does not define what it means by terrorism. It is constructed as the criminalization of a subversive association, which does not define what it means by dictatorship of a social class or elimination of a social class or subversion of the democratic order.

The Italian code punishes the organization, leadership, promotion, or financing, even indirect, of an organization considered terrorist, but also the fact of ordinary membership in such an organization. The fact of giving asylum to or simply transporting persons who have not committed any offenses, but who are condemned for participating in a terrorist organization, suffices for prosecution.

The two laws authorizing prosecution of, on the one hand, the subversive association and, on the other, the terrorist organization, do not define the component parts of the offense. These are determined, on a case by case basis, by the Court of Cassation, which is ostensibly able to determine whether or not the objective of overturning the democratic order through violence can result from the convergence of several components such as "the personality of the members with their known ideological affiliation, the availability of apartments to hold clandestine meetings, the possession of hidden arms in these apartments, the discovery of falsified documents or

---

35   John Brown, "Nous sommes tous des subversifs," available on Multitudes-infos@samizat.net, November 27, 2002.

36   Article 270b of the criminal code.

other objects or instruments that reveal an illegal activity, the possession of leaflets, printed materials or various writings with a clearly subversive content and intended to be used or distributed, the availability of unjustified amounts of money."[37]

The Italian example indicates well the complete change in criminal doctrine that leads to the incorporation of these new crimes into penal codes. They are valuable primarily for the almost unlimited margin of interpretation that they grant to the courts and the police. The interpretation of the law is thus tightly linked to the balance of power at the moment, to the ability of social movements to repulse those attempted interpretations that are the most prone to destroy freedoms. These laws are a method of intervening in the social struggle and aimed at testing the strength of a social movement. They are also flexible instruments of managing, in the very short term, social and political conflicts.

*A Strengthening of Fascist Procedures*

The "Cossiga law," promulgated on February 6, 1980, not only toughens the measures taken from the fascist code, but sets up a new set of exceptions to the normal procedures of the rule of law. It authorizes the police, in the case of a "political conspiracy" or "criminal conspiracy" to conduct preventative arrests lasting 48 hours, increased by a similar length for police custody. During these 96 hours, the person cannot consult with an attorney and thus is at the mercy of all attempts at physical and psychological pressure.

What is more, Article 10 of this law, today abrogated, allowed, at each judicial step, the extension of the preventative detention. That made it possible to extend the latter to a maximum length of 10 years and eight months. Article 9 of the law authorizes, "in case of emergency," searches without a judicial warrant.

The law on informers of May 29, 1982, is an additional element reinforcing this legislation of exception. Thus, numerous accusations have been solely based on denunciations from arrested persons,

---

37  Italian Court of Cassation, February 14, 1985, *Giusticia penale*, 1986, II, col. 85, in Adrien Masset, *La repression du terrorisme*, p. 8, note 21.

whose sentence or release depended not on their acts but their collaboration with the police or judicial authorities.

These exceptions to the investigation and trial stages are coupled with procedures of exception at the detention level. Special prisons were set up by a ministerial decree of May 4, 1977. The network of special prisons rapidly became a space empty of law: total isolation in soundproof cells, continual surveillance, deprivation of all human contact, visits and interviews at the discretion of the administration, unexpected transfers to prevent socializing. Transfer into these prisons did not result from a court order, but were at the sole discretion of the judicial administration. Here also, it is possible to note a toughening of the regulations in comparison to those of the fascist period. During the latter, only the supervising judge had the power to transfer the detainee.

## THE STAKES IN THE ANTITERRORIST LAWS

For those Member States of the European Union who have not developed specific legislation criminalizing terrorism, the ratification of the Framework Decision will lead to profound modifications in their approach to criminal matters, principally concerning different procedures, since it is at this level that the principal transformations in the countries that already had anti-terrorist legislation occurred.

### Primacy of the Procedure of Exception

In his doctoral dissertation, Adrien Masset made a systematic comparison between Belgian criminal law, which has not yet criminalized terrorism, and the penal codes of countries that have developed specific legislation for that purpose. His conclusions indicate that "Belgian criminal law has a huge assortment of crimes that, with a few exceptions (failure to inform the police or communicate useful information, justifying terrorist crimes and offenses, acts of ideological terrorism) make it possible to describe terrorist acts as criminal, acts that foreign legislation sometimes criminalized in a specific manner, sometimes in a mediate manner, in the name of fighting against terrorism."[38]

The author explains the interest in establishing specifically terrorist crimes by the fact that they satisfy the principle of legality but above all because they make it possible to legitimize the recourse to rules of criminal procedure as well as police investigations and prosecutions that deviate from common law. These practices are common to all the Member States of the European Union that have adopted such legislation.

In Germany, different exceptions were established relating to searches and house searches, identity checks, arrests during identity checks, and preventative detention. There are significant exceptions at the trial stage that alter competent jurisdictions and restrict the rights of the defense. The defense attorney can be excluded from participating in a procedure when he or she is suspected of having participated in the act that is the object of the investigation[39] or committed an act that thwarts the investigation. The exclusion is also applied "where circumstances lead to the belief that the defender will commit such an act." This procedure also legalized infringing on the secrecy of correspondence between an attorney and client.[40]

Some measures can also lead to the more or less total isolation of a detainee. They involve significant limitations in the rights of detainees who are declared to be terrorist by authorizing the elimination of contact between detainees or between a detainee and the outside world, including that person's attorney.[41]

Italian legislation also introduced significant exceptions relating to the trial. Merely possessing weapons made it possible to sentence persons for participating in terrorist attacks.[42] It also established a procedure for catching someone in the very act of committing a

---

38  Adrien Masset, *La repression du terrorisme*, p. 34.

39  Article 138a StPO of the German criminal code, added by the law of December 20, 1974 and modified by the laws of August 18, 1976 and the law of April 14, 1978.

40  Article 148a StPO.

41  Introduced by the Kontaktsperregeesetz of September 30, 1977.

42  G. Vassali, "Les orientations actuelles de la politique criminelle italienne," in *Archives de politique criminelle*, 1983, p. 178-179.

crime that eliminated the investigation phase. No investigation was necessary to clarify the nature of such offenses. The law of February 6, 1980, now abrogated, fixed the maximum duration of preventative detention at 10 years and 8 months for terrorist infractions.

The United Kingdom represents a good example of all the exceptions to common law that antiterrorist legislation can engender. Significant powers were granted to the police relating to investigation, arrest, interrogation of defendants and searches.

Article 24 of the Police and Criminal Evidence Act of 1984, linked to the Prevention of Terrorism Act of 1989, allows the police to arrest, without a warrant, any person suspected of being implicated in the commission, preparation or instigation of terrorist acts.

The Prevention of Terrorism Act of 1989[43] speaks of "prohibited organizations" or "banned associations." This legislation applies to a certain number of organizations taken from a black list established by the Home Secretary and approved by Parliament. These laws focus first and foremost on membership in or admission of membership in these organizations, but also deal with support of such organizations, whether it be financial or otherwise, or even preparing or helping to prepare for a meeting.[44] They also punish the non-communication to the police of information useful for preventing a terrorist act.[45]

In Spain, a person prosecuted on the basis of the antiterrorist law does not have the choice of an attorney.[46]

*Generalization of Procedures of Exception*

The procedures of exception introduced by various antiterrorist laws, in quite specific conditions, were not eliminated, although the objective conditions that justified them disappeared. On the contrary, in Germany, some of these measures were extended to other forms of criminality, such as organized crime or drug trafficking. " . . . these ex-

---

43   See Articles 1 to 3.

44   C. Adde Walker, K. Reig, "The Offence of Directing Terrorist Organisations," *Criminal Law Review*, 1993, p. 669-677.

45   I. McLean and P Morrish, *Harris' Criminal Law* (London: Sweet and Maxwell, 1973), p. 429-447.

46   an Fermon, "Les droits démocratiques: dommages collateraux de la guerre contre le terrorisme," *Le Journal des Procès*, n° 423, Bruxelles, 2 novembre 2001.

ceptional regulations have been maintained, although the terrorist threat appears to be less real than in the 1970's, a time in which these particular arrangements increased. A return to a much calmer period in regard to terrorist attacks did not lead the German legislator to move in the direction of a complete return to the classic measures of German criminal procedure; we believe one of the reasons for this lies in the fact that these particular measures were extended to other sectors of criminality."[47]

The persistence in the criminal code of measures undertaken in the context of the fight against terrorism is not unique to Germany. In Italy, the government decree n° 59 of March 21, 1978, specified that the necessary authorization from the examining magistrate or the prosecutor to the police to proceed with interrupting or intercepting communications[48] could be requested verbally, instead of the written procedure previously required. Moreover, the police had the power to request authorization from these judicial authorities to place preventive telephone wiretaps. Telephone wiretaps remain as a means of proof in Articles 266 to 271 in the new code of criminal procedure.

The English laws of exception that criminalize terrorism were described as temporary.[49] They were not repealed, however. The exceptional powers granted to the police, far from disappearing, were then established as rules of common law. Thus the Police and Criminal Evidence Act of 1984 defines the powers of the police by adopting as the norm the regulations taken from the antiterrorist legislation.[50]

The extension of the procedures of exception to the whole criminal field changes the nature of police work inasmuch as its proactive character separates it from judicial work in the strict sense. The English example shows us "that a very small percentage, hardly 15%,

---

47  Adrien Masset, *La répression du terrorisme*, p. 47.

48  Article 226b of the Italian code of criminal procedure.

49  These four laws follow one another under the same heading: The Prevention of Terrorism (*Temporary* [author's emphasis] Provisions) Act: 1974, 1976, 1984, 1989.

50  A. Reid, "Un nouveau départ dans la legislation pénale anglaise," *Revue de sciences criminelles*, 1987, p. 577-587.

of persons interrogated under cover of these laws of exception were later legally prosecuted."[51]

## TERRORIST ORGANIZATION OR CRIMINAL ORGANIZATION

The criminal codes of various European countries were expanded with new crimes aimed at fighting against organized crime. This matter was also an object of concern on the part of international organizations, including the European Union.

In the list of methods for criminalizing terrorism, outside of specific laws, a certain importance should be given to the concept of the criminal organization, of which a terrorist organization is a particular example. The Joint Action of December 21, 1998, relative to the crime of participating in a criminal organization in the Member States of the European Union,[52] makes explicit reference to terrorist offenses.

The two new crimes concerning terrorist offenses and criminal organization have numerous points in common. They seek less to punish criminal behaviors than to criminalize any form of participating in the activities of these organizations, even legal ones. The concept of a criminal organization creates a crime of membership. This measure thus also applies to an organization named as terrorist.

These two crimes owe their existence to the establishment of particular regulations in criminal procedure. The legal definition of the criminal organization limits the exceptions to the investigative level alone. It legitimates "proactive" police investigations, which can take place in the absence of any infractions. Terrorist criminality generalizes the exceptions to all stages of criminal procedure: initial inquiry, investigation, trial, and determination of penalty.

The institution of these two crimes strengthens the primacy of procedure over law properly speaking. It is also clear that the existence of these two crimes is due to police demands. As with the laws

---

51  W. Finnie, "The Prevention of Terrorism Act and the ECHR," *Modern Law Review*, p. 705, cited in Adrien Masset, *La repression du terrorisme*, p. 77.

52  Joint Action of December 21, 1998, *Official Journal of the European Communities*, 29.12.1998, L351, p.1.

dealing with computer crime,[53] U.S. criminal law, and above all the demands of the FBI, played a decisive role. Beyond that, they both present a directly political character since they make destabilization of political and economic power a defining factor of the crime or the criminalized organization.

*United Nations Convention Against Organized Crime*

This past decade, organized crime was a main preoccupation of national States as well as international organizations, such as the United Nations or the European Union. The government of the United States designated international organized crime as a threat to national security.[54] Moreover, it is the U.S. that is behind the principal transformations in the national and international criminal systems engendered by the fight against organized crime.

One can see these modifications in the criminal codes and procedures of various States. Their objective is not to punish the individual commission of a crime, but to take on the very structure of criminal organizations. These legal modifications, as well as the change in police work that is associated with them, were first used by the United States before being adopted by other States.

In November 1994, the World Ministerial Conference on Organized Transnational Crime held in Naples issued a Political Declaration and established a plan of action. One of the principal objectives was to attain greater standardization between different systems of criminal justice in order to make national legislation dealing with transnational criminality compatible.

This project shows the role that international instruments play in the elaboration of global strategies of action against organized crime. This Convention had a double objective. On the one hand, "it would facilitate the bringing of pressure on behalf of the international com-

---

53  Jean-Claude Paye, "La loi relative à la criminalité informatique," *Le Journal des process*, no. 426, 14 décembre 2001; "Criminalisation de l'Internet et Etat de droit," *La revue Nouvelle*, Bruxelles, décembre 2001.

54  Les systèmes pénaux à l'épreuve du crime organisé, Colloque d'Utrecht, 13-16 mai 1998, Rapport des États-Unis, *Revue internationale de droit pénal*, 1er et 2e trimestres 1999.

munity" and, on the other hand, this Convention would also "justify measures taken by each country, including legislative steps."[55]

The policy put forward consists in taking the initiative out of the hands of national executive branches. Parliaments of Member States are transformed into mere chambers for recording decisions taken at the international level.

The fight against transnational crime is a privileged instrument in the conquest of a new legitimacy by international institutions. It also makes possible a transfer of sovereignty from national States towards those institutions. The identification of organized crime as the principal enemy, as the determining factor in the destabilization of national governments, justifies the transfer of initiative from the latter.

The United Nations Conference held at Palermo from December 12 to 15, 2000, carried out the signing of a Convention against organized crime. It criminalizes the laundering of proceeds from criminal activities and corruption. This convention enjoins Member States to establish a liability for legal entities and seeks to promote international cooperation regarding the confiscation of proceeds from crime.

This convention criminalizes the active participation in a criminal group of any person "who has knowledge of either the aim and general criminal activity of an organized criminal group or its intention to commit the crimes in question... ."[56] It provides a particularly wide definition, since it considers any structure "of three or more persons whose aim is to commit a crime or an offense in order to derive a financial or material advantage" an "organized criminal group."[57] The crime is called "transnational" as soon as it involves more than one State.

---

55  United Nations, World Ministerial Conference on Transnational Organized Crime, Naples, 21-23 November 1994. "Crime Prevention and Criminal Justice," p. 15.

56  United Nations. Convention Against Transnational Organized Crime, 2000. Article 5, p. 4. http://www.uncjin.org/Documents/Conventions/dcatoc/final_documents_2/.

57  *Ibid*, Article 2, p. 2.

*The European Union: The Political Idea of the Crime of Membership*

On December 21, 1998, the Council of the European Union adopted a Joint Action,[58] that establishes a definition of common law directed against organized crime. It binds all the Member States without the necessity of ratification by national parliaments. Its aim is to facilitate, among Member States, judicial cooperation in investigations and the prosecution of offenses.

This definition lays the foundation for a new crime, distinct from that of criminal conspiracy. It introduces, as a constitutive element of a criminal organization, the fact of committing an offense as "a means of obtaining material benefits and, where appropriate, of improperly influencing the operation of public authorities." It thus introduces a directly political concept to describe a criminal offense. The work of the criminal investigation department becomes a direct means of stabilizing the State.

Any offense committed within the context of a movement contesting power could fall under this idea of being constitutive of a criminal organization. Does not any social or political organization have the objective of influencing the power of the State? The restriction introduced by the term "improperly" is no guarantee because it is purely subjective and offers a very significant margin of interpretation.

In the same way, defining a criminal organization based on the idea that it is a means of obtaining material benefits offers very significant possibilities for repression that can be expanded to include unions, consumers organizations or any organization for the defense of economic rights.

The European definition creates a crime of membership since it criminalizes, in the absence of any offense, the fact of being part of an organization considered to be criminal. This participation must be active (only Belgium prosecutes passive participation). In order to be prosecuted, participation in the legal activities of such an organization must be done with full knowledge of the fact that it is a criminal organization.

---

58   Joint Action of December 21, 1998, Article 1, *Official Journal of the European Communities*, 29.12.98, L351/1.

However, it is also possible to prosecute the mere intention of the organization to commit crimes. It thus introduces a crime of intention, a purely subjective concept that considerably increases the possibility of police intervention and the judge's power of interpretation.

## The Shadow of the Regional Power

The establishment of a crime on the basis of the legal definition of a criminal organization rests on the German approach to the question. The content of the text is also strongly inspired by the definition used by the Bundeskriminalamt (BKA), the German criminal investigation department. This is a criminological type of definition and aims at legitimizing exceptions at the stage of the police investigation.

As opposed to the criminal approach in the strict sense, a criminological type of definition makes possible a very broad incrimination. Such an approach opposes the principle of legality that requires that the punishable acts be precisely defined. As with the German law, the Joint Action of the European Union clashes with this principle.

Article 129 of the German Criminal Code provides for the specific crime of participation in a criminal organization. Participation, as a member, in an organization whose objectives are to commit crimes is punishable. The organization must have been created for a specific period of time and must have a minimum structure. The mere existence of the organization suffices; it is not necessary that actual crimes have been committed. The German Criminal Code thus creates a crime of membership, but specifically of active membership. Purely passive membership is not sufficient. Active membership means "the integration into, subordination to and execution of activities that make it possible to carry out the criminal activities of the organization." However, in order to be prosecuted, it is not necessary that an active member actually participate in the crimes.

## Criminal Conspiracy or Criminal Organization

The crime of criminal organization or organized crime is new in the French Criminal Code. It was introduced only at the end of 2003 in the Perben II law. Prior to this law, the fight against organized crime was structured around curbing specific activities, such as drug trafficking, by focusing on the existence of aggravating circumstances during the commission of the offense. The incriminating behavior is thus secondary. This is the same type of behavior that is prosecuted in terrorist offenses. The powers of judicial investigation were also strengthened by specific procedural regulations.

In France, the question of organized crime was essentially tackled on the basis of the concept of the "organized gang" introduced by article 132-71 of the new criminal code: "An organized gang in the sense of the law is any group formed or any alliance established with the idea of preparing, in the sense of one or more material acts, one or more offenses."

The concept of "organized gang" becomes the aggravating circumstance of the criminal conspiracy offense. However, this aggravating circumstance can only be taken into account after the execution of the offense and the recognition of the existence of a criminal conspiracy. It is not thus a constitutive element of the offense.

The fact that either definition, that of criminal conspiracy or that of criminal organization, can be used is not without importance as far as the defense of the rule of law is concerned. Article 450 of the French Criminal Code, relating to the concept of criminal conspiracy, stipulates that "a criminal conspiracy is any group formed or alliance established with the idea of undertaking one or more crimes, characterized by one or more material acts, punishable by 10 years in prison." The concept of criminal conspiracy penalizes specific material acts. In France, criminal conspiracy concerning drugs, provided for in Articles 222-233 of the Criminal Code, criminalizes "participation in a group formed or an alliance established with a view to undertake one or more crimes characterized by one or more material acts."

The legal definition of the criminal organization moves away from the materiality of the act and penalizes merely belonging to an organization considered to be criminal, without the necessity of a crime being committed.

The European definition criminalizes "the behavior of any person that consists in having formed [...] an agreement concerning the carrying out of an activity that, if it were implemented, would come down to committing offenses even when this person does not participate in the execution." The text introduces an element of probability in which actually committing a crime is no longer necessary for there to be an offense. That entails a drastic change, not only within criminal law, but also in the substance of police investigation.

The definition of criminal organizations contained in Belgian law is designed to serve as the basis of "proactive" police investigations. This type of investigation has a judicial function, but it concerns acts that have not yet been committed and thus might not be committed. In this case, the investigation will not lead to any legal action, but the filing of information and the investigations will be carried out without an official investigation having been opened and thus without the possibility for the defense to exercise its rights. The "proactive" police investigation is similar to the work of intelligence services.

If the object of such an investigation is to bring the operation of organized crime to light, this police intelligence approach is in contradiction with classic judicial inquiry, i.e., the short-term and focused apprehension of an act. On the contrary, an investigation conducted in the context of the criminal organization approach is carried out in the long term, which brings it closer to the type of investigations carried out by the security services. The similarity between police work and that of the intelligence services will be all the more important when this investigation does not lead to legal proceedings.

If we consider the purpose of these institutions, the protection of property and people in the case of the police and protecting the State in the case of the intelligence and security services, we have to admit that the penal definition of the criminal organization tends to expand the mission of the police to include stabilization of the State.

This double blurring of boundaries between, on the one hand, the mission of the criminal investigation police and that of the administrative police and, on the other hand, between police investigation and the work of the secret services manifests, in fact, the subordination of the judicial function to the executive function. This new orientation of police investigation is not only dangerous for fundamental liberties, but is an indication of a reorganization of police work that incorporates its judicial assignments into the administrative functions. Maintenance of order becomes social surveillance.

All of these conclusions apply to antiterrorist laws because a terrorist group is a type of criminal organization. Laws aimed at combating organized crime apply to terrorism as well. However, the specific criminalization of terrorism establishes exceptions at all stages of criminal procedure and not only at the level of the investigation. At the latter, it develops the tendency begun by the definition of a criminal organization.

## A CHANGE IN ANTITERRORIST POLICIES

The question of the fight against terrorism appeared in the criminal sphere during the 1970's, through the initiatives taken by the United Nations and the Council of Europe. The former encouraged Member States to include sanctions in their criminal codes aimed at specifically punishing certain crimes such as airline hijacking or bomb attacks.

As for the Council of Europe, it removed the political exception clause for a group of offenses considered to be particularly serious. As a result, it is legitimate not to take into account the political motives of the perpetrators of such offenses and to treat these crimes according to classical criminal procedure. Thus, in the Convention of Strasbourg of 1977, any political character is denied to a limited series of crimes and they are treated solely as criminal offenses.

This convention thus excludes certain forms of social struggle from the political sphere by throwing them onto criminal terrain. It treats them as individual crimes and punishes them as such. By doing this, it effects a restriction in the definition of political acts, by excluding actions that do not respect the monopoly of violence that is claimed by institutionalized authority.

### A Revolution in Criminal Law

The current laws that create a specific criminalization of terrorism proceed in the reverse manner. The creation of a specific crime, as well as the establishment of aggravating circumstances for offenses already punished elsewhere, is justified by considering terrorist acts, although analogous to common law crimes, to be different from the latter because of the political motivation of the perpetrator, i.e., the intention of undermining the foundation of the State or the desire to destabilize society.

The characterization of these offenses as political makes it possible to remove them from common law and subject persons suspected of terrorism to procedures of exception at the level of the police inquiry as well as the pre-trial investigation or the trial itself.

These laws are part of a real change in criminal law. The legal definition of the criminal organization, inserted into most national criminal codes, forms the first systematization of this change. This new crime, distinct from that of criminal conspiracy, creates a crime of membership. A person can be prosecuted without having committed a crime or even without having had the intention of committing one based simply on the fact that he/she belongs to an organization defined as criminal. The latter definition includes terrorist organizations.

This new crime, beyond the fact that it not only punishes concrete acts, but sometimes, as in Belgium, a mere intention, establishes a collective responsibility. These laws do not go after individual offenses, but crimes of organization.

### The Antiterrorist Fight and the United Nations

The first measures concerning the fight against terrorism were taken under the auspices of the United Nations, beginning with the Convention on Offenses and Certain Other Acts Committed on Board Aircraft (Tokyo, September 14, 1963). The antiterrorist legislative arsenal from the 1960's to the end of the 1970's is formed of texts that punish concrete acts that are harmful to the free movement of people. Above all it concerns air transport.

Among the conventions and protocols subsequently promulgated, the International Convention for the Suppression of Terrorist Bombings (New York, December 15, 1997) and the International Convention for the Suppression of the Financing of Terrorism (New York, December 9, 1999) are particularly important. The 1997 Convention does not yet give a definition of terrorism. However, while the earlier measures criminalized a definite set of acts, it expands the field to include a general determination of the circumstances of the terrorist act. But that does not yet constitute a specific definition.

Only the later Convention, in 1999, takes the next step and defines a terrorist act by the element of intention, according to a procedure and terms that will be taken up again in the Framework Decision of the European Union. This Convention prohibits the financing of an act "when the purpose of such act, by its nature or context, is to intimidate a population or to compel a government or international organization to do or abstain from doing any act."[59]

The directly political nature and freedom-killing character of this definition did not escape the signatories, which left to signatory national States the responsibility for defending the fundamental rights threatened by the international convention. Thus, Article 6 of the Convention on the Suppression of the Financing of Terrorism establishes a series of safeguards to protect against the arbitrariness of such a crime: "Each State Party shall adopt such measures as may be necessary, including, where appropriate, domestic legislation, to ensure that criminal acts within the scope of this Convention are under no circumstances justifiable by considerations of a political, philosophical, ideological, racial, ethnic, religious or other similar nature."[60]

The September 11 attacks gave a new impulse to the elaboration of an International Convention for the Suppression of Terrorist Attacks, which came into force on April 10, 2002. This Convention is centered principally on the suppression of the financing of terrorist acts and organizations. Resolution 1373 of the United Nations Security Council, adopted unanimously on September 28, 2002, expands the obligation of different States to collaborate by forcing them to cooperate, not only on the suppression of the financing of terrorism but also in areas such as the exchange of intelligence and the establishment of a rapid alert system. It also imposed the obligation

---

59  United Nations. International Convention on the Suppression of the Financing of Terrorism, 1999. Article 2, p. 5. http://untreaty.un.org/English/Terrorism.asp.

60  *Ibid.*, Article 6, p. 7.

on States to adopt legislation specifically focused on acts designated as terrorist.[61]

## The Antiterrorist Fight and the Council of Europe

Under the authority of the Council of Europe, the most significant effort in the fight against terrorism was accomplished with the European Convention for the Suppression of Terrorism (Strasbourg, January 27, 1977). This Convention authorizes suspending application of the traditional clause of refusing extradition for political offenses to certain offenses such as kidnapping or hostage taking. This Convention rests on the idea that "certain crimes are so odious in their methods or results in relation to their motives, that it is no longer justifiable to classify them as 'political offences' for which extradition is not possible."[62]

The text limits itself to an enumeration of crimes, without developing the intentional element. It is the first convention to treat terrorism in a general manner, at least in the sense that it contains a list of acts defined as terrorist.

The first article refers to terrorist offenses relevant to the area of application of the Convention for the Suppression of the Illegal Capture of Aircraft (The Hague, 1970) and the Convention for the Suppression of Illegal Acts Directed against the Security of Civil Aviation (Montreal, 1971). Furthermore, it includes offenses that involve an attack against the life, bodily integrity or liberty of persons having the right to international protection. The offenses include kidnapping, hostage taking, false imprisonment as well as the use of bombs, grenades, missiles, automatic firearms, or letter or parcel bombs, to the extent that their use presents a danger to persons.

Article 2 expands the concept of a terrorist act to other crimes that include an act of violence and that are directed against the life, bodily integrity or liberty of persons and against property, when the act has created a collective danger.

---

61 Pierre Berthelet, "L'impact des événements du 11 septembre sur la creation de l'espace de liberté, de sécurité eet de justice." Partie 1, automne 2002, http://conflits.revues.org.

62 European Convention on the Suppression of Terrorism. Explanatory Report, p. 5. http://conventions.coe.int/Treaty/EN/Reports/HTML/090.htm.

The 1977 Strasbourg Convention was only ratified by national States because it included the safeguard clause that does not make extradition automatic. Judges always have the possibility of deciding on the substance of the case. By refusing automatic extradition, the political branch, signatory to the Convention, left to the judicial branch the responsibility of judging the legality of the acts of organizations accused of terrorism.

The situation established by the European arrest warrant eliminates this judicial control since the return of a suspected person is almost automatic and the judge in the requested State no longer has the possibility of deciding on the materiality of the acts and the legality of the extradition request.

## A Change of Direction

The aim of the first texts was to cultivate international cooperation in the fight against certain particularly dangerous acts of violence. For that purpose, it was important to distinguish them from political acts, by refusing to accord them any political character in order to include them within the scope of common law.

It is thus the non-political aspect of the terrorist act that had to be underlined. For that reason, the only element that distinguishes terrorist acts from common law acts, i.e., the political purpose of the former, had to be systematically set aside. This procedure makes it impossible to establish a general category defining terrorism. Thus, only the acts are punished.

The Framework Decision of the European Union relating to the criminalization of terrorism proceeds in the reverse manner. There are not concrete acts that determine the terrorist character of the offense, but a moral element constructed on the basis of a broad definition that makes destabilizing the State a definition of terrorism.

This generic definition of terrorism requires that a political project be put forward and it is this character that is specifically prosecuted. This procedure offers the possibility of criminalizing any form of political or social struggle.

If the first antiterrorist laws allowed the exclusion of a group of violent actions from the political field, the most recent laws redefine, rather, the political field. It is, on the contrary, the political character that is imprinted on the actions designated as terrorist that justifies the freedom-killing nature of the measures undertaken. However, these actions are defined as such, not because they bear collective demands, but because they are likely to destabilize the State. Politics is reduced to the politician, to the institutional organization of power. The latter is defined in relation to itself and denies any political expression that is partially outside itself.

# 4

## THE EUROPEAN UNION:
## A SPACE OF LIBERTY, SECURITY AND JUSTICE?

The fight against terrorism was explicitly made a part of the European Union's concerns beginning with the Treaty of the European Union, signed at Maastricht in 1992, well before the adoption of the Framework Decision, The Treaty makes explicit reference to terrorism as a serious form of criminality that should be averted and fought.

Three possibilities are envisaged: cooperation between police forces and customs authorities, closer cooperation between judicial authorities and other relevant authorities in the Member States and reconciling the different rules on criminal affairs among the Member States. The adoption of the Framework Decision relative to the fight against terrorism is formally part of the latter possibility.

In 1997, the Treaty of Amsterdam made the creation of a "space of liberty, security and justice" one of the objectives of the Union. The antiterrorist struggle is explicitly a constitutive element of this space. Article 29 of the Treaty of the European Union stipulates that "Without prejudice to the powers of the European Community, the Union's objective shall be to provide citizens with a high level of safety within an area of freedom, security and justice by developing common action among the Member States in the fields of police and judicial cooperation in criminal matters...."

Two solutions are outlined to build this European judicial space: gradual standardization of Member States' legislation and the mutual recognition of judicial decisions. The European Council in October 1999 at Tampere favored the second possibility by indicating that the mutual recognition of judicial decisions could become "the cornerstone of judicial cooperation in both civil and criminal matters."[1] The two poles of the alternative are, however, far from be-

---

1   Communication from the Commission to the Council and the European Parliament: Mutual recognition of final decisions in criminal matters, COM(2000) 495 final, Brussels, 26/7/2000.

ing equivalent. While the standardization of legislation strengthens the primacy of the law in the relations between Member States, the second solution, mutual recognition of decisions, strengthens the domination of procedure.

Formally, establishing a common criminalization of terrorism is part of the first option outlined: gradual standardization of the legislation of Member States. However, the essentials in setting up such a criminalization consist of using exceptional criminal procedures. The adoption of this approach, used jointly with a European arrest warrant that involves an almost automatic handing over of the sought after person, legitimizes and allows the coexistence of different procedures from one Member State to another. The adoption of this criminalization of terrorism is also part of the second option outlined by the Maastricht Treaty, i.e., the mutual recognition of judicial decisions.

### EUROPEAN ARREST WARRANT

The Council of Justice and Home Affairs Ministers adopted on December 6, 2001, a Framework Decision relating to the creation of a European arrest warrant which came into force on January 1, 2004.[2] Although the arrest warrant is not formally limited for use in matters relating to terrorism, it was presented as a measure facilitating its suppression.

The draft of the Framework Decision of the Council on the European Arrest Warrant and the Surrender Procedures between Member States was published by the Commission on September 19, 2001, the same day as the draft of the Framework Decision on the Fight against Terrorism. During the entire Belgian presidency, the two drafts were discussed in parallel. The preamble leaves no doubt about the antiterrorist character of the measure, even if it is clear that the draft does not date from the days following the September 11 attacks and that it had already been brought up at the Tampere summit in 1999.

---

2  Council Framework Decision of 13 June 2002 on the European arrest warrant and the surrender procedures between Member States, *Official Journal of the European Communities*, L190, v. 45, 18 July 2002.

The European arrest warrant replaces the normal extradition proce-dure that rests on the necessity for a double incrimination. Tradition-ally, extradition is possible only if the act being prosecuted is a crime in the country requesting extradition of the person as well as in the requested country. The European arrest warrant abandons this re-quirement. It is sufficient that the act in question be an offense in the requesting country.

Every judicial authority of a Member State recognizes and exe-cutes almost automatically, with minimal controls, the extradition request drawn up by a judicial authority of another Member State. This warrant can be issued for offenses that, had they occurred in the requesting State, would carry a penalty of at least three years imprisonment. There is a non-exhaustive list of 32 crimes, including terrorism, cybercrimes, fraud, money laundering, corruption, hu-man trafficking, first-degree murder and racism.

The European arrest warrant authorizes extradition not only of persons tried but also those merely under investigation. Thus the principle of mutual recognition applies not only to court verdicts but implies de facto recognition of the entire penal legislation of Mem-ber States, including the entirety of the criminal procedures as well as the exceptions from the norm. The Commission also proposes to extend the principle of mutual recognition from judicial proceed-ings to administrative decisions.

The principle of double incrimination had already been circum-vented for some offenses. The Council Act of 27 September 1996,[3] drawing up the Convention relating to extradition between the Member States of the European Union, specifies that extradition of a person cannot be refused, even if the act being prosecuted is not an offense in the requested country, when the requesting State is pros-ecuting a crime on the basis of an alleged criminal conspiracy and that the alleged offense relates to the suppression of terrorism, the drug traffic or other forms of organized crime. The requested State still exercises control over the information appearing on the war-

---

3   *Official Journal of the European Communities*, C313, 23/10/1996.

rant, the sentencing decision or the statement of facts. Any Member State can reserve to itself the right to apply the Convention or to impose certain conditions on its application.

Even if the Convention had already eliminated the requirement for double incrimination for the most serious types of organized crime, including terrorism, the reasons for the institution of the European arrest warrant should be clear from the automatic character of the extradition and the abandonment of control procedures.

The Convention, which was ratified by thirteen Member States, left in place the oversight mechanisms appropriate for extradition. The political authorities make the decision to proceed with an extradition request or not. The European arrest warrant eliminates this prerogative, as well as the supervision exercised by administrative jurisdictions.

In the course of the normal extradition procedure, judicial supervision concerns the materiality of the facts and the legality of the request. With the arrest warrant, judicial supervision is no longer concerned with anything other than the formal legality of the warrant.

Another important change is the abandonment of the principle of explicitness. In the normal extradition procedure, the person handed over can only be prosecuted for the offenses explicitly mentioned in the request. With the European arrest warrant, the requesting country is no longer bound by the specific offenses cited in the warrant.[4]

### The Principle of Mutual Recognition

The elimination of the requirement for double incrimination follows logically from the application of the principle of mutual recognition: "the Decision of the judicial authority of another Member State is recognized in all its effects, ipso facto and without a priori review. It will hardly matter, therefore, if the offence for which the arrest warrant was issued does not exist, or that its components differ in the executing State. Under this principle each Member State not only

---

4    Jan Fermon, "Ben Laden arrête grâce à un mandat européen," *Le Journal des Procès*, no. 422, Bruxelles, 19 octobre 2001.

recognizes the entire criminal law of the other Member States but also agrees to assist them in enforcing it."[5]

Mutual confidence implies that control by the State that executes the arrest warrant is reduced to a minimum because the legality of the request is presupposed. This confidence is based on the presumption that the national judicial systems of the various Member States are sufficiently reliable and independent to avoid the use of a national system for political ends.

Mutual recognition requires that all the articles of the criminal codes and procedures of all the Member States be considered as democratic in actual fact. What does it mean, for example, that elements of the Italian criminal code, issued during the fascist period and still applied, such as the idea of a subversive organization, will be automatically recognized by other European states? Prosecutions undertaken by Italian judicial authorities on the basis of such concepts were not held to be acceptable by French political authorities. With the surrender of Persichetti, the Raffarin government put an end to the tradition of accepting political refugees. It anticipated what is presently the norm with the European arrest warrant.

*A Concrete Example*

The European arrest warrant suspends procedures protecting constitutional liberties. This can be illustrated by a Spanish request for extradition of a Basque couple living in Belgium.

Suspected of being close to ETA, M. Moreno and Madame Garcia took refuge in Belgium beginning in 1992. The couple was accused by a member of ETA, arrested at the end of January 1992, of having housed ETA militants who were alleged perpetrators of murders and abductions.[6] This person retracted the statement several days later, claiming to have spoken under torture. Moreover, his confession will be declared null and void during his trial. On May 19, 1993, following an arrest order accusing them of belonging to an armed gang,

---

5   Proposal for a Council Framework Decision on the European arrest warrant and the surrender procedures between the Member States, Brussels, 19.9.2001, COM(2001) 522 final, p. 16.

6   Martin Buxant et Jean-Claude Matgen, "La prescription opposée à Madrid," *La Libre*, 18 mars 2004.

the couple was arrested and detained on the basis of an extradition warrant. The Brussels criminal appeals court requested and obtained from the Ministry of Justice a refusal to extradite them. After their request for asylum was held to be acceptable, these two persons were freed on December 8, 1993. They were arrested again in 1996, when the extradition request was again examined, following the refusal to grant them the status of political refugees. The new Minister of Justice, favorable to extradition of the couple, had to take into account an opinion of the Council of State favoring suspension of the measure, an opinion backed by a decision of the appeals court. The couple's release led to a momentary suspension of judicial cooperation between Spain and Belgium.

In February 2004, within the framework of the European arrest warrant, Spain again asked for the extradition of its former nationals. The examining magistrate released them unconditionally, after considering the necessary facts. The refusal of the Belgian judge to carry out the European warrant issued against these two persons is based solely on a procedural flaw. If the facts had not been laid out, he could not have opposed their extradition. He could not have put forward obvious basic reasons to oppose the return of the couple, notably that the request was based on confessions that not only could not be guaranteed to be true, but also had been invalidated by a court decision. These facts concerning the basis and legality of the request, which twice led to a rejection of the extradition request, would no longer be relevant to oppose the surrender of persons within the framework of the European arrest warrant.

In this example, the Spanish request was made despite the fact that the accuser retracted his statement and that a legal decision had declared the confession, upon which the request was based, to be null and void. The European arrest warrant thus initiates a suspension of the law.

## Minor Judicial Cooperation

It is not only major judicial cooperation regarding extradition that was profoundly reformed within the European Union. Minor judicial cooperation, allowing a national judicial authority to obtain assistance from an equivalent authority in another Member State, was also completely changed. As far as the Convention on judicial cooperation is concerned, these transformations are essentially the same as those at the level of major cooperation. They make it impossible to refuse to cooperate when the offenses in question are of a political nature and they establish mechanisms of cooperation that are all but automatic, based on the principle of mutual recognition of judicial decisions.

Minor criminal judicial cooperation was essentially regulated by the Convention of the Council of Europe of April 20, 1959 that, like the Convention on extradition of 1957, provides for the possibility of refusing judicial cooperation if the request concerns offenses considered to be political by the requested State.

The Protocol[7] to the Convention of May 29, 2001, on Mutual Assistance in Criminal Matters between the Member States of the European Union eliminates this restriction. It stipulates, on the contrary, that the Member States cannot invoke the political character of an offense as the basis for refusing a request for assistance.

The principle developed by this protocol is thus exactly the inverse of that laid out by the Convention of 1959. However, States still reserve the possibility of limiting this measure to certain serious offenses, those specified in the Convention of the Council of Europe of 1977 on the suppression of terrorism.

The future Framework Decision relative to the execution of orders freezing property or evidence, still in draft at that time, soon made it impossible for a Member State to refuse cooperation with another Member State. The draft[8] was discussed at the time of the Council meeting of Justice and Home Affairs Ministers on February 28, 2002.

As with the European arrest warrant, this proposal is based on the principle of mutual recognition and makes any judicial decision effective anywhere on the territory of the European Union. Further-

---

7   Adopted on October 16, 2001. See, Council Act of 16 October 2001 establishing, in accordance with Article 34 of the Treaty on European Union, the Protocol to the Convention on Mutual Assistance in Criminal Matters between the Member States of the European Union, *Official Journal of the European Communities* C326, 21 November 2001, p. 1.

8   Draft Framework Decision on the execution in the European Union of orders freezing property or evidence, document no. 6552/02, 22/02/2002, COPEN 17.

more, the decision is transmitted directly from a competent authority (not necessarily judicial) in the issuing State to another competent authority in the enforcing State, without first passing through the chancelleries of the respective countries.

### An Extension of National Powers

The establishment of the European arrest warrant should be analyzed in relation to the impact that it could have on problem areas, such as the fight against terrorism and organized crime.

On the one hand, the European arrest warrant cannot only be considered as a procedure of exception in regard to terrorism because it includes other offenses in its field of application. On the other hand, the European arrest warrant was one of the antiterrorist measures adopted by the European Union after the attacks of September 11, 2001. In this context, it is important to note that the system of the European arrest warrant obliterates a series of safeguards that protected persons accused of terrorism. In practice, the principle of explicitness will be totally ineffective for offenses at which the European arrest warrant is directed. The abandonment of this principle could pose very serious problems. What about a country that might request the extradition of a person for theft, linked or not to political activity, and then might describe the same acts as terrorist, obviously punishable in a completely different manner from the offense for which the European arrest warrant had been issued? Can we be certain that, in the context of the fight against terrorism, Member States will never use the strategy of describing the acts in question at a lower level of seriousness in order to get its hands on someone and then define the acts differently? Recent experience in Spain, Italy or the Federal Republic of Germany does not allow us to dismiss this possibility. In a matter such as terrorism, the absence of oversight and safeguards leaves room for the arbitrariness of States and their police and intelligence services.

With the European arrest warrant, any political and administrative oversight is abolished and judicial oversight is not truly strengthened. On the contrary, even if formally the judiciary only had the power of issuing an opinion in the earlier system and now has the power to issue an order, the margins of the latter at this point are so narrow that it becomes a pure formality.

The establishment of a European warrant rests on the existence of mutual confidence in criminal systems of the Member States. It is presumed à priori that these systems are based on the principles of liberty, democracy and the rule of law. The implementation of warrants can only be suspended when a Member State "is suspected of serious and repeated violations of fundamental rights …"[9] The existence of the rule of law would no longer result from the establishment of oversight mechanisms to monitor acts of the government, but from the presupposed legality of the latter.

The framework decision is the instrument used for the creation of the European arrest warrant, as well as for the definition of a terrorist offense. The use of this means clearly indicates the intention to move quickly. According to the terms of article 34 of the Treaty of the European Union, framework decisions "shall be binding upon the Member States as to the result to be achieved but shall leave to the national authorities the choice of form and methods." They do not entail any direct effect and require a modification of national legislation. Contrary to conventions, framework decisions do not require that a certain number of Member States have to place these measures in their national legislation in order to be able to take effect.

The European arrest warrant does not lead to a unification of legislation and criminal procedures. On the contrary, it permits the coexistence of profound disparities between Member States. The same thing is true regarding the creation of a common crime defining a terrorist act. With the definition adopted by the European Union, it is less a question of unifying national legislation than of justifying the use of rules of criminal procedure, different in each Member State, that deviate from common law.

These two Framework Decisions result in extending the sovereignty of Member States in criminal matters to the entire territory of

---

9   Proposal for a Council Framework Decision on the European arrest warrant and the surrender procedures between the Member States, Brussels, 19.9.2001, COM(2001) 522 final, p. 23.

the European Union, while eliminating various political and judicial controls.

AN ATTACK AGAINST SOCIAL MOVEMENTS

A proposal of the Spanish presidency of the European Union in February 2002 makes it clear which groups are the intended targets of the various antiterrorist measures.

### The Proposal of the Spanish Presidency

Spain had requested that, by means of a Council decision, a standard form be drafted to facilitate the exchange of information about terrorist incidents.[10] However, the presidency gave a biased interpretation to terrorist acts, limiting them to urban violence. "This would provide a very helpful tool in preventing and, where appropriate, prosecuting violent youthful urban radicalism, which is increasingly being used as a cat's-paw by terrorist groups in order to achieve their criminal aims."[11]

The goal is to criminalize legal organizations by considering them to be just social fronts for terrorist organizations: "by which we mean groups taking advantage of their lawful status to aid and abet the achievement of the aims of terrorist organizations recognized as such within the European Union."[12]

When presenting the grounds for the proposal, the Spanish presidency expressed some purely formal reservations concerning guarantees of freedom of assembly and expression: "The information will not relate to people exercising their constitutional rights to express their views and demonstrate at such events [...], but rather to members of actual organized groups run by terrorist organisations for the purpose of achieving their own destabilisation and propaganda

---

10  Council of the European Union. Presentation of a Presidency initiative for the introduction of a standard form for exchanging information on terrorist incidents, 5712/02, ENFOPOL 18, Brussels, 29 January 2002.

11  Council of the European Union. Initiative by the Kingdom of Spain for the adoption of a Council Decision introducing a standard form for exchanging information on incidents caused by violent radical groups with terrorist links, 5712/1/02 rev. 1, ENFOPOL 18, Brussels, 13 February 2002, p. 2.

12  *Ibid.*

aims."[13] These considerations were not intended to be integrated into the text of the Framework Decision. Furthermore, they do not explain at which level of organization citizens who are using their freedom of expression can be considered to be part of groups directed by terrorist organizations.

The information exchanged would be extensive and could concern anyone since it could involve any person "with a police record in connection with terrorism, although any country may, in accordance with its national law, exchange information on individuals not fulfilling that requirement."[14]

*A Technocratic Decision-Making Process*

The Spanish proposal, initially rejected by several Member States, will be presented in six versions. The first two make explicit reference to "violent radical groups with terrorist aims." The first draft refers to events in Gothenburg and Genoa.

Despite the absence of terrorist attacks during G8 or EU summits, the texts, the last of which is dated May 29, 2002,[15] speak of "terrorist organizations carrying out their criminal actions at international events" as well as "terrorist organizations seeking to expand their propaganda and destabilization aims" during European summits and international events.

The last version indicates that the information exchanged cannot concern persons who exercise their constitutional rights as defined by Article 6 of the Treaty of the European Union. But this is a purely formal clause that does not succeed in hiding the fact that protesters are specifically targeted by this text. This proposal was finally adopted without debate as an "A" item at a meeting of the Council of the European Union on November 14, 2002. The subject of that meeting was the competitiveness of member countries.[16] This procedure of

---

13  *Ibid.*

14  *Ibid.*

15  Initiative by the Kingdom of Spain for the adoption of a Council Decision introducing a standard form for exchanging information on incidents caused by violent radical groups with terrorist links, 5712/6/02 rev. 6, Brussels, 29 May 2002.

16  http://www.statewatch.org/news/2003/apr/16spainterr.htm.

making politically embarrassing decisions, without discussion, by including controversial proposals as subsidiary items on the agenda of a meeting ostensibly about other matters seems to be currently alive and well in the Council.

The proposal was adopted as a Recommendation rather than a Framework Decision. The latter requires ratification by national parliaments, but the former does not. Member States that wish to adopt it can do so without having to reach a consensus at the parliamentary level. This Recommendation legitimizes the actions of the most overtly liberty-killing governments in exchanging information concerning political movements.

The "Working Party on Terrorism" was formed within the structure of the Council, uniting experts chosen by Member States. These representatives are answerable to various justice and interior ministers. This group is behind the presidency's statement to the Council that "the Working Party has noticed a gradual increase, at various European Union summits and other events, in violence and criminal damage orchestrated by radical extremist groups, clearly terrorising society, to which the Union has reacted by including such acts in Article 1 of the Framework Decision on combating terrorism, where the offence is defined."[17] These supporting arguments allow us to clarify what the Framework Decision on the definition of terrorism understands by the phrase "seriously intimidate a population."

### The Expansion of the Shengen Information System

The proposal to modify the Shengen Information System (SIS) gathered pace after the September 11 attacks. As a document of the European Council indicates, "the idea of using the SIS data for other purposes than those initially foreseen, and especially for police information purposes in a broad sense, is now widely agreed upon and even follows from the Council conclusions after the events of 11 September 2001."[18]

---

17  Council of the European Union, 13 February 2002, *op. cit.*, p. 1.

18  Council of the European Union, "Requirements for SIS," document no. 5968/02, Brussels, 5 February 2002, p. 2.

The new database could put on file suspected protesters, in order to deny them access to countries where an international demonstration is scheduled. The new system, already called SIS-II, particularly targets anti-globalization demonstrators, who are defined as "persons likely – in the context of certain international events, especially those linked to demonstrations in the context of European summits or comparable events or to sporting events – to be violent troublemakers, posing a threat to public order."[19]

The new database could also include all foreigners coming from a third country and entering into the Shengen area, thereby facilitating verification of their having left the Shengen area upon expiration of their visa.

SIS-II includes very broad categories of data: bank and medical information as well as what Member States already have in their national databases, including genetic fingerprints, fingerprints, photographs and biometric fingerprints.[20]

The Shengen system is fundamentally changing from an instrument for monitoring the movement of people within common frontiers to a police instrument for managing immigration and social conflict. This database, to which intelligence services will surely have access, will be useful for "proactive" police investigations. As with intelligence on airline passengers handed over to American authorities, this new system will be concerned with outlining "virtual personalities," those with a high risk of being potential terrorists.[21]

After the Salzburg, Genoa and Barcelona summits, hundreds of activists were placed on the SIS list, in order to stop them at the borders during the next international events. Another illustration of the use of the Shengen system in the struggle against social protest movements is the recording of intelligence on demonstrators participating in the pacifist action of Greenpeace at Anvers on February 17, 2003.[22]

---

19  *Ibid.*, p. 15.

20  http://www.statewatch.org/news/2003/feb/15.

21  Jelle van Buuren, "Les tentacules du système Schengen," *Le Monde diplomatique*, mars 2003.

22  http://www.statewatch.org/news/2003/feb/15.

# 5

## SURVEILLANCE OF PRIVATE LIFE

Surveillance of the Internet falls within the context of the war against terrorism. It is the latter that determines the meaning of the new criminal procedure regulations that make this surveillance possible.

The current measures in the fight against terrorism differ from earlier laws, such as those that already existed in certain member countries of the European Union, by the fact that they are not reactive but preventative. The object is no longer to react to specific acts, but to prevent a potential threat. This involves anticipating such threats through an exploratory surveillance of the population. Thus it is the antiterrorist fight that justifies organizing systematic surveillance procedures that, often, were already established before the attacks.

The latest English measures that require telecommunications companies to store the content of their clients' messages, while allowing financial criminals and terrorist groups to evade such monitoring, demonstrates quite well, to those who still doubt it, that it is above all a question of establishing a generalized surveillance of the entire population.

American and British antiterrorist laws make simple intrusion into a computer system a terrorist offense. With regard to this offense, these laws carry out their traditional penal role, namely, the conquest of a social space by its privatization and the establishment of disciplinary rules that ensure the reproduction of this stranglehold. However, laws specifically targeting email have generally accompanied the introduction of new crimes linked to the new economic sectors. Modifications to criminal procedure regulations, which allow the preventative retention of computer data or the exploratory surveillance of the content of electronic messages, were introduced by specific legislation or could, as in Belgium, be integrated into laws that create new crimes linked to computer use.

Laws introducing new criminal procedures that authorize the monitoring of the Web and Internet users must be studied in relation to antiterrorist laws.

## AN AMERICAN INITIATIVE

The unique role of the United States is due to the dominant place of American multinationals in the new economy. The privatization of the Web is also something that concerns the United States as a superpower. In fact, it is a constituent part of its imperial management.

American laws, as well as their British clones, increasingly act as models for other national laws. However, it is necessary to note that, given the weaker resistance of English society to attacks against respect for private life, English laws surpass or anticipate, in many respects, U.S. measures.

The most recent laws relating to generalized wiretapping of electronic communications are the concretization of much older proposals, most often secret or at least negotiated in the greatest confidentiality.

Statewatch, an organization for the defense of public liberties based in England, revealed that, already at the time of the European Union/United States summit held in Madrid on December 3, 1995, an agreement was established aimed at enlarging the role of national security agencies in maintaining order in Europe. The content of this agreement was not subject to any debate in the Justice and Home Affairs Council. It was adopted, without debate, as an extra agenda item at a meeting of the European Commission on fishing on December 20, 1996.[1]

In February 1997, a "security" commission of the European Union, created within the framework of the third part of the Maastricht Treaty, had accepted in secret the creation of an international network of telephone wiretapping. According to the Guardian of February 25, 1997, this agreement stipulates that the countries of the European Union should agree on international norms concerning interception, in order to permit the decoding and reading of en-

---

1    Rapport STOA, "Una valutazione delle technologie di controllo politico," p.11, http://www. tmcrew.org/privacy/STOA.htm.

crypted communications by government agencies. According to Statewatch, providers of telephone networks and services are obliged to install systems that make it possible to wiretap and place under surveillance any person or group, from the moment that a request for interception is presented. This proposal was never submitted to any European government nor to the Committee on Civil Liberties of the European Parliament. It led to a protocol, still classified as secret, signed by Member States on December 25, 1995.[2]

The surveillance plan of the European Union-United States exists outside of the third part of the Maastricht Treaty. It is negotiated among twenty countries, the fifteen members of the European Union plus the members of the UKUSA.[3] This group is accountable to no one, neither to national States nor to the European Parliament nor to the Justice and Home Affairs Council of the European Union. Decision-making powers are exercised by autonomous groups of functionaries that carry out police functions and act as intermediaries for American demands, as we will see.

### An Autonomous and Unsupervised Police Group

Since 1993, representatives of the police of most countries of the European Union and the nations of UKUSA organize, once a year, a forum in order to talk about their needs concerning communications interception. These high functionaries are invited by an organization created by the FBI called ILETS (International Law Enforcement Telecommunications Seminar).

The meetings of 1993 and 1994 resulted in the clarification of police requirements. These were noted in an ILETS document called IURI. This document is based on a FBI report published in 1992 that is devoted to the "requirements of police organizations concerning surveillance of electronic communications."[4] It takes up all the FBI

---

2   ENFOPOL,1121-037/95.

3   Group of electronic eavesdropping networks set up secretly in 1947 between Great Britain and the United States, to which were later added networks in Canada, Australia and New Zealand. Stations in these countries form a single integrated network.

4   Duncan Campbell, *Surveillance électronique planétaire* (Paris: Éditions Allia, 2001), p. 107.

demands except one concerning cryptography, which called for "a system for storing or recovering cryptographic keys."

These proposals were adopted by the U.S. Congress in October 1994 and taken up again in 1998 by a new version of IURI.

*From Functional Weaknesses to Police Surveillance*

For Whitfield Diffie,[5] the idea of monitoring the identity of Internet users as well as their movements is linked to the fact that the large e-commerce servers as well as the access providers opted for less secure configurations. He also deplores the lack of security offered by the majority of computers on the market.

Wayne Madsen, former official of the National Security Agency, revealed the existence of weaknesses (backrooms) in a large number of commercial software applications that allow intelligence services to carry out their surveillance activities. The development of a police space on the Net is closely linked with the lack of security in the system. This deficiency results from a deliberate choice of the principal access providers and manufacturers.

Thus, since the discovery of a function called "NSA key," Microsoft is suspected of having implanted such a flaw in its system.[6] Microsoft and Intel, leaders in the "personal" computer industry, were implicated regarding the identifiers placed, without the knowledge of the user, in the Windows 98 operating system and the Pentium III processer.[7]

It can be inferred from this that the providers of computer equipment anticipated the needs of the intelligence services. Moreover, the American government ordered companies to modify their software in order to make it possible for intelligence services to read protected messages.

---

5   American mathematician who revolutionized cryptography in the middle of the 1970s by creating an encryption system used on the Internet to ensure the encoding of electronic mail and to secure electronic commerce transactions.

6   Joël Auster, "Le FBI nous prend pour des naïfs," *Libération*, 7 octobre 2000.

7   Denis Duclos, "Ce petit château de l'âme, cerné de toute part," *Manière de voir*, no. 56, mars-avril 2000, p.28.

The vulnerability of these systems is essential for carrying out surveillance of Internet users. The institutions responsible for the security of the State must then coordinate a double objective: ensure the protection of the technical infrastructure of the United States while making possible the surveillance of the population. This double purpose is the basis for the most recent reforms, such as setting up the Department of Homeland Security (see Chapter 1), part of whose responsibility is to protect "critical infrastructures."

Information on these critical infrastructures, supplied by companies to the new Homeland Security Secretary, will not be subject to the Freedom of Information Act, the law covering freedom of information. This information will be held secret. It concerns intelligence about the search for viruses, flaws in software and vulnerabilities in operating systems. The fact that this information is not available to the public can lead one to assume that securing networks and the reliability of software or operating systems is not the objective sought after, but rather the ability of police and intelligence services to exploit these weaknesses.

This choice complies with the policy developed by the Bush administration concerning "cybersecurity." Richard Clarke, special counselor to the President, stated at the time of the government report on Internet security in September 2002 that it was not a question of taking legal measures to reduce this vulnerability.[8] Responsibility for security on the Net is transferred to companies and users. The computer manufacturers and the telecoms are simply asked to strengthen the security of the products that they sell.

A decree signed by President Bush in March 2003, moreover, permits keeping sensitive information secret, such as that concerning "critical infrastructures" of the Net. In this Executive Order, intelligence on so-called critical infrastructures is put on the same footing as intelligence concerning "weapons of mass destruction" or "defense against international terrorism." In relation to the preceding decree

---

8    Robert Lemos, "Government Unveils Cybersecurity Plan," *CnetNews.com*, September 18, 2002. http://news.com.com/Government+unveils+cybersecurity+plan/2100-1023_3-956353.html; Robert Lemos and Declan McCullagh, "Cybersecurity Plan Lacks Muscle," *CnetNews.com*, September 19, 2002. http://news.com.com/Cybersecurity+plan+lacks+muscle/2100-1023_3-958545.html.

signed by President Clinton in 1995, the new text reclassifes information already released to the public as a defense secret.[9] It is indeed a question of limiting to the maximum extent possible all availability of information that would make it possible to limit the vulnerability of the Web and the possibilities for eavesdropping.

## AN INTERNATIONAL PROMOTION

On April 24, 2001, the parliamentary assembly of the Council of Europe in Strasbourg adopted an international convention on cybercrimes in support of long-standing police demands. This convention involves not only the 41 member countries of the organization but also the United States, Japan and South Africa, which participated in the drafting of the text. On November 5 of that year, the Foreign Ministers of the member countries of the Council, in turn, adopted the proposed law.[10] This convention contains a series of measures that involve integrating new offenses into various national criminal codes and new regulations into national criminal procedure codes.

The new offenses, all intentional in nature, are listed in four categories. There are computer crimes, such as falsification and fraud; offenses against confidentiality, such as illegal access; illegal interception and attacks on the integrity of data or a computer system; and offenses concerning content, such as child pornography and those linked to intellectual property.

Classic rules of criminal procedure are overturned by the introduction of new methods, which aim at increasing police investigative powers. The convention supports the retention of connection data, search of computer systems and data capture. It also recommends the capture, in real time, of data related to network traffic and the content of email messages.

The European Union Parliament had already criticized this convention at the draft stage. On September 6, 2001, the deputies had adopted a recommendation indicating strong opposition to this

---

9   Declan McCullagh, "Bush Order Covers Internet Secrets," *CnetNews.com*, March 26, 2003. http:// news.com.com/Bush+order+covers+Internet+secrets/2100-1028_3-994216.html.

10  Convention on Cybercrime (ETS no. 185), http://conventions.coe.int/Treaty/EN/Treaties/ Html/185.htm, November 23, 2001.

text, above all concerning the new rules of criminal procedure. Parliament refused the general principle of data retention as well as the obligation of citizens, under court order,[11] to allow the decoding of their coded messages or to hand over their cryptographic keys.

The text of this convention is the concretization of a report on cybercrime drawn up by the Council of Europe and approved on October 2, 2000 at Strasbourg. It had received the support of the G8 during the meeting of October 24, 2000 in Berlin. This was long a preoccupation of the G8 since, during their meeting at Mont-Tremblant in Canada in May 2002, the G8 Justice and Home Affairs ministers approved a document in preparation since 1999, "Recommendations for Tracing Networked Communications Across National Borders in Terrorist and Criminal Investigations." This text elaborates upon the principle of preventive retention of data in order to fight against terrorism by identifying a user and his/her activities on the Net.

Ten concrete measures are put forward. Among them is the necessity of "having traffic data available," that is, "logs" that make it possible to reconstruct the history of an Internet user's activity. In order to do this, it is necessary to "ensure the expeditious preservation of existing traffic data regarding a specific communication whether one or more service providers were involved in its transmission, and the expeditious disclosure of a sufficient amount of traffic data to enable identification of the service providers and path through which the communication was transmitted, through the execution of a single domestic judicial or similar order where permitted by domestic law."[12]

This document is accompanied by a list of technical data for IP networks to take into consideration.[13] This list goes beyond the requirements of the fight against cybercrime to cover all the police demands concerning surveillance of the Web.

---

11  Thibault Verbiest, "Le Parlement européen critique le projet de convention sur la cybercriminalité," 16 septembre 2001, http://www.droit-technologie.org.

12  "Recommendations for Tracing Networked Communications Across National Borders in Terrorist and Criminal Investigations."

13  "Principles on the Availability of Data Essential to Protecting Public Safety." http://www.g8.gc.ca/2002Kananaskis/data_essential-en.asp.

*The European Union*

The protection of privacy on the Net has been governed since 1995 by a general directive on the protection of personal data, the main principle of which was the automatic erasing of connection data. Preservation of data beyond what is necessary for transmission or billing purposes was not authorized. A new proposed directive, coming out of the Council of the European Union, was started with the aim of eliminating this principle. The European Parliament and the European Commission were opposed on this proposal.

In July 2001, the Citizens Freedom and Rights Committee adopted the Cappato Report. Parliament followed the proposals of the radical Italian deputy, who wished "to oppose the attempts of Member States to give carte blanche into intrusion into the private life of citizens, deviating from human rights and fundamental liberties."[14]

Amendment 20 to the Cappato Report stated that the limitation of rights protecting privacy "[...]constitutes a necessary, appropriate, proportionate, and temporary measure [...] ."Specifically, it stated that "these measures shall be entirely exceptional and based on a specific law which is comprehensible to the general public, and shall be authorised by the judicial or other competent authorities on a case-by-case basis. Under the European Convention on Human Rights and the EU Charter of Fundamental Rights and pursuant to rulings issued by the European Court of Human Rights, any form of widespread general or exploratory electronic surveillance is prohibited."[15]

On November 13, 2001, European deputies adopted this report and thus validated the principle of prohibiting any form of general or exploratory surveillance. They took a stand in favor of a strict framing of the right of access by police forces to the logs collected by telephone companies and Internet access providers.

---

14 Estelle Dumont, "Le Parlement européen dit non à la surveillance des connexions," ZDNet.fr-Actualités, 12 juillet 2001.

15 Amendment 20, "Recommendation for the Second Reading on the Council common position for adopting a European Parliament and Council directive concerning the processing of personal data and the protection of privacy in the electronic communications sector," (15396/2/2002-C-0035/2002-200/0189(COD)), FINAL A5-0130/2002, 22 April 2002.

The document "Respect for Privacy of Communications," drafted by the Parliament, provided for mechanisms of protection against the use of new "intrusive" technologies. It particularly opposed the possibility of precisely locating the user of a mobile telephone or the installation of spy software in personal computers that makes it possible, without the user's knowledge, to follow his/her movement on the Net or record the content of his/her electronic communications.

*Abandonment of the Principle of Protecting Privacy*

While Parliament had unanimously passed an amendment prohibiting any form of general surveillance, the Council abandoned its proposal for joint regulations and proposed to give carte blanche to the Member States. Implicitly, a mandate would be granted to each national State to monitor its citizens.

The Council of the telecommunications ministers of the fifteen had not, however, abandoned its objectives. On December 6 and 7, 2001, it amended this proposed directive by eliminating the comment "any form of widespread general or exploratory electronic surveillance is prohibited." It thus called into question the amendment supported by Parliament to the initial proposed directive. Consequently, it ratified the position adopted confidentially by the working group COROPER (Committee of Permanent Representatives), a group of functionaries delegated by Member States to assist ministers in preparing for European councils.

Following the reservations expressed by the European Parliament, the Member States had given preference to their participation in the Council of Europe, rather than pursue further action on the European Union level. The liberty-killing context that followed the September 11 attacks made it possible to put an end to the isolated resistance of Parliament. On May 30, 2002, European deputies abandoned their earlier position and passed article 15 of the proposed directive, that stipulates "Member States may adopt legislative measures to restrict the scope of the rights and obligations provided for in Article 5, Article 6, Article 8(1)(2)(3) and (4), and Article 9 of this Directive when such restriction constitutes a necessary, appropriate and pro-portionate measure within a democratic society to safeguard nation-al security, (i.e. State security) defence, public security, the preven-tion, investigation, detection and prosecution of criminal offences or of unauthorised use of the electronic communication system [...]. To this end Member States may inter alia adopt legislative measures providing for the retention of data for a limited period justified on the grounds laid down in this paragraph."[16]

They thus adopted, in opposition to their previous position, the principle of retaining private data that opens the way to a general and exploratory surveillance of communications.

*A Police Demand*

These modifications meet the demands of the ENFOPOL group, which put forward the necessity of preserving, for years, connection "logs" as well as the complete list of protocols used, such as email, fo-rums, etc., the list of contacts and the content of exchanged messages. The "ENFOPOL" group (Enforcement Police) brings together experts from various Interior Ministries of the European Union countries.[17] Beginning in 1995, the activities of this group concerning monitor-ing of telecommunications were revised when the Council adopted a recommendation that extends the principle of telephone wiretaps to electronic communications. This recommendation was the subject of a Parliamentary vote in May 1999. Since then, telecommunication companies must design their systems to facilitate access to unscram-bled data.[18]

The Council of the European Union had adopted a resolution con-cerning the legal interception of telecommunications on January 17,

---

16 Position of the European Parliament adopted at second reading on 30 May 2002 with a view to the adoption of European Parliament and Council Directive 2002/58/EC concerning the processing of personal data and the protection of privacy in the electronic communications sector. P5_TA(2002)0261. A5-0130/2002, Article 15, Line 1.

17 "Data protection or data retention in the EU, Statewatch report on EU telecommunications surveillance," www.statewatch.org/news/2001/may/03/Centopol.htm.

18 Jérôme Thorel, "L'Europe à nouveau tentée par les écoutes en tout genre," *ZDNet.fr-Actualités*, 19/5/2001.

1995.[19] However, this resolution, binding on those States that ratified it, was not published in the Official Journal of the European Communities until November 4, 1996. It sets out the particulars that have to be integrated into national laws. It stipulates that "authorized services" must have access to numbers called or to the number of the caller and to all the telecommunications sent to or from the number used by the subject of the interception.

It specifies that authorized services must have the possibility of surveillance in real time. Network operators or service providers must provide one or more interfaces from which intercepted communications can be transmitted to surveillance installations.

Point 6 of the annex, which defines the particulars authorizing the Member States to carry out a legal interception of communications, states: "Based on a lawful inquiry and before implementation of the interception, law enforcement agencies require: (1) the interception subject's identity, service number or other distinctive identifier; (2) information on the services and features of the telecommunications system used by the interception subject and delivered by network operators/service providers; and (3) information on the technical parameters of the transmission to the law enforcement monitoring facility."[20] Network operators must also make provisions for implementing a number of simultaneous and multiple intercepts by several authorized agencies.

The vote of the European Parliament in May 2002 authorizing the preservation of data thus appears as the result of a whole set of long-standing police demands. Thus, at the beginning of the 1990s, the TREVI group, made up of the Interior Ministers of the European Union, as well as police experts temporarily assigned to the group by Member States, had begun the liberty-killing process. In December 1991, this group, assembled at the request of the FBI in order to coordinate the fight against organized crime and terrorism, decided that "a study should be made of the effects of legal, technical and market

---

19  This resolution is not binding. However, it will be ratified by a certain number of countries that will form an ENFOPOL space. It will be imposed on any new member of this space.

20  Council Resolution of 17 January 1995 on the lawful interception of telecommunications. *Official Journal of the European Communities*, C329, 4 November, 1996.

developments within the telecommunications sector on the different interception possibilities and of what action should be taken to counter the problems that have become apparent."[21]

*Surveillance Carried Out by Autonomous Police Forces*

The authorization granted by the European Parliament for retaining data leaves the door wide open to a generalized surveillance of private life. In the Member States, this surveillance will be carried out by police forces unaccountable to judicial authorities and autonomous from ministerial supervision.[22]

It is the same at the level of the European Union. The European Police Office (EUROPOL) has a significant amount of autonomy. It enjoys immunities that ensure its independence. The Protocol of the Council of Ministers of June 19, 1997 grants its agents immunity from legal process concerning responsibility for any act involving the illegal or improper treatment of data as well as exemption from searches, seizures, requisitions, confiscations and any other form of constraint on its possessions, funds and assets.

Article 8 of the Europol convention also grants to its members "immunity from legal process of any kind in respect of words spoken or written, and of acts performed by them, in the exercise of their official functions" as well as "inviolability of all their official papers and documents and other official materials."[23]

If Europol evades judicial supervision, national as well as European, political control proves to be just as insufficient. At this level, Parliament has a purely consultative role. As far as the Commission is concerned, it can attend meetings of the Administrative Council of Europol, but without voting rights.

---

21  *Ibid.*

22  Jean-Claude Paye, "L'État policier, forme moderne de l'État," *Les Temps Modernes*, no. 605, Octobre-Novembre-Décembre 1999.

23  Protocol drawn up, on the basis of Article K.3 of the Treaty on European Union and Article 41 (3) of the Europol Convention, on the privileges and immunities of Europol, the members of its organs, the deputy directors and employees of Europol. *Official Journal of the European Communities*, C221, 19 July 1997.

This autonomous police force, which already carries out investigations without judicial supervision, also demands a legal extension of its field of operation to the Net, taking up the recommendations of the G8 to its advantage.

In a confidential document, introduced at a meeting at the Hague on April 11, 2002, Europol also proposed a list of data that must be retained by telecommunications companies. This list contains data connected with the Internet protocol, included in the document drafted by the experts of the G8. This data include references to each subscriber's telephone number, identifiers and bank account numbers. It also includes data relative to tracking SMS messages: date, hour, numbers dialed, as well as the geographic coordinates of the calls. The type and length of data retention would be up to each Member State.

In an oral question to the European Parliament, Mario Cappato, who revealed the existence of this confidential document, maintained that the documents is the result of a questionnaire sent to each Member State. For him, "it seems that the Council is in the process of making a general decision that aims at introducing common regulations concerning the retention of data."[24]

### THE EXAMPLE OF GREAT BRITAIN

The British antiterrorist law, the Terrorism Act 2000, which entered into force on February 19, 2001, places computer pirates into the same category as terrorists. It includes in its definition of terrorism any "act consciously designed to hinder or seriously disrupt an electronic system" with the intention "of influencing the government or intimidating the population" for "a political, religious or ideological cause," including "acts outside the United Kingdom." What is more, it makes no distinction between ordinary intrusion into an electronic system, "hacking," and true computer piracy.

This law replaces the 1973 "Prevention of Terrorism" law and thus extends to the new technologies the powers already conceded to the police concerning terrorism. The 1973 law had been formulated to

---

24  Jérôme Thorel, "Communications sous surveillance," http://news.ZDNet.fr-Actualités.

fight against the Irish Republican Army, but it had already been used in a much larger framework.

The new law offers to the British government the possibility of quelling a number of different acts of political opposition. According to Paul Mobbs, official of GreenNet, an Internet host for numerous opposition sites, "if a group leads an opposition campaign aimed at the Prime Minister and overloads an email system, this can be interpreted as terrorism."[25]

### The Legalization of Electronic Surveillance

In July 2000, the British Parliament passed a law requiring the retention of connection data: the Regulation of Investigatory Power Bill (RIP). The RIP Act provided for the installation of black boxes in the equipment of Internet access providers. These boxes must be connected to a police observation center. It also requires users of encoding software to hand over their encryption key at the request of a judge.

This law gave rise to lively opposition that led to the adoption of an amendment providing for criminal sanctions in case of any police misconduct concerning the decryption of court exhibits, but without setting up any mechanisms for supervising the work of the police.

In relation to Belgian and French laws, the English legislation represents a step forward in the legalization of social surveillance, since the law not only allows limited and specific eavesdropping, which would justify the creation of data collections, but institutionalizes a system of global eavesdropping in real time by the police. Only Russia goes further, by setting aside the justification of a criminal investigation, since the Storm 2 program legalizes the installation of black boxes directly linked to the secret services.

In June 2002, the British government planned to institute an extension of the RIP Act, in order to allow local and national administrative authorities to access records of Internet and telephone traffic. The Home Secretary quickly withdrew this edict following criticisms

---

25 Christophe Guillemin, "Les hackers british sont des terroristes en puissance," *ZDNet.fr-Actualités,* 22 février 2001.

from civil liberty defense groups and the opposition of numerous deputies, But the Home Office has not abandoned its proposal and has called for a "broad debate" on the RIP Act. It is thus interesting to analyze the content of the proposal.

If the initiative of the minister were accepted, administrative agencies would be authorized to check data without a legal warrant. There would be no independent examination of the request for interception. The requests for an inquiry would simply be approved by a designated person within each administration. The persons under surveillance who, by chance, might know about the investigation and consider themselves wronged, would merely have the possibility of taking the complaint before the Investigatory Tribunal, a tribunal already called into question by the Intelligence and Security Committee for its structural inability to fulfill its mission, considering "the ridiculous size of its staff."[26]

The Home Secretary also expressed his desire for governmental agencies themselves to determine the length of time to retain information: "It all depends on why they need the information. The retention period must be adequate to permit investigations and judicial prosecutions."[27]

## A Selective Surveillance

The British government, however, was not stopped by this setback. Beginning on August 1, 2002, it required telecommunications companies, including Internet access providers, to intercept and store, upon the demand of an administrative authority, the content of communications by certain subscribers. This data included emails and faxes as well as information concerning web sites visited. This measure required service providers to carry out the surveillance of the targeted person as soon as they receive a legal order for interception. This measure, called Maintenance of Interception Capability Order, was linked

---

26   Matthew Broesma, "Inquiétudes face aux nouveaux pouvoirs de surveillance aux États-Unis," *ZDNet.Uk*, 13 juin 2002.

27   *Ibid.*

to the RIP Act[28] and presented by the government as intended to fight against terrorism. But it concerns only the largest access providers, those with more than ten thousand subscribers. Smaller telecoms, such as those that work with financial institutions, are not subjected to this obligation. Terrorists would thus have no difficulty in avoiding the recording of the content of their communications.

This measure indeed appears as an attempt to monitor the population. Since the surveillance does not concern capital movements nor the holders of that capital, it would be possible for organized crime as well as terrorist organizations to elude it.

*Access Providers as Assistants to the Police*

The obligation put on Internet access providers is the completion of an old project. In November 2001, the Home Secretary had already expressed a desire to amend the RIP Act, by introducing a clause that would legally allow the police to use connection logs for investigations that are not part of the fight against terrorism or organized crime. It was a question of introducing a voluntary clause, a Code of Practice, which would permit access providers to give the police information, in complete legality, on their clients. This code would urge these operators to preserve communications data over a longer period of time than provided for in the law when national security is at stake. The data preserved would be complete files of logs on a person's Internet sessions as well as traffic data that would make it possible to locate an individual.

The government expected the access providers to communicate this data voluntarily so that various administrative agencies could obtain the information without having to seek a legal warrant. This collaboration would be voluntary, but leaving nothing to chance, the government also foresaw the need to regulate this voluntary participation. Clause 102 of the antiterrorist law, Terrorism Act 2000, specifies that if the principle of voluntary participation turned out to be ineffective, the public prosecutor's office would have the right to

---

28  Matt Loney, "Royaume-Uni : les opérateurs télécoms bientôt auxiliaires de justice," *ZDNet Uk*, 12 juillet 2002.

obligate the communications service providers to collaborate with the authorities and preserve connection data.

Just like at the European level, such laws as the Anti-Terrorism, Crime and Security Bill or the RIP Act, as well as their successive adjustments, are in contradiction with all of the preceding laws passed to protect the rights of users, such as the Data Protection Act of 1988. The latter is intended to prevent the disclosure of personal data, stipulating that traffic data must only be preserved long enough for billing purposes, while anticipating exceptions for the prevention and detection of crimes.

## IN FRANCE

In France, the government has guarded against the effects of such contradictions. With the agreement of the great majority of deputies, the Prime Minister and the President of the Republic, the proposed Law Governing Everyday Security, finally promulgated on November 15, 2001, was not submitted to the Constitutional Council, which made it possible to limit the debate to Parliament.

This law establishes a whole series of exceptional procedures, such as searching vehicles at the preliminary inquiry stage and long-distance interrogations by videoconference. It also initiates a "slide towards the privatization of security," as the National Consultative Committee on Human Rights remarked.[29] In addition, it substantially weakens the rights of the defense. In the appendix, it introduces measures that require the preventive preservation of connection data on the Internet for a period of twelve months.

One month after this law's adoption, the retroactive law on finances for the 2001 fiscal year extended its area of application. The law on finances provides agents of the fiscal administration with the possibility of accessing the preserved data authorized by the Security law.

The proposed Law on the Information Society of the Jospin government also allowed for access to the content of electronic messages, under a judicial or administrative warrant. It sought to complete the

---

29   Jerôme Thorel, "La LSQ adoptée après un débat précipité," *ZDNet.Fr-Actualités*, 31 octobre 2001.

regulation of cryptology by requiring service providers to hand over their encryption keys to the Justice Ministry. This measure is in total opposition to another measure taken by this government in 1999 concerning the liberalization of the use of encryption that was presented as the only means of maintaining the confidentiality of correspondence.[30]

*Alignment with the English Model*

The Law on the Direction and Planning of Internal Security, proposed by Nicolas Sarkozy and adopted on August 29, 2002, determines the direction of the government for the next five years. Most of the concrete measures provided for in this framework law must be the subject of other proposed laws, notably concerning the surveillance of computer networks. Here it is a question of permitting remote access by the police to data preserved by the telecommunications companies and Internet access providers, as well as implementing the crosschecking of data from police files. In the appendix, it is indicated that "a proposed law will be developed that will make it possible for the criminal investigation police, acting within the framework of a judicial investigation under the authorization of a magistrate, to access computer files directly and seize remotely, by telematic means or by computer, information that appears necessary to ascertain the truth."[31]

In relation to the Law Governing Everyday Security and the directive of the Council of the European Union on the protection of data in the telecommunications sector, this law represents an additional step in the surveillance of entire populations. It makes it possible to evade the required procedure of sending a requisition to a telecommunications operator. Formally, this procedure imposes the necessity of getting judicial verification of the legality of the request sent to an operator. This procedure, which requires a letter rogatory, forces officials to respect pre-trial investigative procedures and provides for

---

30  Jerôme Thorel, "LSI : la cryto libre et ses accents liberticides," *ZDNet.Fr-Actualités*, 14 avril 2001.

31  Estelle Dumout, "Informatique et sécurité intérieure : un projet de loi pour muscler la LSQ," *ZDNet.Fr- Actualité*, 19 juillet 2002.

possible recourse against the measure.[32] Once again it is the ramparts of the rights of the defense that are collapsing.

The obligation to send a request to an operator also encourages a certain monitoring of the police's work. It makes it possible to establish the number of requests sent and to know their content and purpose. By abandoning the necessity of sending a request to a judicial authority for review, the August 2002 law constitutes an additional step in the merging of police investigation into intelligence work.

The pilot study provided for "direct access by investigators to computer files, seized remotely by telematic means and through searches of computers on networks"[33] as well as "the extension of recourse to telephone wiretapping to pursue criminals on the run," but these measures had to be referred to the Perben Law on reform of the Justice Ministry.

Through a series of decrees specifying how already existing laws concerning encryption should be enforced, the Raffarin government blurred the distinction between police investigative work and the work of the security services even more, while simultaneously trying to transform the providers of encryption services into auxiliaries of the Justice Ministry and the police. Thus the decree of July 16, 2002 that specified enforcement mechanisms for the law of July 10, 1991, relating to the secrecy of correspondence transmitted via telecommunications methods, places in danger the confidentiality of data belonging to users of encryption tools. It asks service providers to implement the "conventions on the decoding of data," i.e., to install back doors in their products and become "reliable third parties" for their clients, by possessing a copy of their key.

What is more, the decree of August 7, 2002 specifying enforcement mechanisms concerning Article 30 of the Law Governing Everyday Security made official the creation of a technical assistance center, the aim of which is to unscramble encrypted information. Since this law anticipates that the work of code breakers "will not have a legal

---

32  Meryem Marzouki, "Fichages, écoutes et interceptions : Raffarin rime avec Jospin," 16 juillet 2002, www.iris.sgdg.org.

33  http://www.assembllee-nat.fr/12/dossiers/securite-interieure.asp.

nature and is not susceptible to any appeal," no judicial supervision is possible.

Under the pretext that the hijackers of September 11, 2001 had entered the United States by regular flights originating in Europe and had done so under their true identities, the American authorities demanded that all air passengers arriving in the United States be identified beforehand. Following an interim agreement with the European Commission, American customs officials have, since March 5, 2003, access to the passenger reservation systems of airline companies located in the European Union. Canada and Australia also concluded similar agreements.

This collection of information is added to a database called CAPPS II, Computer Assisted Passenger Pre-Screening System. The information could be retained for up to seven years. Thus the American immigration and naturalization service is able to detect possible suspects before their arrival in the United States.

The information transmitted, called Passenger Name Record, includes surnames, forenames, address, telephone number, date of birth, nationality, passport number, sex, address during the passenger's stay in the U.S., complete itinerary of the trip, ground contacts, as well as medical data and dietary preferences. The requested information can also include a credit card number or precise reason for the visit. In fact, as formulated by the Americans, the intelligence provided can include "any other data deemed necessary to identify persons traveling [and to] implement regulations on immigration or protect national security and safety."[34] The files already contain 40 distinct entries per client.

*An Unmonitored Surveillance*

The objective is, as we saw, to establish "high-risk profiles." Thus it becomes possible to detect persons presenting a set of characteristics

---

34  "EU Working Party report on passenger data access by USA" http://www.statewatch.org/news/2003/feb/11usdata4.htm.

that would "justify" special surveillance or even preventive arrest upon arrival on American soil. Recall that the USA Patriot Act allows the arrest, without any charge, and detention, without any trial, of any foreigner suspected of participating in any activity of an organization designated as terrorist. The European Commission gave its agreement for the airline companies to provide intelligence on their passengers to American authorities without any means of limiting the information transmitted. The program does not explicitly mention information contained in the "passenger files." The agreement made by the European Commission for the transmittal of data on airline passengers is an agreement in principle that is not based on an exhaustive list of information. That makes it possible for the American authorities continuously to pose new demands.

American authorities have access to the online and check-in reservation systems of the airline companies. The information transmitted will be stored in a database in the Department of Homeland Security called "Arrival/Departure Information System." A filtering system was to limit the information only to flights coming into the United States. In the absence of such a system, American customs authorities would have access to all the data, even of those people who are not passing through their frontiers.

The not easily controllable extension of American demands is not without its problems since, as opposed to the European Union, the United States does not have legislation to protect personal data nor independent organs for the defense of privacy. To put this in perspective, however, it is necessary to note that the European directive concerning the protection of privacy was emptied of all substance by a restrictive clause that mandated the maintenance of order and the security of the State.

### A Consensual Violation of Legality

The law, which requires each airline company to provide all the information that it has on passengers traveling to or from the United States, provides for significant sanctions for recalcitrant companies. In particular, it includes a fine of up to $10,000 per flight.

Moreover, the possibilities for American customs officials to put pressure on airline companies are significant. They have the capability of denying recalcitrant companies from access to the American market. The German company Lufthansa, which had protested against this measure, subsequently saw one of its planes subjected to extensive monitoring. "It is obvious that if passengers from a British Airways flight get through customs in twenty minutes while Lufthansa passengers must wait three hours, the client will ultimately choose British Airways," notes a functionary of the European Commission.[35]

After six months of negotiations, the European Commission permanently yielded to Washington's demands. Various American agencies obtained the right to consult and store the Passenger Name Record data of passengers flying from European Union countries, while various European police forces must get a judicial warrant. Thus a person classed as dangerous could be denied access to American territory. There is no possibility for foreigners to correct the data, even if it is not based on any genuine facts. The ban on entering U.S. territory will last for fifty years for persons classified as "high risk." In general, information is preserved for three and a half years and for seven years for foreigners who have been the subject of a manual search.[36]

The acceptance by the European Commission to have the Aviation and Transportation Security Act applied to European passengers has a twofold consequence. First, it introduces the Union and the Member States into a system of unilateral engagements without the possibility of controlling or enforcing them. Second, it forces Member States of the European Union to violate common regulations, as well as their own laws. After a boycott of Delta Airlines by American passengers, the U.S. Congress stopped the application of these same regulations to American citizens. Hence they apply only to non-Americans.

The European Parliament adopted a resolution on March 13, 2003 condemning the backing given by the European Commission to

---

35  Christophe Lamfalussy, "Sous l'oeil du douanier américain," *La Libre Belgique*, 21 février 2003.

36  Jean Quatramer, "Le Parlement européen condamne le Big Brother aérien," *Libération*, 1 avril 2004.

these regulations. For the Parliament, the transmittal of information on airline passengers violates the European directive on the protection of personal data. Reticence appeared within the Commission itself. The internal working group on the protection of individual data, called Article 29, issued a very critical opinion on these regulations.[37] The Parliament renewed its opposition to this agreement in a new resolution on March 31, 2004,[38] by declaring that access by American authorities to personal data is "illegal in terms of national law and European law on private life." The deputies were particularly worried by the fact that the United States wants to transmit the information it collects to third countries for verification purposes.

This negative opinion did not prevent the European Council from again submitting to the orders of the American authorities in a decision of May 17, 2004.[39] Having a purely consultative role in the matter, the Parliament referred it to the European Court of Justice in order to nullify this agreement. However, in a ruling dated September 21, 2004,[40] the Court refused to apply the expeditious procedure to the examination of the Parliament's complaint. Consequently, the request would be examined only after a waiting period of two to three years, allowing free rein to the transmittal of information on airline passengers. This situation is a good example of how European institutions function. While the representatives elected by universal suffrage operate in a mere advisory capacity, Coroper, the group of permanent members of the European Council, conclude the agreement on widespread recording of passenger information, with the support of the full Council. The overall command structure is essentially administrative. The American authorities negotiated directly with a specialized corps of functionaries. The formal structure of executive authority, be it on the national or European level, essentially

---

37 Matthieu Auzan, "Les passagers des vols transatlantiques sont bien fichés par les États-Unis," www. transfert.net , 9 juillet 2003.

38 "Observatory on the exchange of data on passengers (PNR) with USA," http://www.statewatch. org/pnrobservatory.

39 *Official Journal of the European Communities*, L 183/83, 20/5/2004.

40 http://www.statewatch.org/news/2004/oct/ecj-pnr-orders.pdf.

fills the role of ratifying decisions, without the power, or often even the desire, to weigh in on them.

*Expansion of Surveillance of Passengers in the Union*

While the Parliament was opposed to the transmittal of PNR data to American authorities, the Council of Justice and Home Affairs ministers, during its meeting of March 30, 2004, envisaged carrying out such surveillance for flights departing from or arriving in member countries. The final decision was made during the summit in June 2004. This objective was part of the proposals developed since the beginning of 2003. The proposal was first presented by the Spanish presidency. Surveillance was envisaged for all airline passengers. Then, it was designed to apply only to persons arriving in a country of the Union. The reason put forward was the fight against illegal immigration. At the beginning of 2004, before the March 11 attacks in Spain, the proposal was modified again to cover all passengers.[41]

The plan envisages three classes: green, yellow and red. A person presenting a yellow risk will be subjected to a more thorough evaluation, while the passenger classified as "red" will be prohibited access and probably arrested. This is an administrative decision. The procedure is secret and, of course, there is no possibility for appeal. Persons classified as "yellow" represent the "high-risk" category. It is these people who are the real object of this measure. It is not necessary to resort to this procedure in order to bring in for questioning individuals already sought after or under a summons. The object of this measure is not specific individuals or groups, but to develop a process to stigmatize large parts of the population. The American practice of categorizing individuals demonstrates that the "high-risk" idea can involve 5 to 15% of all travelers.

The March 11 attacks in Spain allowed the British government to introduce two modifications to the initial proposal. Personal data would not be erased and there would be no time limit after which a request from authorities would no longer be acceptable. Access to the data would also be extended to the immigration services. This

---

41  http://www.statewatch.org/news/2004/mar/27eu-pnr.htm.

system could then be used to control migration into the European Union.

## A Strategy of Tension

At the beginning of 2004, the American government had decided to elevate its alert level, after intercepting information that led them to believe that Al-Qaida was preparing "massive attacks" in the USA. Thus, in the space of several days, two flights of the company Aero Mexico connecting Mexico and Los Angeles were canceled and a third was forced to turn back in mid flight because the American authorities concluded that there was a terrorist threat. They claimed that the passengers had not been monitored enough at departure. A British Airways plane coming from London was searched for several hours, after having been escorted by American fighter jets. All the passengers, after having been interrogated and searched, were only allowed to leave the aircraft five hours after landing. According to the FBI spokesperson, the federal police believed that there were on board "people with whom the American authorities wanted to talk,"[42] clearly demonstrating the disproportion between the means employed and the declared objective. American fighter jets also escorted other civilian airliners, including two aircraft of Air France, without any justification other than vague and unverified intelligence. Moreover, six Air France flights were cancelled during the Christmas period in 2003 because the FBI had detected the presence of six names of persons who appeared likely to hijack the planes in order to crash them on American territory. The FBI acknowledged its error. The Wall Street Journal disclosed that the suspect persons were in fact three French citizens, a three-year old child whose name was taken to be that of the leader of a terrorist group based in Tunisia, as well as a Welsh police officer and an elderly Chinese woman.[43]

The unconditional support for the American position or the absence of reactions on the part of other nations allows American authorities

---

42  "La crainte des menaces terroristes demeurent intactes aux États-Unis," *Yahoo! Actualités*, 2 janvier 2004.

43  Jacky Durand et Fabrice Rousselot, "Sarkosy soutient les craintes américaines," *Libération*, 3 janvier 2004.

always to go much further in pursuing the unilateral character of their actions. Moreover, these actions are based not on facts, but on intelligence of which they are the sole holders. The mere possibility of a terrorist action suffices to justify any measure, even if the information quickly turns out to be erroneous or unfounded. The collaboration of other nations is thus based on a common vision of the terrorist context and not on the basis of shared intelligence. Minister Sarkosy thus stated: "We share the analyses of the American services that we live in a period of tension that requires increased vigilance. We have information on the context, but not on the precise action."[44]

GENERALIZED BIOMETRIC SURVEILLANCE

Beginning January 5, 2004, the FBI also has had access to biometric data on airline passengers. In fact, all foreigners entering the United States must allow themselves to be photographed and fingerprinted. This information is digitized and stored. They are compared with police files before authorizing entry into U.S. territory. At the end of 2004, travelers will also have to report their departure from American territory, by scanning their prints at terminals provided for this purpose.

These measures, first operational in airports, will be extended, beginning in 2006, to all border posts. This procedure is an extension of measures already in force, on a case by case basis, since the attacks of September 11. The Department of Homeland Security had the authorization to proceed with taking fingerprints and photographs of all foreign visitors. The use of this right was left to the discretion of the police; now, this procedure becomes systematic.

There is a twofold objective. The procedure facilitates the identification of criminals or presumed terrorists and thus makes it possible to turn them back or arrest them. It also makes it possible to detect persons who have remained on U.S. territory longer than authorized.

The new program, called U.S. Visitor and Immigration Status Indicator Technology would make it possible, at the beginning, to put 24

---

44 "Sécurité sur les avions : Sarkosy défend les exigences américaines," *Yahoo! Actualités*, 3 janvier 2004.

million visitors on file.[45] The U.S. General Accounting Office contests the effectiveness of this program. A very small percentage of errors, of persons wrongly identified as undesirable, would lead to the failure of this procedure. Since this fact is known to all, the Office concludes that the objective of this program is above all to "intimidate people."

*An American Initiative*

The citizens of 28 "friendly" countries, including France, who can enter the United States without a visa, are exempted from this surveillance. But this exemption is coupled with the obligation for citizens of these countries to have, by the end of October 2004, a passport secured by optical scanning in order to enter onto American territory.[46] The passports will be provided with a silicon chip containing the holder's photograph and biometric data: either scanned fingerprints or a reproduction of the iris.[47]

These various American measures concerning the biometric surveillance of foreigners entering into U.S. territory were accepted without opposition by third countries. Only Brazil introduced in its airports a similar measure for American citizens. In fact, the political will to set up such a surveillance system is shared among various European authorities.

In France, the Minister of the Interior, Nicolas Sarkosy, said on January 2, 2004, while visiting Charles de Gaulle airport, that a preliminary test of biometry would be carried out at the beginning of the year. At the European level, "the visas are going to be issued with two biometric components beginning in 2004-2005: digitized photographs of faces and fingerprints."[48] The American demands concerning entry into U.S. territory by citizens of friendly countries only anticipate and justify the measures planned by the authorities of other nations.

---

45 Jean-Marc Manach, "Les USA instaurent le fichage biométrique systématique des étrangers," www.transfert.net/a9518.

46 Pour entrer aux États-Unis, il faudra un passeport sécurisé," www.transfert.net/a9051.

47 Pascal Riche, "Aux frontières américaines: souriez, vous êtes fichés.," *Libération*, 6 janvier 2004.

48 "Biométrie testée ce printemps pour les passagers réguliers," *Yahoo ! Actualités*, 2 janvier 2004.

*Within the European Union*

The fact that various European authorities, at both national and community levels, have submitted to American measures permits them to accelerate their own reforms concerning the establishment of biometric surveillance of populations. The European approach, which consists in unconditionally yielding to American demands, is similar to that taken relative to surveillance on the Net. U.S. initiatives and demands design the strategy undertaken by all national authorities. France anticipated similar surveillance measures. A law of November 26, 2003 already authorizes the government to collect, store and process automatically the fingerprints and pictures of foreign visitors.

The attacks of March 11 in Spain allowed the European Union to accelerate things and no longer justify its projects by putting forward American demands. However, the decision was officially taken before the attacks. On February 18, 2004, the Commission adopted a proposed regulation obliging Member States to introduce personal data, facial picture and fingerprints on passports that they issue. This information, placed on a silicon chip, will also be entered into national databases, to which the police forces, customs authorities as well as immigration services will have access. The national databases will be supplemented by a European register of passports also containing fingerprints. This register would have to link up with the VIS (visas and residence permits) database integrated in the future into the SIS II system (the new Schengen Information System).

Just as with surveillance of airline passengers, the measures were first justified by the necessity of facing up to illegal immigration.[49] Thus such a silicon chip was placed on entry visas and residence permits. It is only in March 2004 that it was officially proposed to extend this measure to all passports and identity documents issued to citizens.

---

49  "EU: Everyone will have to have fingerprints taken to get a passport," http://www.statewatch.org/news/2004/feb/-biometric-passports.htm.

The introduction of new crimes authorizing surveillance of the Net attack fundamental liberties. The new legislation is particularly incompatible with the constitutional principle of legality. These are framework laws that leave a wide margin of interpretation to the judge and above all an almost total freedom of action for the police. The principle of legality is also emptied of its content by the secret character of international measures that act as the basis for national legislation or resolutions of the Council of the European Union. As for the removal of encryption processes, it represents a flagrant violation of the principle of proportionality that a criminal investigation must maintain. In effect, it makes possible an unsupervised extension of police investigations outside the field of a judicial inquiry properly speaking. The legal measures concerning computer crime call into question the autonomy of judicial authority relative to the executive and confirm the overwhelming power of the police.

The requirement that access providers constitute a database on users of their services seems to be the principal objective of these laws. This requirement is part of the current tendency that privileges criminal procedure over the law.

National laws as well as recommendations, resolutions and international conventions relative to computer crime and the retention of data are particularly representative of the new form of the State. They are part of an evolution in legislative practice that violates the constitutional principles that guarantee individual and collective rights.

In relation to recent reforms in the police and judiciary that also restrict individual liberties,[50] these legal acts go much further still in calling into question the rule of law. They attack not only its formal structure but also its material base, the separation of private life from public life.

Surveillance of the Internet highlights the disappearance of private space in comparison with the growing fields of political and economic power, as well as the elimination of a collective space that

---

50   See Jean-Claude Paye, "L'État policier, forme moderne de l'État," cited above.

181

partially escapes the commodification of social relations. The privatization of public space is accompanied by the disappearance of private space.

The implementation of generalized biometric surveillance of populations complements the elimination of mechanisms that protect private life. Police surveillance of population movements is a condition for the integration of their whole existence, including their daily life, into market mechanisms.

### Primacy of the Police Function

The integration of private life into market mechanisms is accompanied by police surveillance, which is no longer limited to the public domain but is now part of daily life. The central role that the police play in managing databases preserved by telecommunications companies appears clearly in the English law that offers to the police the possibility of reading in real time the content of all email messages. In other legislation, this power is camouflaged by the necessity of obtaining a warrant from the examining magistrate before proceeding to seize a particular message. However, the removal of encryption keys permits an extension of investigative power without any effective control on the part of the judiciary or the supervising authorities of the police.

The weakening of the judiciary and its subordination to the police, an increasingly autonomous part of the executive, is a structural element in the extinction of the form of the rule of law. As opposed to England, where the police have a monopoly over judicial inquiries, countries such as France or Belgium, while reducing the prerogatives of judges, still make ritual reference to the necessity of having judicial supervision over police investigations. However, the English model is rapidly being imposed, as the development of French legislation demonstrates.

At the level of the European Union, the resolution of 1995 concerning cybercrime again links the formation of databases to the necessity of responding to the needs of the judiciary. But the proposal to update this resolution is much closer to the Anglo-Saxon model.

In the absence of any control, be it judicial, legislative or executive, there is an increasing autonomisation of police operations at the national, European (Europol) or world levels. This process places the police at the center of the structures of the national State[51] and gives it a central role in the organization of the world market.

The American federal police (FBI) plays a decisive role in elaborating the norms as well as in giving itself the power to apply them, be it in surveillance of the Net or the fight against organized crime or terrorism. The FBI has not only taken the initiative to promote, at the international level, legislation concerning these matters but has also had the ability to influence the content of such legislation, since the various proposed laws respond closely to the specifications demanded by this American organization.

The influence of the FBI is also   manifested in its ability to ensure directly the coordination of its services with the various police forces of the Member States of the European Union, Canada, Australia and New Zealand. Here it is a matter of defining police priorities concerning interception of communications. This supranational police organization is autonomous. It is not controlled, in countries of the European Union, by any judicial, legislative or executive body, be it national or community.

*A Crisis of National Sovereignty*

Control over private life is one of the last prerogatives that remain within the competence of national States. However, this power structure exists within an international context that dictates its actions. Following American demands, various laws instituting new crimes concerning computer use and allowing the retention of electronic information were promulgated by international organizations. The predominance of American demands is explained by the important place occupied by American companies in the new economy. A strong correlation exists between the demands of the FBI and the creation of less secure software by American manufacturers. Police surveillance of the Net is justified and facilitated by the choice of vulnerable con-

---

51   *Ibid.*

figurations on the part of access providers and electronic commerce servers and by the lack of security in computers.[52]

The control exercised by the United States over the organization of police forces and the orientation given to criminal laws and codes of procedure within the European Union is connected with the power of U.S. manufacturers and telecommunications companies to control the market. Software is created as a function of the interception needs of the National Security Agency.

Reforms in criminal law concerning computer crime and the preventive retention of connection data and the content of email messages are emblematic of the crisis of national sovereignty. They challenge the particular mode of organizing power linked to a specific territory, where judicial, legislative and executive competence is exercised by a sovereign State.

Reforms of this nature no longer require a legitimation process in relation to the sovereignty of a "people."[53] Not only are the decisions made at the international level, they are not the subject of any debate and no control is exercised by the formal structures of power established at the national level. What is more, these legislative acts do not appear as the result of political negotiations, but are presented as necessary adaptations to purely technical problems. Hence it is possible for the particular interests of the monopolistic companies of the new economy to be imposed as the only conceivable rationality.

---

52  Cf. Jean-Claude Paye, "Internet: autorégulation du marché et autonomie du contrôle policier," La Pensée, no. 331, juillet-août-septembre 2002.

53  On the question sovereignty, see Étienne Balibar, "Prolégomènes à la souveraineté : la frontière, l'État, le peuple "et Paul Alliès : "Souverainistes versus fédéralistes," Les Temps Modernes, no. 610, Septembre-Octobre-Novembre 2000.

# 6

## REORGANIZATION OF THE NATIONAL STATE

There has been a profound transformation in the national State over the last several years.[1] Significant reforms in the police and the judiciary display a great consistency. They favor the public prosecutor's office over the examining magistrate, while weakening the ability of all judges to monitor the police. They have also strongly reduced the autonomy of the judiciary in relation to the executive.

The various reforms have completely eviscerated the remaining powers of Parliament and sanctioned the primacy of executive power. The Houses of Parliament appear as no more than the organ that ratifies, in an increasingly expeditious manner, decisions made elsewhere. As for executive authority, even if it be strengthened, it is now autonomous bodies, such as the police, that fulfill this function more than the formal structure of the executive branch itself.

### THE POLICE: CENTRAL BODY OF THE STATE

Small urban crime is made into a major problem through the policy of "zero tolerance" and the procedures associated with immediate trial. The strategy of intervention is defined on the basis of the notion of high-risk groups, such as the young, foreigners or the poor. The central actor in these policies is the police apparatus that, in this context, obtains a near monopoly on judicial inquiries. It already occupies a decisive place in formulating the social policies directed at these groups.

The reorganization of power is based less on the law than on procedure, and more particularly on the procedure that is an exception to common law. The role played by the exceptional procedure underlines the central place occupied by the police in the management of populations.

---

1  Jean-Claude Paye, "L'État policier, forme moderne de l'État national," cited above,, and *Vers un État policier en Belgique?*, (Bruxelles: EPO, 2000).

Legislation concerning computer crime, organized crime and terrorism also exhibits a great consistency. Such legislation strengthens the exploratory character of police investigations and brings the latter closer to the work done by intelligence agencies. It also weakens judicial monitoring and the legal protections that guarantee individual liberties.

The importance assumed by the police is thus considerably increased by the adoption of this legislation. The same thing is true of the new laws punishing terrorist acts. One of the objectives of these new crimes is to promote the use of exceptional criminal procedures.

The police, freed from administrative as well as judicial supervision, become the central body of the national State. They not only carry out the function of domination, as the instrument for maintaining order and social control, but they also have a hegemonic function through their mobilization of the population in the implementation of security policies.

The concept of community policing, to which policies of police reorganization invariably refer, goes beyond the framework set up by the idea of a local police force. It is less a question of curbing crimes than of preventing the latter and securing the participation of the population in that effort. This strategy encourages, as in Germany[2] or Belgium,[3] the creation of neighborhood networks bringing together citizens who are anxious to aid the police. This also allows the police to play an important ideological role in mobilizing citizens in the fight against violence. In Germany, the approach is essentially reactive. In Belgium, it is preventive. These groups are particularly directed towards assisting police investigations.

The law on Internal Security of March 18, 2003, proposed by Nicolas Sarkozy, is exemplary. Its objective is to expand the recording of information on the population, of persons simply suspected of offenses. It also aims at increasing the links between files of different

---

2   H.Kurth, G. Groll, "Diffusion de la sécurité à la société civile ou policisation du social," *Les Cahiers de la sécurité intérieure,* juin 1999.

3   Thierry Hendrickx, Sybille Smeets, Cedric Strebelle, Carol Tange, "La police de proximité en Belgique : un bilan des connaissances," *Les Cahiers de la sécurité intérieure,* juin 2000.

police forces. Ulrich Schalchli of the Syndicat de la Magistrature[4] estimates that there will be files on 15 million people, instead of 7 million, in two or three years. Access to the information is open to judges and the police, but also to employers of the public or private sectors who are associated with the department of defense or who use products of a dangerous character. These files could also be consulted to screen entry to a sporting event or to screen applicants for citizenship or renewal of residence permits.

The law also aims at expanding the files on sexual offenders to include crimes against persons and envisages the inclusion of mere suspects. According to the Minister of the Interior, the objective is to record 150,000 genetic prints in 2004.[5] The preamble to the law lays down the methods used for the creation of these files by specifying what will happen when "one or several plausible reasons for suspicion" are encountered. The level of legal protection is strangely similar to the requirements established by the USA Act for the determination of proof, i.e., that it must simply be "convincing for a reasonable person." A ministerial decree will establish how long genetic prints will be preserved.

Parallel to these measures, the Interior Minister's proposed law provides for a whole set of specific measures targeting particular social groups, such as street people, drug addicts or prostitutes. The whole population is seduced into acquiescing to the undermining of the mechanisms protecting privacy by establishing specific discriminatory measures aimed at particular groups in the population. Hegemony is constructed by the use of the scapegoat, the creation of specific relations of domination over particular social groups, which are thus criminalized and excluded from social space.

This procedure is analogous, in both its objectives and its method, to American procedures that eliminate all constitutional guarantees to persons who are not American citizens and to legal measures restricting the individual and collective liberties of the whole population. The exercise of domination over target groups is used as a way

---

4  http://www.lsijolie.net/sq  "L'ère du soupçon," 24 octobre 2002.

5  Jacky Durand, "Petits délinquants au fichier génétique des tueurs et violeurs," *Libération*, 31 décembre 2003.

to exercise hegemony over the whole population. The blurring of the distinction between functions of domination and functions of hegemony or, more precisely, the use of the relation of domination for hegemonic ends is a characteristic of totalitarian regimes.

As far as the preventive retention of connection data and the interception of the content of email messages are concerned, the interim draft of the proposed law anticipated a series of measures that were referred to the Perben Law on reform of the Justice Ministry. These measures provided for "direct access by investigators to computer files, remote seizure by telematic means and searches of computers on networks."[6] The objective of future legislation is thus clearly established.

THE "PERBEN" LAW

In France, the predominance of procedure over law is clearly apparent in the increase in reforms of criminal procedure: 23 modifications in 22 years, including 10 in the last four years.[7] The Perben Law, adopted on November 27, 2003 and entitled Adaptation of Justice to New Forms of Criminality,[8] is the latest example, and not the least, of this transformation.

*The Concept of Organized Crime*

It proposes a broad definition of organized crime. The declared objective is to attack the mafia and trafficking in human beings. However, the list of concrete crimes likely to be identified under this concept does not include any economic, financial or fiscal infractions. On the contrary, it includes new crimes, such as "damage to property," "aid to people staying in the country illegally," and committing offenses in "an organized group."

These choices confirm that, for the government, financial crime is far from being a priority and that it has no relation to organized

---

6   http://www.vie-privee.org/comm55.

7   Jean-Denis Bredin, "Un droit d'exception qui tient les droits de l'homme à l'écart," *Libération*, 20 janvier 2004.

8   Loi du 9 mars 2004 PERBEN II, http://lexinter.net/loi4/LOI_du9mars_2004.

crime. The new idea of damage to property appears in the context of the definition of a terrorist organization, promulgated by the European Union. It could also apply to social actions. As for aiding illegal residents, it demonstrates the national State's redefinition of immigration policies and its desire to criminalize any humanitarian act in this area.

Interpreting acts through the prism of organized crime, a concept that can even include an association of only two people, makes it possible to justify a whole set of exceptional procedures at the investigatory and trial stages. The "organized crime" characterization is particularly extendable. Any crime committed with an accomplice could be characterized as an organized crime. Thus, the techniques of exception used in this context can quickly become the norm.

The Perben Law expands police powers and modifies investigative procedures by increasing the potential for police custody, searches and wiretaps in cases of organized crime. Persons taken in for questioning could thus remain in police custody for 96 hours instead of the 48 hours provided for under common law. From the very beginning of an inquiry, the means available to the police for investigation and coercion are expanded.

It authorizes a preliminary investigation that is arranged without the knowledge of the person concerned. This is a secret procedure, without a due hearing and of unlimited duration. Contrary to usual procedures, the police will be able to implement special investigative techniques, such as wiretapping, undercover operations, and close surveillance by placing microphones and cameras in private spaces. This espionage would be authorized for a period of four months and possibly renewable. In the absence of the suspected persons, the police will be able to proceed with searches at night and seize pieces of evidence. Police investigations become similar to the work of the intelligence services, with the same absence of judicial monitoring and protection for privacy.

The expansion of police powers at the level of the investigation is coupled with an increase in its scope of activities at the trial stage. The accused could be judged solely on the anonymous testimony of an undercover police officer and could be confronted with this testimony only by means of a videoconference.

If the concept of an organized group is used to describe the facts of the case, then it could be treated by a special jurisdiction, a tribunal covering several regions. This new authority, which has yet to be defined, would have a much closer relationship to the police,[9] increasing the subordination of the judiciary to the police even more.

*Weakening the Investigating Magistrate*

Generally speaking, the Perben Law advocates a procedure, the "plea bargain," called "appearance in court upon prior recognition of guilt." In the United States, this procedure has become quite common. It has become the least risky choice for the accused. In exchange for an admission of guilt, it is possible to obtain a reduction in the charges by amending them (for example, a murder charge changed to manslaughter) or a recommendation of clemency to the judge.[10] It formally introduces a type of contract between two unequal parties and a way of negotiating that is opposed to the principle of legality.

The promotion of plea bargaining is coupled with another procedure introduced in 1999: restitution, by which the perpetrator of a crime can escape prosecution in exchange for compensating the victim and performing community service work. At the beginning, this procedure was reserved for crimes with a maximum penalty of fewer than three years imprisonment; the law on criminal reform moves the threshold to five years. As a result, crimes such as aggravated theft, fraud, influence peddling, misuse of company property and breach of trust are included. These offenses, commonly linked to financial crime, could be the subject of negotiations that would allow the perpetrator of the acts to avoid going to trial.

Nicolas Sarkozy's intention, expressed on September 26, 2002 before the police association, of attacking what remains of the law of presumed innocence is expressed in a justice of one rule for some

---

9  Jacqueline Coignard, "La parole est à l'accusation. Le projet de loi Perben renforce les pouvoirs du parquet et de la police," *Libération*, 27 novembre 2003.

10  Pascal Riche, "Plaider coupable, modèle américain," Libération, 27 novembre 2003.

and another for the rest. On the one hand, there is a presumption of guilt for those who will be introduced as such by the police and, on the other hand, the possibility of evading the law for the perpetrators of economic and financial crimes. This privilege is legally written down. It is made part of the legal order.

By means of this law, the Minister of Justice is introduced into the criminal code. As such, he claims the power to intervene into individual files. In effect, he records in the law itself the end of the formal separation of powers. The French Minister of Justice presents himself as a judge with extraordinary prerogatives that are given to him by the law. The choice of what to prosecute will be carried out by a public prosecutor strongly controlled by the executive authority. The strict dependence of the prosecutor is assured by the reorganization of the indictment process, now structured around general prosecutors named by the Council of Ministers. Parallel to the powers accrued by the police, the balance of power within the judiciary is profoundly changed. The role of the prosecutors is formally strengthened. They legally oversee the preliminary police investigations.

As in Belgium, with the creation of the "mini-investigation"[11] the moment when an investigation can begin is delayed and, as a result, the moment when the rights of the defense can be exercised. As regards organized crime, the prerogatives of the examining magistrate are reduced to the advantage of the State prosecutor, who reports directly to the Minister of Justice and, in practice, favors the police. The prosecutor, in fact, does not have the means to supervise closely the particular investigative techniques employed within the context of this procedure. Most of the measures undertaken during the preliminary inquiry are placed under the supervision of the "judge of release and detention."

---

11  The 1998 law on the Improvement of Criminal Procedure at the Investigation Stage gives the King's prosecutor the job of managing the inquiry. The prosecutor can demand that the examining magistrate carry out certain acts that fall within the competence of the latter alone without opening an investigation. This runs the risk of confining the investigation itself only to acts excluded from what is already called the mini-investigation. The transfer of power from the examining magistrate to the prosecutor's department delays the moment when the investigation begins. During the investigation, the prosecutor retains a right of inquiry.

The magistrates' associations opposed these measures. For Dominique Barella, president of the Union Syndicale des Magistrats, "the authority of the examining magistrate is emptied of all substance by shifting responsibility for supervising the work of the police to an apparent judge, a judge of release and detention."[12] For Évelyne Sire-Marin, president of the Syndicat de la Magistrature, the plan "ratifies the expansion of exceptional procedures relating to lengthy police custody. The examining magistrate is marginalized and the role of the prosecutor is enhanced. This only strengthens again the weight of the executive power in the operation of justice."[13]

The subordination of the function of the investigating magistrate, resulting from the Perben law, is also clearly seen in the introduction of productivity bonuses called adjustable bonuses. The use of these bonuses to control the pay of magistrates makes it possible to take into account "the manner in which the magistrates carry out their functions"[14] that is, the manner in which these judges submit to the orders of the executive authority. These measures, made in the context of the fight against organized crime, increase the power of the police by restricting the area of the investigating magistrate's competence. They anticipate future changes in the French criminal code since, as we have already seen, as opposed to neighboring countries, the legal concept of organized crime did not exist in France. The legal definition of a criminal organization separates prosecution of a crime from the commission of a crime. The definition of this new crime aims at legalizing the proactive approach of the police.

The weakening of the investigating magistrate in France appears within a European context in which the powers of the police are strengthened at the investigation stage. Countries such as Italy or Germany have pushed things even further, since the investigating magistrate has disappeared and been replaced by the magistrate of

---

12  Cécile Prieur, "Le projet Perben sur la criminalité fait la part belle aux policiers," *Le Monde,* 13 décembre 2002.

13  *Ibid.*

14  Dominique Simonot, "Perben 2 braque juges et avocats," *Libération,* 20 janvier 2004.

the investigation.[15] The latter no longer has jurisdiction over the investigation. The assignment, rather, is to carry out a certain number of acts for which that magistrate alone is competent: the arrest warrant, surveillance measures and searches. Above all, the primary role is to be the guardian of the legality of the procedures in question. As for England, the problem is reduced to its simplest expression: the police simply have a monopoly on judicial investigations.

THE NATIONAL STATE: A STRUCTURE INTEGRATED INTO THE EMPIRE

The legal definitions of criminal organization and terrorism, as well as the laws that deal with cybercrime and authorize the legal retention of computer data, completely change the criminal law of national States. As seen above, these measures have their origin in American initiatives, mainly in the specific demands of the FBI. On these matters, the FBI also has the possibility of directly organizing the police forces of other States. The European Union and the Council of Europe, which have drawn up various conventions enjoining their members to make legislation quickly concerning these matters, have served as relays for American demands.

Thus the central place of the police in the structure of the national State is not only the consequence of isolated policies. It also results from the reorganization of power at the world level. The fight against terrorism forms the decisive factor in this restructuring and is the privileged instrument of the Americans for strengthening their domination.

This change in the exercise of power goes beyond the simple modification in the juridical form of the State to affect its material constitution, its mode of organization, as much internal as external.

*Control over Populations: Basis of the National Form of the State*

The change in criminal law (the domination of procedure, including the procedure of exception, over the law) is accompanied by a structural change in the organization of power. It implies an instru-

---

15 Damien Vandermeersch et Olivier Klees, "La réforme Franchimont," *Le Journal des Tribunaux* no. 5886, 23 juin 1998, p.442.

mentalization of the judicial apparatus by the executive power, more precisely the subordination of the Justice Ministry (or Department) to the police. In practice, judicial authority no longer exercises any control over police work. It only appears afterwards, as a sort of guarantee or support for the prosecution decisions made by the police.[16]

Police forces, be they national or European (Europol), have the capability of negotiating agreements and organizing their collaboration with one another independently of the national or European executive structures to which they belong and outside the control of national or European legislative and judicial authorities.

The national State finds its specific place within the imperial structure as administrator, not of the police forces, which are partially international, but of a judiciary that is strongly instrumentalized by the executive power.

Up to now, the only point of resistance from the national State against the relinquishment of sovereignty resulting from globalization was the preservation of the formal structure of the judicial apparatus. The management of populations and the surveillance of individuals are the prerogatives that specifically define the national form of the State. This resistance of the national State appears particularly clearly at the internal level of European construction and in the relations between the latter and the American superpower.

However, the results of intergovernmental negotiations are moving in the opposite direction concerning the creation of a European judicial space or police and judicial cooperation with the United States. Through the institution of a European arrest warrant, the European Union proves to be a developed form of the national States that compose it, while the latter begin to abandon a significant portion of their sovereignty over their populations to the American State.

---

16   Jean-Claude Paye, *Vers un État policier en Belgique?*

The national form of the State is articulated around a border that marks the place where the normal juridical order is suspended. According to Schmitt, the border is "the antidemocratic condition of democracy" in the modern State. As Étienne Balibar interprets it, it is "the place where the monopoly of legitimate violence takes the form of preventive counter-violence."[17] The management of population movements through immigration and asylum policies is a perfect example.

If the sovereignty of the national State is exercised over a specific territory, the American State eludes this limit. It is the only one to free itself from the border as a limit on its power. In the war against terrorism, American courts gave themselves an extra-territorial jurisdiction that evades international law. This self-attribution of jurisdiction is a function of the legalization of police operations outside the United States or of military operations conducted without a declaration of war.

The agreement on extradition and judicial cooperation between the United States and the EU gives a new dimension to the U.S.'s extra-territorial scope of activities. The possibility of having European citizens handed over to the United States for trial outside of any constraint defined by the rule of law gives the American judicial system a particular place in the maintenance of the world order. The whole of this agreement records in the law the specific role of the American national State as world police. If the national form of the State is related to the function of maintaining order, the American State plays a directly imperial role at this level.

Thus the national State of the United States occupies a particular place. Its executive structure remains an integrated whole and is not diminished to the advantage of one of its components, such as the police. The American federal police have an international function of organizing the national police forces of other countries.

The USA Patriot Act brought out a second aspect of the course of action pursed by the United States: the domination of one particular

---

17  Étienne Balibar, "Prolégomènes à la souveraineté: la frontière, l'État, le peuple," p.56.

power over other States. The exercise of imperial domination proceeds through the specific prerogatives that the superpower grants itself. It remains the only particular nation to have an outside: the rest of the world and non-Americans.

If the Patriot II Act is passed by Congress, the distinction between Americans and foreigners (since the withdrawal of citizenship can lead to extradition) at both the criminal and administrative levels will no longer be a constraint on the executive power of the United States. However, this distinction will still be imposed for foreign institutions. The citizens of the United States will remain protected from the actions of an outside judicial authority, national or supranational, if their act is protected by the executive power of their country. Various bilateral treaties, as well as the agreement obtained by the United States at the United Nations, prevents any prosecution of American citizens engaged in "actions of maintaining the peace." Here also, the benefit of the privileges attached to American citizenship is linked to behaviors that conform to government policy.

The articulation of this proposed law with the treaties mentioned above leads to a result characteristic of an imperial power: it eliminates the internal/external distinction for the American government, while preserving the privileges of American citizenship in relation to foreign judicial and administrative authorities.

# 7

## AN IMPERIAL STRUCTURE

It is the fight against terrorism that provides the link between the reorganization of the national form of the State and the restructuring of power at the global level. It makes possible the establishment of an integrated world political command in which the national State, refocused on questions of maintaining order and social control, acquires a new place.

Criminal law plays a decisive role, both in the change at the national level and in the establishment of a global order. It is the component of the system used by political power to emphasize the central place occupied by the police at these two levels of the imperial structure.

The influence of the United States over control of the Internet, as well as over the transformations in criminal codes and procedure and in the conduct of police forces, represents one of the aspects of the exercise of imperial power concerning the regulation of the market and control of a globalized society. The other aspect lies in the exercise of direct domination by a superpower that has the possibility of regulating international political relations as a function of its particular interests.

The war against terrorism therefore structures the two aspects of the exercise of imperial power: hegemony and domination. It is the context for the new agreements on judicial and police cooperation between the United States and the European Union. These agreements allow the American executive power to force other States to recognize the powers of exception that it arrogates to itself.

Before the Patriot Act, adopted after the September 11 attacks, various American laws already included a definition of terrorism. They authorized U.S. courts of law to extend their competences outside of the United States itself.

The adoption of these laws was always the occasion for the American lawmaker to claim liberties with international law. Thus, the Omnibus Diplomatic Security and Terrorism Act, passed on August 12, 1986 by Congress, grants universal competence to national courts. Prosecutions must be authorized by the Attorney General, who must certify in his decision that this offense was committed with a view to "constrain, intimidate or exercise reprisals against a government or a civilian population."[1]

The extension outside U.S. territory of American judicial prerogatives is coupled with the possibility for the FBI to seize individuals wanted by the U.S. in foreign countries without authorization by local authorities.[2] The U.S. Supreme Court effectively decided, in an arrest of February 28, 1990, that American authorities had the right, in the absence of a legal warrant, to carry out searches of the homes of foreign citizens and seize them outside the territory of the United States.[3]

However, the new antiterrorist measures have another significance than the generalization of privileges, which the United States already had the habit of claiming for itself in criminal matters. They are the occasion for completing a reorganization of police and judicial systems at the international level. It is a question of setting up an asymmetric structural relation in which American institutions would occupy the role of the party who gives the orders.

The last agreement on extradition and judicial cooperation between the United States and the European Union, signed on June 25,

---

1   United States Code Annotated, Title 18, 1990, Cumulative Annual Pocket Part (St. Paul, MN: West Publishing Co.), § 2331, p. 72-73.

2   See C. Rousseau, "Pouvoirs exceptionnels accordés au FBI par le département américain de la Justice," "Chronique des faits internationaux," *Revue générale de droit international public*, 1990, p. 491-492.

3   "Verdugo-Urquidez Case, Decision of the Supreme Court on February 28, 1990," 110 S Ct, 1056(1990), *Harvard International Law Journal*, vol. no. 1, 1991, p.295-301.

2003, gives a new dimension to the extraterritorial jurisdiction of the United States. The possibility that a European citizen can be handed over, as well as put on trial, outside of any constraint imposed by the rule of law, grants the American judiciary a special place in the maintenance of world order. This agreement represents an additional step in the establishment of an imperial structure. It constitutes the moment when the European countries abandon the power of assuring that court appearances of their citizens will occur according to the legal guarantees granted to them in conditions determined by a particular national State. There exists a significant difference between the right claimed by the strongest to exercise the privileges they grant to themselves and the inclusion of this prerogative in the law of other countries.

This agreement on extradition plays a decisive part in carrying out the demands formulated by the United States to the member countries of the European Union in the aftermath of the September 11 attacks. On October 16, 2001, the American government had sent to the President of the European Commission a list of sixteen action proposals. The demands of the United States addressed to the European Commission were an attempt not only to increase their power, but to carry out a veritable reorganization of police and judicial cooperation. This involved allowing the police authorities and magistrates of each Member State to negotiate directly with American judicial authorities, while short-circuiting national procedures as well as the various levels of controls that they imply. Judges were also authorized to demand legal files orally or invite witnesses to appear in court.

Washington solicited "rapid access" to "critical" financial and bank files and demanded that Europol transmit directly intelligence on persons linked to terrorism or organized crime.

American and European expectations concern different matters. The United States particularly insists on the ability of its administration and courts to obtain the extradition of European citizens or foreign residents in Europe, as well as the necessity of defining a "modern approach" to terrorism. This would involve, notably, establishing a common list of crimes that could not be considered political.

European negotiators want to strengthen cooperation in the area of computer crime. They also desire to establish a joint approach to interception of telecommunications and organize joint investigative teams.[4]

These intersecting demands are actually complementary. Each camp represents one aspect of imperial sovereignty. The Europeans demand that the United States exercise its hegemony in organizing control of the Internet and of all means of communication. American expectations are the demands of a superpower that grants itself particular rights. These privileges are the counterpart of its political control.

## THE EUROPOL-UNITED STATES AGREEMENT: AN AUTONOMOUS NEGOTIATION

On December 20, 2002, the agreement on cooperation between Europol and the United States was instituted. Its aim is to facilitate information exchanges between the two parties, particularly of data of a "personal nature." These data are intelligence on the "physical, physiological, mental, economic, cultural and social characteristics" of persons suspected of belonging to a terrorist organization or of taking part in organized crime.

This agreement stipulates that data relative to "race, political opinions, religious or other beliefs, sexual life style"[5] will be exchanged, if these steps are considered "appropriate" to the development of an investigation.

Handing over this data is not, however, necessarily intended to curb any criminal offenses. Operating with the idea of detecting and preventing offenses makes it possible to be freed from having a particular judicial aim in mind or even needing the existence of a particular crime. What is more, Article 5 includes handing over data relative to procedures concerning immigration. Concerning terror-

---

4   "Secret EU-US agreement on criminal cooperation being negotiated," *Statewatch Analysis no. 12*, www.statewatch.org/news/2002/jul/11Auseu.htm.

5   Council of the European Union, "Draft supplemental agreement between the United States of America and the European Police Office on the exchange of personal data and related information," 4 November 2002, 13689/02.

ism, the exchange of intelligence also involves steps to seize and restrain assets or confiscate goods, "even where such seizure, restraint or confiscation is not based on a criminal conviction."[6]

After the September 11 attacks, a provisional agreement on cooperation between Europol and the United States was signed on December 6, 2001. It provided for the exchange of strategic and technical information, but explicitly excluded personal data. Thus, this new agreement goes much further. It includes personal data and eliminates any protection mechanism. It includes no mention of principles of protection for the forwarded information or of specific rules of access for such information.

In accordance with the Europol Convention of 1995,[7] the European Office of Police undertook negotiations with the American authorities with complete autonomy. A decision of the Council on March 27, 2000,[8] gives the Europol director authorization to engage in negotiations with third States not linked to the European Union, i.e., with the United States.

Europol conducts the discussions directly, not the Council of Justice and Home Affairs Ministers or its permanent groups of functionaries, such as Coroper and the Article 36 Committee. The role of the Council is limited to giving its agreement for the beginning of negotiations and to ratifying the result.

The European Court of Justice has no possibility to rule on the validity of the agreements nor the power to interpret them. The European Parliament is not consulted. There is no obligation even to inform it. No ratification by national parliaments is required. A number of documents bearing on certain conditions in the Europol-U.S. agreement are secret.

---

6   Council of the European Union. Note from the Presidency to the Council. "Consolidated Version of the Exchange of Letters Related to the Supplemental Agreement," 5 December 2002, 15231/02 ADD 1, Europol 104, Article 5, p. 3.

7   Convention based on Article K.3 of the Treaty on European Union, on the establishment of a European Police Office (Europol Convention), *Official Journal of the European Communities*, C316, 27 November 1995, p. 2-32.

8   "Council Decision of 27 March 2000 authorising the Director of Europol to enter into negotiations on agreements with third States and non-EU related bodies," *Official Journal of the European Communities*, 13 April 2000, 200/C106/01.

During the preliminary discussions, several Member States were troubled by the absence of control over the use of the information handed over. It appeared that an indeterminate number of American institutions, judicial, police and also administrative, would have unlimited access to the data forwarded by Europol. The European party insisted, moreover, on introducing a clause allowing Member States and Europol to lay down restrictive conditions for the use of forwarded data.

States that were hesitant about some conditions in the agreement, including Germany, in the end, gave in on the question of forwarding information without any possibility of being able to control its use. However, initially, they remained inflexible on the question of extradition. On the other hand, the conditions posed by the United States concerning the exchange of information were accepted. The U.S. demanded that there be no changes in existing national laws. They had indeed just passed two particularly restrictive laws concerning the protection of personal data: the USA Act and the Cyber-Security Enhancement Act. The United States also demanded that there be no change in the procedure allowing automatic access to the data by various American institutions. American authorities were, furthermore, unable to be specific about how many agencies would have access to the information forwarded by Europol.[9]

DELAYED JUDICIAL COOPERATION

While the joint police teams, working with the FBI, were already operational in European Union territory, American demands in the area of judicial cooperation were not satisfied. Control over the work of the justice ministries was the only point where the European countries still demonstrated their national sovereignty. The discussions between the American Department of Justice and the Council of Justice and Home Affairs Ministers concerning a cooperation agreement were suspended by a Council decision on February 28, 2003.

The United States wanted to be treated as a Member State of the European Union on questions of extradition and mutual judicial

---

9  "Proposed exchange of personal data between Europol and USA evades EU data protections rights and provisions," 27 novembre 2002, http://www.statewatch.org/news/2002/nov/12eurousa.htm.

cooperation. This implies, as with the European arrest warrant, the application of the principle of the mutual recognition of judicial decisions and thus the abandonment of the principles of political and judicial control over extradition demands from the United States.

Since September 11, several demands for handing over suspects residing in the European Union to American authorities had been refused by the member countries concerned.

The concern brought up by the EU that led to the suspension of negotiations was the reticence of several Member States to hand over persons who could be condemned to death or be tried before special courts in the United States. Some countries, including Germany, remained inflexible on the question of extradition. The Danish Presidency did not succeed in successfully concluding the projected agreement between the European Union and the United States concerning judicial cooperation and extradition.

Progress was made in the discussions at the meeting in Copenhagen on September 13, 2002, which took place in the absence of any intervention on the part of the European Parliament and the assemblies of Member States.

The negotiations between the European Union and the United States concerning cooperation in criminal matters are based on Articles 38 and 24 of the Treaty of the Union. It is on this basis that the Council of Justice and Home Affairs Ministers gave a mandate to the President of the Council to open negotiations. Coroper, a permanent group of functionaries attached to the Council, conducted the negotiations. This facilitated the confidentiality of the negotiations, as well as the absence of control on the part of various national and community legislative and executive authorities.

On May 8, 2003, the Council of Justice and Home Affairs Ministers reluctantly accepted the results of the negotiations. The agreement was signed once and for all in Washington on June 25, 2003. This agreement will have to be ratified by the U.S. Congress as well as the national parliaments of the Member States of the European Union, which explains why the final documents became accessible.

The text contains two parts: an agreement on extradition and an agreement on judicial cooperation.

The text also applies to Member States that already have bilateral agreements with the United States. Until now, these bilateral negotiations were the preferred means for the United States to impose its demands on questions of security and justice. A comprehensive agreement at the level of the European Union was too visible and likely to cause resistance. The new political context after the September 11 attacks allowed the United States to negotiate directly with the European Union.

The finished agreement assures a minimum level of cooperation. If bilateral treaties between some Member States and United States go further concerning mutual obligations, then they continue to be applicable, complementing the agreement negotiated by Coroper.

*A Broad Scope*

The proposal was justified by the necessity of taking on the most serious crimes, such as terrorism and organized crime. However, the agreement's field of application is very broad. It covers the great majority of crimes prosecuted by various criminal codes. Thus, an offense can lead to an extradition if it is punishable, in the requested and requesting States, by a penalty of more than one year in prison.[10]

The agreement negotiated by Coroper departs from the measures found in the bilateral treaties that authorize extradition for only a limited list of specific offenses. On this point, the text promoted by the Council of the European Union is substituted for the language found in the national treaties. There exists, however, a great difference between the two procedures. The European text makes it possible to generalize the extradition procedure, formerly circumscribed to the most significant offenses. The European agreement also considers that an extradition can take place for the mere attempt or "conspiracy" to commit an offense, as well as participation in the commission of a crime.

---

10   Article 4, "Draft Agreement on Extradition between the United States of America and the European Union," Council of the European Union, 8295/1/03, Rev. 1, 2 June 2003.

The refusal of some member countries to hand over suspects to the United States in cases of a capital offense could be circumvented due to a clause that stipulates that "the requested State may grant extradition on the condition that the death penalty shall not be imposed on the person sought, or if for procedural reasons such condition cannot be complied with by the requesting State, on condition that the death penalty if imposed shall not be carried out." These stipulations were criticized on May 3 by the European Parliament, which considered that the question of the death penalty should be an explicit consideration that would prevent an extradition. Referring to the European prisoners held at Guatanamo, it also expressed its desire that "the agreements explicitly exclude any form of judicial cooperation with American exceptional and/or military courts."[11]

*An Implicit Recognition of Exceptional Jurisdictions*

The European arrest warrant permits an almost automatic handing over of a wanted person, without control over the appropriateness and legality of the demand. This procedure is based on mutual recognition of legal decisions.

Since the United States wants to be treated by European countries as a Member State of the Union, it also wants extradition to the United States to be deprived of all political or judicial controls. This is the fundamental issue underlying the agreement. It is not possible to determine from the text itself just where this objective is met. Nothing is dealt with concretely. The text is only the visible portion of an iceberg of secret negotiations. National parliaments will have to support a type of framework-agreement, in which the modes of enforcing the agreement will determine its real scope.

The agreement is, moreover, constructed in such a manner that the American authorities can exert pressure on European countries so that constitutions or judicial decisions present no obstacles to their demands. The agreement specifically states that "where the constitutional principles of the requested State may pose an impedi-

---

11   European Parliament. "Report containing a proposal for a European Parliament recommendation to the Council on the EU-USA agreements on judicial cooperation in criminal matters and extradition (2003/2003(INI)), FINAL A5-0172/2003, 22 May 2003, p. 6.

ment to fulfillment of its obligation to extradite, and resolution of the matter is not provided for in Agreement or the applicable bilateral treaty, consultations shall take place between the requested and requesting States."[12]

In fact, this agreement is the first step towards satisfying American demands. Given that the text of the agreement does not exclude judicial cooperation with a military tribunal and does not explicitly oppose extradition demands for persons who are going to be tried in exceptional jurisdictions, it actually constitutes recognition of the legality of these special courts. Remember that a Presidential decree, made within the framework of the USA Patriot Act, establishes special military commissions to try foreigners accused of participating in the activities of presumed terrorist organizations. Nothing prevents European citizens, handed over by their national authorities, from being tried by these jurisdictions. These military courts eliminate any possibility of assuring a fair defense and function with a particularly less demanding burden of proof than regular courts. Remember that around 20,000 immigrants, who have not been accused of any crime, are currently in prison in the United States.[13]

These agreements assume the form of a mutual undertaking. In fact, for European countries, it will be, above all, a matter of satisfying demands coming from the United States. The demands laid down by George Bush on the Belgian presidency, i.e., the possibility for an American judicial authority to approach an equivalent European institution directly, without any political or judicial control on the part of the State in question, could now be about to happen. Article 5 stipulates simply that the request "…shall be admissible in extradition proceedings in the requested State…"[14] American authorities are going to take action again at the level of bilateral agreements in order to adapt them to accelerated handover procedures.

---

12  Article 16a, "Draft Agreement on Extradition between the United States of America and the European Union."

13  http://www.examiner.ie/pport/web/ireland/Full_Story/did-sg46g7KsOcvBEsg70WirlStPSk.asp.

14  Article 5, "Draft Agreement on Extradition between the United States of America and the European Union."

The agreement established between the European Union and the United States is a significant step in the organization of an imperial structure. While the United States already had the possibility of directly organizing European police forces, this was not the case with European judicial systems. The latter had a certain autonomy in relation to the globalization of the political command structure. This relative independence defined the national form of the State. This obstacle formed, up to now, the only point of resistance on the part of European countries to American demands. This last constitutive pillar of the sovereignty of national States is in the process of collapsing.

## The Agreement of Judical Cooperation

The second part of the agreement concerns judicial cooperation. This covers a very broad area: from exchange of bank information to surveillance and the interception of communications, as well as the formation of joint investigation teams.

Article 4 requires the requested State to ascertain if banks located in its territory possess information on "whether an identified natural or legal person suspected of or charged with an offence is the holder of a bank account or accounts."[15]

The information must be related to an investigation or a criminal prosecution but can concern any type of crime or the mere suspicion of the existence of an offense. The demand for information must contain "sufficient" detail to allow the authority of the requested country "to have reasonable grounds" to believe that the information concerns a criminal infraction.

## Absence of Protection for Forwarded Data

While a legal purpose is usually put forward to justify the exchange of personal data, the text of the agreement provides for an almost unlimited possibility of using the exchanged information. The information obtained can also be used in non-criminal administrative procedures or "for any other purpose, only with the prior consent of

---

15 Article 4, "Draft Agreement on Mutual Legal Assistance between the United States of America and the European Union," Council of the European Union, 8295/1/03, Rev. 1, 2 June 2003.

the requested State." The requesting State can, without the explicit consent of the requested party, use the forwarded information "to prevent an immediate and serious threat against its public security." The requested State may impose specific restrictive conditions on use of the data, but may not impose "generic restrictions with respect to the legal standards of the requesting State for processing personal data." That means that a European State may not refuse to hand over information to the United States just because the latter does not have legislation for the protection of personal data.[16]

In a general manner, the orientation of the agreement is that there be the fewest possible restrictions on the demands of a requesting State. Thus when a bilateral treaty imposes fewer restrictions on the use of information, these measures can be applied in the place of the relevant clauses of this agreement.

Also remember that there are no rules for accessing forwarded data nor any possibility of correcting the information, as Directive 95/46 of the European Union guarantees. The absence of such protections is also a violation of the Charter of Fundamental Rights, which follows this directive. Article 8 of this Charter places the protection of data as a fundamental right on the constitutional level.

What is more, the agreement contains no clause specifying what authority can have access to the information nor any condition regulating the forwarding of data to a third party. The American authorities offered, moreover, no guarantee that this data would not be handed over to private companies.

*Legalization of Joint Investigative Teams*

Article 5 concerns the formation of joint police investigative teams. Indeed, this clause ratifies an already existing situation: "The Contracting Parties shall, to the extent they have not already done so, take such measures as may be necessary to enable joint investigative

---

16 Article 9, "Draft Agreement on Mutual Legal Assistance between the United States of America and the European Union."

teams to be established and operated in the respective territories of the United States and each Member State..."[17]

These police teams organize themselves. Their actions are formally limited to investigations and criminal prosecutions. However, no provision is made for judicial supervision of their work. "The procedures under which the team is to operate, such as its composition, duration, location, organization, functions, purpose, and terms of participation of team members of a State in investigative activities taking place in another State's territory shall be as agreed between the competent authorities responsible for the investigation or prosecution of criminal offences, as determined by the respective States concerned."[18] Thus no judicial monitoring, be this at the level of the examining magistrate (when one exists) or the prosecutor, is set up over the operation of these investigative teams. Although intended for use in the prosecution of criminal acts, this procedure can also be set in motion by an administrative authority.

Thus that part of the agreement concerning judicial cooperation turns out to be, above all, an agreement on police cooperation around formally criminal investigations. This is, first of all, a legalization of joint police teams already active. The text of the agreement also makes it possible to go beyond just the framework of information sharing and provides a legal opening for existing practices of police collaboration. Above all, it institutionalizes existing practices such as the possibility, already used by the FBI, of promoting investigations and managing joint police teams operating outside the territory of the United States.

THE BILATERAL TREATY BETWEEN IRELAND AND THE USA

The Mutual Legal Assistance Treaty between Ireland and the United States,[19] which was just signed in July 2005, is a good example of a bilateral agreement constructed entirely to the advantage of the dominant power. This treaty, signed by the Irish Minister of Justice, Michael

---

17  Article 5, "Draft Agreement on Mutual Legal Assistance between the United States of America and the European Union."

18  *Ibid.*

19  http://www.statewatch.org/news/2005/aug/ireland-usa-mlat.pdf.

McDowell, is a concrete application that falls within the scope of the agreements on extradition and legal assistance signed in June 2003 between the European Union and the United States. First presented as an obligation to assist the United States in its fight against terrorism, it was then made part of the broader and more innocuous framework of cooperation where crime is concerned.

Normally, the judicial authorities of the U.S. can request of their Irish equivalents to carry out the arrest of a person in Ireland and to transfer that person, under Irish control, to the United States. However, this treaty goes much further in satisfying American demands. It allows the Irish police to conduct investigations and to seize evidence upon the request, not of a judicial authority, but of the American government. The latter, then, is granted the authority of a magistrate. It also authorizes American investigators, who can be secret service agents, such as the CIA, to interrogate Irish citizens secretly in Ireland. Persons designated as suspects will not only have to give their testimony, but may be investigated and, if necessary, seized by the Irish police, even if they are not suspected of any crime in Ireland. This agreement also allows American judicial and administrative authorities to have access to secret bank information concerning Irish citizens. Upon the request of American authorities, this procedure must remain secret.

This bilateral treaty thus introduces a triple level of exception. It transfers the police authority belonging to the Irish authorities to foreign authorities. It grants police authority to secret services and it confers a secret character on police procedures, thereby bringing them into line with the practices of the intelligence services. As the Irish Council for Civil liberties stated, this agreement between Ireland and the USA goes even further in the dismantling of judicial protections than the agreements signed between the Member States of the European Union do.

Secrecy characterizes the deliberations that led to this treaty. However, in order for these new procedures to take effect publicly, they must have a legal basis in Ireland. Hence, they will have to be authorized by the clauses introduced into the new law regulating mutual assistance concerning criminal justice.[20]

AN ASYMMETRICAL RELATIONSHIP

The extradition agreement has effects similar to those of the European arrest warrant.[21] Handing over wanted persons entails recognition of court orders, verdicts or investigations made by the requesting country. Thus, in effect, this is a process of recognizing, à priori, the democratic character of the judicial apparatus and political system of the requesting State.

While the European arrest warrant implies, for example, that articles from the Italian criminal code, such as the criminalization of a subversive organization, which comes from the Fascist code, are considered to be democratic, the recent agreements reached with the United States result in accepting that the laws and exceptional measures made by the United States conform to human rights.

There is, however, an important difference. The European arrest warrant is a system of exchange and mutual recognition. The agreement on extradition between the UE and the United States is reciprocal only in form, since it is combined with other bilateral treaties that proscribe bringing American citizens to trial. It is enough to consider agreements, imposed on certain partners of the United States, which prohibit the extradition or transfer of American citizens before the International Criminal Court. Remember that Great Britain, Italy and Spain blocked any joint European reaction against this type of agreement. Thus the American executive power will gradually be able to impose this kind of clause on a number of member countries of the European Union. This asymmetry will first be revealed in actions before being assuredly transcribed into treaties, as American demands become increasingly pressing and European surrender more and more obvious.

---

20   Dan Buckley, "Treaty gives powers over Irish citizens," http://www.examiner.ie/pport/web/ireland/Full_Story/did-sg46g7KsOcvBEsg70WirlStPSk.asp.

21   Jean-Claude Paye, "L'Union européenne : un espace de liberté, de sécurité et de justice?," *La Pensée*, no. 334, juin 2003.

The United States has the capability of imposing its own criteria concerning forwarded data, as well as its special courts for trying foreigners. By relinquishing their own legality, the European countries accept the subjection of their citizens to procedures laid down by the United States. The latest agreements on extradition thus place European citizens into the American system of exceptions to the law.

These agreements contribute then, as with other agreements, to the organization of an imperial structure. The international recognition of the status of the exception imposed by the United States makes possible the reorganization of the judicial system at the international level. Thus, the American executive power exercises world sovereignty. It is the American executive that sets the boundaries between the norm and the exception and inscribes the latter into the law.

During the month of May 2002, the Bush administration demonstrated overt opposition to the International Criminal Court. It accused it of infringing on American national sovereignty. The United States thus denied that the ICC has the power to judge its soldiers.

*An Imperial Sovereignty that Evades International Law*

On June 30, 2002, the American ambassador to the United Nations justified the decision to deny the jurisdiction of the International Criminal Court over American citizens in these terms: "What we do not want to see is American peacekeepers going forth into the world undertaking substantial risk in the pursuit of international peace and security be subjected to the jurisdiction of a Court to which the United States is not a party."[22] He had previously stated that any attempt to take in an American citizen for questioning "would be considered illegitimate and would have serious consequences." The United States had threatened to withdraw their troops from Bosnia if they were not granted immunity from prosecution before the ICC.

United Nations resolution 1422 of July 12, 2002 satisfied the United Sates. It prohibited the International Criminal Court from prosecuting American citizens taking part in peacekeeping operations for a

---

22   Fabrice Rousselot, "Les États-Unis s'exemptent de justice," *Libération,* 2 juillet 2002.

period of one year. Formally, the resolution requests that the Court, "if a case arises involving current or former officials or personnel from a contributing State not a Party to the Rome Statute over acts or omissions relating to a United Nations established or authorized operation, shall for a twelve-month period starting 1 July 2002 not commence or proceed with investigation or prosecution of any such case ..."[23] The United States is not a signatory to the Rome Statute. The Security Council expressed its "intention" to renew this request every twelve months for as long as necessary.

John Negroponte, US ambassador to the UN, announced that this resolution "constituted only a first step." He also declared: "we are going to take advantage of the coming year to look for additional protections."[24] Indeed, the United States has also turned to bilateral agreements on immunity and non-extradition in order to undermine the authority of the International Criminal Court. They obtained from Israel, Colombia, Argentina, South Africa and Rumania agreements not to transfer American citizens to the ICC. What is more, Congress passed a law in August 2002 called ASPA (American Service-Members' Protection Act) that permits the imposition of sanctions on those countries unwilling to meet American demands. Such countries could face the end of American military assistance if they do not promise to never extradite an American citizen to the jurisdiction of the ICC.

As far as these bilateral treaties are concerned, the European Union does not have a common position. That leaves open the possibility that such agreements could be drawn up between different Member States and the United States. Great Britain blocks any consensus in this context and, as we have seen, is joined by Spain and Italy in its opposition to any joint agreement.[25]

---

23  http://www.un.org/News/Press/docs/2002/sc7450.doc.htm.

24  *Ibid.*

25  "La lutte antiterroriste n'autorise pas le viol des droits de l'homme," entretien avec Kenneth Roth, secrétaire exécutif de Human Rights Watch, *Le Soir*, 23 janvier 2003, p.13.

Six days after the September 11 attacks, President Bush signed a Presidential Finding giving broad powers to the CIA in the antiterrorist struggle, including the authorization to kill, capture and detain, anywhere in the world, individuals considered to be part of al-Qaida, Thus the agency can, with or without the cooperation of foreign security services, arrest suspects outside of American territory, keep them in detention in these countries or transfer them to other regions. It can also use interrogation techniques that are prohibited by American law and that contravene international agreements concerning the prohibition of torture to which the United States is a party.[26]

More recently, it has been revealed that the CIA has chartered six planes for secret flights. According to Amnesty International, the CIA has carried out 800 flights since 2001, of which around 430 alone have been above German territory. These flights have been used to convey prisoners to their country of origin (extreme rendition) as well as to transport detainees from one center to another.[27]

Numerous examples confirm the existence of torture in these centers. Craig Murray, British ambassador to Uzbekistan from 2002 to 2004, was forced to tender his resignation following publication of information establishing links between Great Britain and the United States concerning the program of "extreme renditions" to Uzbekistan. When he denounced these crimes to the government, the latter responded that "it was perfectly legal to obtain intelligence by means of the torture chambers of Uzbekistan."[28]

---

26  Dana Priest, "Covert CIA Program withstands New Furor – Anti-Terror Efforts to Grow," Washington Post, December 30, 2005.

27  Philippe Grangereau, Pascal Riche et Marc Semo, "La lutte antiterroriste ébranlée," Liberation, 7 décembre 2005.

28  Patricia Lombroso, "Prisons et tortures CIA: l'Union européenne savait, affirme un ex-ambassadeur britannique," Il Manifesto, 9 février 2005, http://www.ilmanifesto.it/Quotidiano-archivio/09-Febbraio-2006/art80.htm.

Following a request from the American secret services to clarify the rules on the amount of pain they are allowed to inflict on prisoners, the Department of Justice issued a report on August 1, 2002 that gave a very narrow definition of torture. The latter was defined only as physical pain that "accompanies serious physical injury such as death or organ failure."[29] In December 2004, the Department of Justice abolished these regulations. However, the American administration's definition of torture remains quite restrictive. For the Bush administration, to deprive a detainee of sleep, to beat him or her, provide him or her with unhealthy food, subject him or her to loud noise, cold, or heat, to simulate his or her execution or threaten him or her with drowning are not torture, but are "strong interrogation techniques" or "moderate physical pressure." However, these strong interrogation techniques are indeed similar to torture such as it is defined by the 1984 Convention that prohibits "acute physical or mental suffering" intentionally inflicted to obtain information. The "renditions" are also a violation of international law. Article 49 of the fourth Geneva Convention explicitly prohibits such actions. American law also prohibits such "renditions" when they involve returning a detainee to a country that is suspected of practicing torture.

Vice President Dick Cheney unsuccessfully fought to have the CIA excluded from the provisions of the McCain Amendment to the 2006 military spending bill, which prohibit torture. However, the Boston Globe revealed that the American president has reserved to himself the possibility of ignoring this amendment under certain conditions.

The export of torture outside of U.S. territory is one of the methods developed by the administration. Several former officials, some of whom occupied positions of responsibility, have provided information in interviews about the implementation of the procedures used. Within the structure of the CIA's clandestine sites, each center has a specialty. According to Robert Baer, former CIA agent: "If you want a serious interrogation, you send a prisoner to Jordan. If

---

29   Cécile Chambraud, "Des pays européens accusés de collusion avec la CIA," *Le Monde*, 18/11/2005.

you want them to be tortured, you send them to Syria. If you want someone to disappear - never to see them again - you send them to Egypt.[30]

*A Globalized Organization*

According to the Washington Post, more than 100 prisoners have been transferred into secret prisons created by the CIA in eight foreign countries. As a matter of urgency, the CIA first entrusted prisoners to Jordan and Egypt. By the summer of 2002, two new black sites had appeared in Thailand and in an eastern European country.[31]

There are two components to the CIA program. First, there are the black sites, the secret prisons where about thirty prisoners are detained and interrogated. These detainees live in total isolation. They have no legal rights and no one can be in contact with them. Then there are the extraordinary renditions of prisoners to foreign governments where the latter deal with them. It is this program that the New Yorker explained in detail in February 2005. These prisoners, around 70 in number, are in Egypt, Syria, Jordan, Morocco, Saudi Arabia, Afghanistan and Uzbekistan.

The "black sites," where the most important prisoners are kept, are directly operated by the CIA. The other camps, where the other 70 less important detainees are kept, are organized by the host countries with the financial assistance of the CIA and sometimes under its command.

The Washington Post first revealed the existence of these "black sites" set up by the CIA on European territory in an article on November 2, 2005.[32] According to journalist Dana Priest, who, acceding to the demand of American authorities, promised not to reveal their identity, several European countries are involved. Because of their involvement with the American army in Iraq, Hungary, Bulgaria, Poland and Rumania were immediately suspect. Four cases of

---

30  Stephen Grey, "America's gulag," *The New Statesman*, May 17, 2004, http://www.newstateman.com/200405170016.

31  Pascal Riche, "La CIA délocalise ses prisons pour la lutte antiterroriste," *Liberation*, 3/11/2005.

32  Dana Priest, "CIA Holds Terror Suspects in Secret Prisons," *Washington Post*, November 2, 2005.

"rendition" involving European countries are known: the transfer to Egypt of two Egyptians, Ahmed Agiza and Mohammed Zeri, picked up by the CIA in Stockholm in December 2001; a former imam by the name of Abu Omar, sent to Egypt from Milan via the American base in Ramstein, Germany; and the case of a German of Lebanese origin, Khaled al-Masri, kidnapped by the CIA in Macedonia in December 2003, detained for several months in Afghanistan, then released in Albania.[33]

While all European countries proclaim their innocence, the reaction of the European Union is to feign astonishment. The European Commissioner of Justice threatened to suspend the voting rights of any country belonging to the Union that harbors illegal detention centers. The "request for clarification" presented by the British minister, Jack Straw, on behalf of the European Union betrays the same attitude of denial. Indeed, it is enough to remember that, for the British government, confessions extracted under torture by foreign agents would be sufficient proof to expel the individuals in question. The English executive authorities are not the only ones to openly share this interpretation. Witness the statements of the new German Interior Minister that justify the use of information obtained under torture, so long as German officials do not commit these acts themselves.[34]

On the other hand, on November 22, 2005, the Swiss Senator, Dick Marty, President of the Committee on Legal Affairs and Human Rights of the Parliamentary Assembly of the Council of Europe, was charged with preparing a report on the question of the violation of European air space by flights transferring prisoners to torture sites as well as on the existence of CIA secret detention centers in Europe.[35] In his preliminary memorandum, he states" drawing on all this concordant information and evidence we can say that there is a great deal of coherent, convergent evidence pointing to the existence of a system of "relocation" or "outsourcing" of torture... set up by the

---

33  "Sur la piste des activités cachées de la CIA en Europe," *Le Monde*, 9/12/2005.

34  "Spiegel online" December 16, 2005.

35  "Le Conseil de l'Europe ouvre une enquête sur les éventuelles prisons secrètes de la CIA," *Le Monde avec AFP*,23/11/2005.

CIA in defiance of international law and the European Convention on Human Rights." According to him, even if it is difficult to obtain concrete proofs, several facts exposed for the first time by American media, on the basis of American administration documents or documents of certain NGOs, are today well established.

During an interview on Télévision Suisse romande, Marty confirmed that all European countries are implicated, to varying degrees, in the CIA's system of relocating torture. He stated that "for three years, all countries have known full well what has been happening. Some have actively collaborated, others have tolerated it and the rest have simply looked the other way."[36]

The good faith of the European countries can be pleaded only with great difficulty because, while NATO allows the CIA to land planes on one of its bases without the authorization of the local government, the secret services of member countries of the European Union work in close collaboration with their transatlantic colleagues. The position of the European governments can be summarized in the question posed by the rapporteur: "Is it enough for one's own secret services not to be physically present at the place of interrogation and to pretend to have no official knowledge of this practice to state that the law is not being broken?"[37]

The reorganization of the CIA's work is not limited to the establishment of a global structure of secret detention camps. The agency is also involved in setting up a secret structure of intelligence agencies in cooperation with European, Asian and Middle Eastern agencies. According to the Washington Post of November 18, 2005,[38] CIA centers, jointly managed with local intelligence services, exist in more than twenty countries. For its part, France is home to a multinational general headquarters called "Alliance," which mounts operations throughout the entire world.

---

36 "Les gouvernements européens auraient été au courant des prisons secrètes de la CIA," *Le Monde*, 14/01/2006.

37 Parliamentary Assembly of the Council of Europe, Committee on Legal Affairs and Human Rights. "Alleged secret detentions in Council of Europe member states." Information Memorandum II. AS/Jur (2006) 03 rev 22 January 2006, http://assembly.coe.int/Main.asp?link=/CommitteeDocs/2006/20060124_Jdoc032006_E.htm.

38 Dana Priest, "Foreign Network at front of CIA's terror Fight," *Washington Post*, November 18, 2005.

In closed testimony before the US Congress, a CIA official explained that practically all of the captures or eliminations of suspects since September 11, 3000 in all, were made in cooperation with foreign intelligence services.[39]

These centers are independent of national intelligence services. They are formed with the participation of local agents, specially named by the governments concerned.

The former CIA director, George Tenet, who made major changes in the American agency by organizing cooperation with foreign services, set up these centers. They thus appear as part of a fundamental and permanent change in the mission of the CIA, which occurred a little after the 2001 attacks. Whether it is a question of secret detention centers or intelligence, the American agency is no longer a tool only for foreign intervention by the superpower. It has become, like the FBI in police affairs, a tool that plays an imperial role, one that is directly involved in the function of maintaining world order, an order that also, despite their denial, is supported by the member countries of the European Union.

THE POLICE FUNCTION AS BASIS OF IMPERIAL SOVEREIGNTY

The antiterrorist campaign is the outcome of a widespread process of restructuring politics, organized on the basis of international police cooperation that is autonomous from national authorities and directly managed by the United States.

The place taken by the police in the imperial structure is due to the fact that it is situated at the intersection of control over various markets and surveillance of populations. In a period of interpenetration between finance capital and various criminal gangs,[40] the police play an important role in the regulation of markets. In fact, it is police action, and not the law, that determines what is criminal or not, that

---

39   "La CIA aurait créé des centres antiterroristes à l'étranger," Le Monde avec AFP et Reuters, 18/11/2005.

40   See Jean Ziegler, Les Seigneurs du crime, les nouvelles mafias contre la démocratie, Le Seuil, Paris, 1998, Les nouveaux maîtres du monde, Fayard, Paris, 2002 ; Jean de Maillard, Le Marché fait sa loi, Mille et une nuits, 2001 ; "La tentation mafieuse," Le Monde Initiatives no. 14, décembre 2002. Also refer to Vladimir Ivanidze et Sophie Shilab, "Rusal, numéro un mondial de l'aluminium, mis en cause pour ses liens avec les mafias russes," Le Monde, 13 février 2003.

distinguishes crimes, which should be prosecuted, from acts that, although illegal, should be considered as part of the normal reproduction of the dominant class.

The police play an essential role in the exercise of domination as well as hegemony. Currently, the mechanisms of power operate less through the discipline imposed by the organization of the labor process than through control exercised over the entire process of existence, including private life, of all individuals in both the dominated and dominant classes.

The fight against terrorism has made it possible to divide the world into two axes: the "axis of good and the axis of evil." External sovereignty is no longer established as a function of the power to make war. That prerogative is reserved to the American superpower. Conflicts are no longer thought of as simple police operations conducted against "rogue States," such as Iraq, or against terrorist populations, as in Chechnia.

Hence, there is no more exterior in the management of the Empire. The distinction between internal and external sovereignty is no longer applicable. The antiterrorist fight integrates various territories and populations under the universal of imperial domination. As for what is still called foreign policy, it is defined as nothing more than an accompaniment to these police operations.

If the police apparatus is at the center of the national State, the police function is at the center of imperial policy. The fight against terrorism leads to a change in the very nature of sovereignty. War is no longer constitutive of the latter. International relations are completely contained within the maintenance of the imperial order as control over various populations.

The strategy developed to deal with social movements is similar to that developed in the war against Iraq. Iraq did not attack the United States. There was not even an imminent threat. The war is presented as a mere anticipation of a seemingly inevitable conflict. The launch of military operations was justified by the necessity of facing "a gathering threat,"[41] according to the expression of President Bush. In the absence of all proof and against any likelihood, it was a question of

---

41  Patrick Jarreau, "Les défis de George W. Bush," *Le Monde,* 25 mars 2003.

averting any possibility of cooperation between the Iraqi regime and Islamic terrorism, since Baghdad was suspected of retaining chemical arms of mass destruction. Antiterrorist legislation proceeds in a similar manner. It attacks organizations that are designated terrorist by the executive power. It also aims at anticipating a potential threat, most often created by the actual policies of the constituted government. Preventive war is coupled with a "proactive" repression.

# 8

# THE FIGHT AGAINST TERRORISM:
## A CONSTITUTIVE ACT

The criminalization of terrorism is part of a long tendency of the "proceduralization" of law. Legal formalization is affirmed first of all by the increasing importance of jurisprudence as adaptation, as instrument for the subjection of the universal to the particular.[1] The increasingly extensive use of jurisprudence in the management of social conflicts is part of a wider issue: the regulation of society on the basis of procedure.

If the intervention of the law is increasingly present everywhere, it is expressed in the form of the procedure, so that it is possible to speak of a "proceduralization" of social relations. Antiterrorist laws form the last element of this process. They establish a law exploited by an autonomous apparatus of the executive power, the police.

## A CHANGE IN CRIMINAL LAW

The reasons that justify establishing a specific crime of terrorism lie in the idea that terrorist offenses differ from offenses found in common law. In order to differentiate the two kinds of offenses, a criminal act specific to terrorism introduced an element of intentionality, the wish to destabilize political and economic power or to intimidate society. It is the subjective part of the offense, its moral element, which is decisive for characterizing it as a political crime. The terrorist characteristic does not stem from material acts — homicides, attempted assassinations or murders, airline hijacking, etc. — but from the claimed or presumed intention of the offense's perpetrator. The meaning given to this motivation is provided by the policies of the antiterrorist struggle. They codify which actions are acceptable to established authority as legitimate political opposition and make a distinction between the latter and acts designated as terrorist.

---

1   Jean Robelin, *La petite fabrique du droit*, Kimé, Paris, 1994, p.48.

222

The function of criminal law is displaced. Normally, criminal law is concerned with prosecuted persons as individuals. The new crimes related to criminal organizations and terrorist organizations create illegal acts of collective responsibility and focus on organized groups. Simply belonging to an organization designated by the executive authority as criminal or terrorist is punishable, separate from committing any offense or from the intention of doing so.

The subjective character, which is decisive for defining a terrorist offense, plays a role that is all the more important because it does not necessarily concern only specific acts, but also participation in the legal activities of a prosecuted organization or mere membership in or support of the latter. In this case, there is a maximum margin of interpretation. The crime of complicity, put forward by the European Framework-Decision on terrorism, is a good example of the vague and shifting character of this idea. It allows the government to define the concept of terrorism in the short term and, when needed, to adapt its interpretation of that concept and thus decide whom it wants to prosecute.

While the criminal law of countries that have not created specific legislation to punish terrorism is sufficient to prosecute such offenses, it appears that the reasons for creating such a crime are found in the elaboration of justifications for practices and rules that depart from the traditional rules of criminal procedure.

These exceptions occur at each stage of the criminal law process, from inquiry to trial. The exceptions include special investigative techniques such as wiretapping. The criminalization of terrorism also justifies exceptional measures of preventive detention or administrative imprisonment, sometimes directed at mere witnesses, as in the United States. Particular rules concerning communication between the accused and his or her attorney are imposed, as well as the establishment of exceptional jurisdictions.

Exceptional procedures linked to the fight against terrorism are generally extended to other crimes and thus contaminate everything connected with criminal law. Thus the traditional role of criminal procedure is reversed. Instead of being the framework for protecting various public and private liberties, it becomes the means by which the latter are systematically violated. By neutralizing various constitutional guarantees, it effects a suspension of the law.

## SUSPENSION OF THE LAW

While the primacy of techniques of exception over constitutional liberties entails a suspension of the law as well as a change in the judicial order, pure anomie, the exception set down outside any system of law, leads us into another form of the political organization of society. It places us into a new type of political system.

In the United States, the antiterrorist law, the USA Patriot Act of October 26, 2001, authorizes the Attorney General to carry out the arrest and detention of any foreigner suspected of putting national security in danger. These measures were extended by the Military Order of November 13, which makes it possible to subject non-American citizens suspected of terrorist activities to special jurisdictions and keep them in indefinite detention.

These two measures create zones of non-law. They suspend or suppress the legal status of these persons. The latter are totally in the hands of the executive authority and are outside of any judicial supervision. In the same way, the prisoners captured in Afghanistan and incarcerated in Guantanamo do not have the status of prisoners of war, as the Geneva Convention defines it. This suspension of the law is carried out inside U.S. territory as well as outside, since the detention is first preceded by capture through a police operation. Designed to eliminate any protections for arrested foreigners, these measures suspend the law of the United States for individuals who are not U.S. citizens.

This discriminatory law is coupled with a suspension of international law, which privileges American citizens. Any American nationals engaged in "peacekeeping" missions are protected from any prosecution before the International Criminal Court in The Hague.

Whether it be to eliminate any protection for foreigners or to protect Americans from any prosecution before international institutions, the whole aim is to set up prerogatives that privilege individuals who have the good fortune of being American citizens. Such discrimination is the clear manifestation of relations of imperial domination.

The suspension of the law is the expression of a pure balance of power. It is the judicial representation of the exercise of pure violence. However, it is coupled with a hegemonic function through its insertion into American law and acknowledgement by the United Nations. Further, it is accompanied by the acknowledgement on the part of other governments and various populations of the special status accorded to the United States in relation to international law.

The examples of the American and English antiterrorist laws show that the possibility offered to seize foreigners outside of any judicial protection is coupled with proposals to extend this possibility to the whole population, including citizens. The suspension of the law for non-citizens is indeed the first step in a worldwide suspension of the legal order.

CRIMINAL LAW AS CONSTITUTIVE ACT

The new function of criminal law is situated not only at the level of civil society, but also at the ethico-political level, at the level of the State apparatus strictly speaking. Criminal law is currently part of the organic moment of State formation, the organization of the parts in the whole. Criminal law also becomes the means by which various governments redefine the relation between public authority and the citizen. The relation between the sovereignty of the people and the sovereignty of the State is reversed. The proposed American law, Patriot Act II, is the most explicit reform, since it grants the executive branch of government a discretionary power concerning the recognition of citizenship.

Criminal law becomes a tool for reorganizing power at the global level. It is a constitutive relation in the establishment of an imperial State structure as well as the legitimation of the latter. The agreements on judicial and police cooperation between the European Union and the United States are good examples of the role of criminal law in this process.

The place of criminal law in breaking up social movements forces us to examine its function in the process of restructuring power. It is not only now that criminal action plays a significant role to counter the emergence of a social or political opposition. The rule of law in the 19th century was also a rule of non-law. It authorized employers' organizations while prohibiting workers' organizations. However, criminal law in this time period was an objective law, it punished a set of delimited acts, precisely defined. Legal action was essentially re-active. It took place once a crime occurred. Police investigations had an exclusively judicial function and were overseen by magistrates.

Today, we are witness, on the contrary, to a subjectivization of criminal law that makes the courts into auxiliaries of the police. Al-though similar in certain respects to criminal law policies in the 19th century, for example the policy of locking up the poor, particularly prevalent in the United States and growing in Europe,[2] the crimi-nal policies of the contemporary State are fundamentally different. Within the framework of the rule of law, criminal law was a tool for controlling individuals. Now, as an instrument of social decomposi-tion, it is a tool for an internal restructuring of politics.

In the 19th century, criminal law targeted the "dangerous" so-cial classes. It was a question of forcing the proletarians to work and keeping them in their condition of worker objects by preventing them from achieving any social gains and any political recognition. Criminal law protected the rule of law for the possessing classes. As for current criminal law, it is an attack against the social State, the modern form of the rule of law, which guarantees a minimum of public and private liberties to all individuals, including members of the dominated classes.

The revolution in criminal law, established with the definition of the terrorist act, no longer has the purpose of denying the political character of protest actions, of reducing the role of politics in crimi-nal law, but of dividing politics between, on the one hand, legitimate action and, on the other, terrorist crime. The criminal law policy of the contemporary State focuses, not on an organized social force, but on "high-risk groups." It creates a real war against a potential enemy, constantly redefined. It is not a defense of the State against a

---

2    Loïc Wacquant, *Les prisons de la misère*, Raisons d'agir, Paris, 1999.

social movement outside of the State. On the contrary, it is an internal transformation of the structure of power.

### The Identification of Enemy with Criminal

The fight against terrorism abolishes the distinction between enemy and criminal. It is not simply a question of criminalizing the enemy. The two terms result from the same process. The enemy is created as criminal.

War is reduced to a simple police operation against rogue "States." In the same way, any social movement, as internal enemy, can be criminalized in the name of the struggle against terrorism. While the new criminal procedures are similar to the suspension of the law specific to the state of exception, the new crimes create a new order of law. Thus, criminal law becomes formative. Currently, criminal law is part of the organic moment of the formation of the state. Criminal law becomes the means by which various governments redefine the relation between the public authorities and the citizen. The relation between the sovereignty of the people and sovereignty of the State is reversed. The proposed Patriot II law shows us the way: the government establishes the "people."

Criminal law also becomes a tool for reorganizing power at the global level. It has a formative connection to the establishment of an imperial State structure, as well as the legitimation of the latter. While, traditionally, war indicates the external sovereignty of the national State, the "war against terrorism" denotes the imperial order. It allows the President of the USA to redefine permanently the potential border between the "camp of good and the camp of evil." By integrating the police and judicial systems of other nations under the command of the executive power of the United States, international criminal law is constitutive of the internal sovereignty of this imperial structure over whole populations.

The exceptional procedures that lead to a suspension of the law are characteristic of the state of exception. This idea is quite suitable for making sense of historical events, such as the suspension by the Nazi government of all articles guaranteeing individual liberties found in the Weimar Constitution. The idea is also useful for understanding the present situation.

Within the context of the antiterrorist struggle, the type of government characterized by the state of exception is not temporary. It is part of a long-term war against a constantly changing enemy.

The concepts of rule of law or state of exception do not yet allow us to pose the question of the concept of power itself. These ideas simply point to opposing forms of government, alternative modes for the State to organize society, without being able to establish the organic character of their relation. These ideas are, in fact, incapable of conceiving of the State simultaneously as condensation of social relations and as a structure distinct from this society. They are a first approach to the problem. They make it possible to indicate and classify the different changes that we have detected in the methods of the political management of society.

## The Concept of the Rule of Law

The concept of the rule of law is in itself double. On the one hand, in rational theories of law, the rule of law is synonymous with the juridical order. Any State is an example of the rule of law. Thus for Kelsen, it is a simple pleonasm. On the other hand, this form of political organization refers to a set of private and public rights guaranteed by this juridical order. The formal concept is thus coupled with a material base.

The change that we have outlined at the level of criminal codes and criminal procedure calls into question the rule of law, its form as well as its content.

The rule of law also refers to a separation between civil society and the State strictly speaking. More precisely, one can say that this concept represents the mode in which civil society is organized by the State, while keeping the two levels separate. According to Norberto

Bobbio,[3] this public-private distinction is the basis of the very idea of a juridical order.

The concept of the rule of law is, however, only used to designate a particular type of government, whose internal organization guarantees a threshold of individual liberties. The primacy of legislated acts over other forms of producing the legal order establishes the latter as systematized and hierarchical. The distinction between public and private domains is assured by a relative separation of powers, in which the judicial system is guaranteed a certain autonomy.

In the 19th century, the existence of the rule of law applied only to a part of the population, which constituted the society. The non-possessing classes were placed outside the mechanisms of social recognition. The structure of the rule of law could be applied to them only in its pure form, that is, respect for procedures and abstract rights.

In terms of content, the rule of law was also a rule of non-law. The public liberties of the laboring classes were strictly limited. While employers' organizations were permitted, workers' organizations were prohibited. A domestic worker was a legal minor.

The hierarchical relation between the different authorities, legislative and executive, was already greatly modified by the establishment of the social State. The latter is more a rule of law by content than by form. The management of democratic rights, extended to the whole population, is organized in a bureaucratic manner. This form of State is already characterized by the larger share of power given to the executive than to the legislative authorities. The process of governmental decision-making, controlled by the party system, is substituted for parliamentary debate.

The current dismantling of the social State is based on the extension of the supervision exercised by the executive power over parliament. The novelty resides in the narrow instrumentalization of the judiciary by the executive and, in fact, by the subordination of the departments or ministries of justice to various police entities.

---

3   Norberto Bobbio, *Dalla struttura a la funzione. Nuovi studi di téoria del diritto*, Comunita, Milan, 1977.

*The Concept of the State of Exception*

The formal conception of the State conceives of the rule of law as a hierarchical order of juridical norms. Each norm finds its basis in a higher norm, while serving as the foundation for a rule lower down in the hierarchy. This is a complex montage, where any juridical act, while drawing its validity from belonging to this hierarchical order, "is simultaneously the application of a higher norm and the creation, regulated by this norm, of a lower norm."[4] Thus, the formal theory of law makes the Constitution the fundamental juridical act, placed above the other norms and determining their conditions of production. However, it is unable to give an account of the formative act itself as well as of pure acts of constraint. The theory of the state of exception developed by Carl Schmitt integrates this second aspect.

Considered as a purely political fact, the concept of the state of exception is not easy to define juridically since it usually refers to an unusual situation, not covered by the law. It is situated in "an ambiguous and uncertain zone, at the intersection of the juridical and the political."[5] The specificity of this author's approach, a politically committed theoretician of the Nazi State, consists in the reintegration "of pure violence," of non-law, as organization of the real, into the juridical domain.

The theory of the state of exception, constructed by Carl Schmitt in opposition to the formal theory of the law, proves to be, in fact, complementary to the latter. Schmitt founds sovereignty, not on the power to impose a norm, but on the decision freed from any normative obligation. "The exception reveals most clearly the essence of the state's authority. The decision parts here from the legal norm, and ... authority proves that to produce law it need not be based on law."[6] The sovereign is the one who determines an exceptional situation.

In Schmitt, the sovereignty of the State is defined not, as in Max Weber, as the monopoly over the means of coercion or domination,

---

4   Jacques Chevalier, *L'État de droit*, Montchrestien, Paris, 1999, p. 44.

5   A. Fontana, "Du droit de résistance au devoir d'insurrection," in *Le droit de résistance: XIIe–XXe siècle* (Paris: ENS-LSH Editions, 2002), p. 16.

6   Carl Schmitt, *Political Theology: Four Chapters on the Concept of Sovereignty*. Translated by George Schwab (Cambridge, MA: MIT Press, 1985), p. 13.

but as the monopoly to decide. Whereas this definition appears reductionist as a characterization of the nation State, it is particularly appropriate to the imperial structure.

Schmitt is thus incapable of accounting for the organic character of the sovereignty of the nation State, of the interdependence existing between internal and external sovereignty, as well as the articulation of the various institutions and levels of power. In fact, he defines politics on the basis of the "friend-enemy criterion." Such an approach leads to a privileging of foreign policy over internal government.

Following the disarticulation of the nation State and the integration of this now residual structure into a form of imperial power, the problematic developed by Schmitt presents a new interest.

For Schmitt, the decision concerning the exception appears within a juridical order. The exceptional situation is not chaos. If the State suspends the law, it is in the name of its preservation. Within this perspective, the decision on the exception is above all a decision on the conditions of applying the norm. "For a legal order to make sense, a normal situation must exist, and he is sovereign who definitely decides whether this normal situation actually exists."[7]

Thus the theory of the state of exception is presented as a theory of sovereignty, in a double movement. The decision on the exception is the mark of power, but the sovereign, who determines the state of exception, guarantees its insertion into the juridical order.

## Pure Violence and the Juridical Order

The debate between Walter Benjamin and Carl Schmitt on the relation between violence and law, as recounted by Giorgio Agamben,[8] allows us to go further. While Benjamin gives pure violence an existence outside of the law, Schmitt wants to reintegrate its effect into the juridical order.

In fact, the opposition rests on different evaluations of the distinction between a fictitious state of exception and a real one. This dif-

---

7    Ibid.

8    Giorgio Agamben, State of Exception. Translated by Kevin Attell (Chicago: University of Chicago Press, 2005).

ferentiation is found in both authors. Schmitt calls a state of exception that is regulated by the law fictitious. He relies on the opposition made by Theodore Reinacht between real state of siege (or military) and fictitious state of siege (or political).[9] Benjamin takes up this distinction in order to reject it more effectively. For him, the fictitious state of exception is itself a simple fiction, since it is impossible, when the exception has become the rule, to distinguish the norm from its exception. For him, the Nazi State is the very example of the impossibility of the law reintegrating violence into itself. The latter becomes pure violence and exists outside of the juridical order. Thus, the state of exception does not guarantee the separation, in time and space, between the legal order and exception to it. This form is not, as in the rule of law, the articulation between an outside and an inside, between norm and anomie. It becomes a zone of absolute indetermination.

When the elements of this discussion are compared with the analysis of the current situation, one indeed sees a zone of indetermination between law and exception. This vagueness is situated in time as well as space. The fight against terrorism is a mobilization, for an indefinite length of time, against an enemy that is periodically redefined. However, we must speak of a relative indetermination and not an absolute one.

The relations between the norm and its exception, as well as the respective content of each of these terms, are constantly adjusted. These changes depend on the most immediate change in the balance of power. The vote on the Patriot II law is suspended due to the resistance of American society, in the first instance, to the ability of civil liberties organizations to stand effectively against such projects. The boycott of American airline companies, such as the one announced against Delta Airlines, made it possible to suspend, for American citizens, surveillance measures to which other airline passengers must submit.

---

9    *Ibid*, p.4-5, 58.

## THE EXCEPTION: BASIS OF A NEW JURIDICAL AND POLITICAL ORDER

The concept of the state of exception developed by Schmitt is useful for the analysis of the current reforms in criminal law and its enforcement procedures. The crimes and procedures that are exceptions to common law are part of a global change in the exercise of power. This drastic change can, for the time being, be viewed as establishing a form of a generalized state of exception, which does not consist simply in the temporary suspension of the law, as in the state of siege, but is part of a radical modification in the juridical order.

While the state of exception is not the establishment of a special law, like the law of war, but the suspension of the existing legal order, it is also the establishment of a new legal order. The decision to suspend the norm remains within the juridical domain. It is integrated into a global change in the law. It is the most advanced point, as well as the tool, of this change.

When the American executive authority, instead of resorting to the law of war by using courts martial, creates special military courts to try foreigners accused of terrorism and removes any legal status from arrested persons, it totally suspends existing law, including the law of exception. However, the exception is the basis on which new laws are created. The proposed Patriot II law, which includes a provision to strip American nationality from any citizen accused of terrorism, is not only the extension of the suspension of legal guarantees to the whole population, but the inclusion of anomie itself into the law.

The international recognition of the status of the exception also serves to restructure the judicial system at the international level. The latest extradition agreements signed between the European Union and the United States insert European citizens into the system of exception to the law, imposed by the United States.

In this double evolution, the exception to existing law plays a decisive role. It is the center of gravity, around which a new political order is constructed, as well as its juridical transcription. This role occurs at two levels. The turning of criminal procedures into a system to neutralize constitutional guarantees operates from within the existing legal order. It is the internal dismantling of the rule of law. The Patriot Act and the English law, the Antiterrorism, Crime and Security Act, place the exception outside of the legal system. The exception becomes pure violence and serves as the basis for the establishment of a new political order.

## From the National State to the Empire

Schmitt's reading of dictatorship as the highest form of the state of exception turns out to be, again, pertinent to decipher current affairs. The effectiveness of the suspension of the law, its integration into criminal law as constitutive act, is confirmed at all levels of the imperial structure, at the level of the American executive power as well as at the level of the subaltern forms of the integrated command structure, those entities that continue to be called national States.

The context posited by Schmitt is the national State. His analysis appears clearly within the structure of the nation, the real synthesis of the people and the State. The paradigm is the border. It is there that sovereignty is established. It is the place of demarcation between internal and external, the articulation of which serves as the basis for the double Western legal system, integrating the rule of law and the law of exception. The border is thus the place where the guarantees of the rule of law are suspended and where a preventive counter-violence can be carried out.

This observation still applies to the modern form of the State. Globalization of the economy and trade is accompanied by a tighter control over the circulation of people. Immigration policies made possible the development of camps, discreetly called secured centers, for asylum seekers and foreigners whose papers are not in order. The detained persons are subjected to a law of exception of a purely administrative nature.

The last reference for Schmitt in the history of modernity concerns the imperialist struggle among the great powers. However, his conceptual apparatus takes on new operational force when used for the study of the establishment of an integrated structure of political organization at the global level and when the emphasis is shifted from his paradigm of the border and the imperialist struggle to the formation of the Empire. The relation that he constructs between politics and the State makes this analytical shift possible. Politics is not reduced, as in formal theories of the law, to a general, i.e., a juridical, theory of the State. Politics is formed on the basis of the relation between friend and enemy. This explains why sovereignty is achieved on a defined territory delimited by borders. Schmitt conceives of an extension to this demarcation with the concept of an internal enemy.

## Rogue States

Étienne Balibar[10] emphasizes that Schmitt already noted the evolution of the national form of the State, as well as the change in public law guaranteeing equality between sovereign nations. By designating certain States as enemies of all of humanity, the distinction between enemy and criminal is abolished and the concept of just war is rehabilitated. "The danger in this change, according to Carl Schmitt, is that it [...] imposes on politics the fatal illusion of a perpetual peace that has every possibility of being transformed into endless war."[11] Here the author anticipates what, through changes in the organization of national States, would become imperial rule.

The evolution towards a globalized society, where just wars are made in the name of human rights, leads to the creation, by the American administration, of the "camp of good" opposed to the "camp of evil." Imperial power no longer has to face enemies, but "rogue States."

This criminalization of the enemy, against which one does not make war but which one neutralizes by a police operation, modifies the very nature of sovereignty. Imperial sovereignty is not constructed along the border, it does not fight against an external enemy but against criminals subjected to its jurisdiction. Criminal law becomes a doctrine of sovereignty. It establishes an international balance of power. By suspending the concrete liberties of citizens, it also transforms the sovereignty of the people into abstract human rights.

---

10  Étienne Balibar, "Prolégomènes à la souveraineté : la frontière, l'État, le peuple." *Les Temps Modernes*, no. 610, Septembre 2000, pp 47-75.

11  *Ibid.*, p. 55.

The conception of sovereignty founded on the decision, such as Schmitt develops it, is opposed to legal normativism, which reduces the State to a set of legal relationships. This perspective, of which Kelsen is the best-known representative, thus affirms the identity of the State and the law. The law is "this very coercive order as which the state appears...."[12] The State, as political organization, is reduced to a legal order, to the single legitimate and sovereign order of the law. The institutive process thus moves from the law to the State.[13]

While for Kelsen, "the law regulates its own creation," for Schmitt, the Constitution does not rest on a higher norm, but on the political decision, expression of the will of a constitutive power. The Schmittian conception of sovereignty is articulated around a central point, the exception. It is at that point that the legal order is overturned so as to neutralize the limits that constrain all power.

For Schmitt, legal normativism cannot think the decision. He is opposed to theories of the law for which "a decision in the legal sense must be derived entirely from the content of a norm."[14] He thus reverses the institutive relation, which moves from the State to the law.

## Two Sides of the Same Coin

These two conceptions of sovereignty are formally opposed. In fact, however, they are partial and turn out to be complementary. Each one puts forward only one aspect of the State's role. The normative theory makes it possible to think the relation between society and State, to conceptualize the manner in which, normally, the State controls the former. It allows us to construct the State as the condensation of social relations. While it makes it possible to determine the norm, it is incapable of integrating the exception to the rule and the way in which the latter is established.

---

12  Hans Kelsen, *Pure Theory of the Law*. Translated by Max Knight (Berkeley, CA: University of California Press, 1967), p. 318.

13  Jacques Chevalier, *L'État de droit*.

14  Carl Schmitt, *Political Theology* p. 6.

Decisionism, on the contrary, begins with the exception and constructs the legal order on that basis. This theory cannot integrate the aspect of State governance, which functions as a synthesis of society. However, it does allow us to perceive the State under its second aspect, as an autonomous apparatus opposed to society.

The organic theory of the State, as developed by Hegel,[15] integrates the two moments. The object of this theory, the national form of the State, allowed the articulation of these two aspects in the direction taken by the sovereign.

Currently, organic sovereignty, appropriate to the national form of the State and founded on the organization and control of the people's sovereignty, has disappeared. It has given way to the duality of a globalized civil society, split between a mechanical and external moment of political order, symbolized by the concept of governance, and an autonomous political and military command structure. The fight against terrorism thus makes it possible, as the agreements on police and judicial cooperation between the United States and the European Union confirm, to establish an imperial system of political command, built around the executive branch of the United States.

Paradoxically, the shattering of the sovereignty of the national State provides a new dimension to these two theories. Each one, through its partial character, succeeds in clarifying one aspect of the political organization of the Empire. Instead of pointing to a lacuna in the normative theory, the critique made of it, that "this normativism ends up at the extreme limit of a State that administers but does not govern,"[16], demonstrates, on the contrary, a new function-

---

15   The concept of organic sovereignty is Hegel's (see *Elements of the Philosophy of Right*. Edited by Allen W. Wood; translated by H. B. Nisbet (New York: Cambridge University Press, 1991)). It interests us insofar as it articulates, while also distinguishing, the political organization of civil society as external State, as legal-administrative State, and the ethico-political State, the internal State, the organic moment, thereby assuring the adherence of the citizen to the whole state structure. The current situation is characterized by a crisis of organic sovereignty since it is a matter as well of calling into question the distinction between the two moments, private and public, civil society and political State. This must lead to a new articulation between the two moments as well as the establishment of a new form of imperial political system, which maintains control over the entire new structure as well as hegemony over various populations.

16   Jean-Louis Schlegel, "Introduction," *in* Carl Schmitt, *Théologie politique* (Paris: Gallimard, 1988)., p.VIII.

ality for the theory. The national State, integrated into the system of world governance, as well as various supranational political organizations, become institutions that do not exercise sovereignty, that administer but do not govern. Conversely, decisionism allows us to apprehend the central role played by the American executive power in setting up a comprehensive structure of command at the world level. Sovereignty is exercised by the one who decides what the exception is and uses it to change the legal order.

Due to the collapse of the organic character of the modern form of the State, the Empire is based on a dual structure. On the one hand, the networked organization of multinational companies, international institutions and national States administer the planet as if it were a company. On the other hand, the executive branch of the United States, a political apparatus in the fullest sense of the term political, in contrast to globalized society, exercises imperial sovereignty.

The two opposed theories, legal normativism and decisionism, each give an account of one of the two distinct and fragmented aspects of the contemporary political order. They both demonstrated their inability to think the organic character of the national State. The shattering of the latter gives these theories, paradoxically, a new lease on life as tools that allow us to apprehend the establishment of an integrated command at the world level, not by providing the concept of this new phenomenon, but by highlighting the duality of this structure.

## THE SUSPENSION OF THE LAW: CONSTITUTIVE ACT OF THE EMPIRE

The antiterrorist struggle makes the exception and the suspension of the law the founding acts of an imperial constitution. The establishment of such a legal order provides a new dimension to Schmitt's fundamental thesis: the decision on the exception as constitutive act of sovereignty.

Current affairs demonstrate that the decision concerning the exception is part of the order of law. Recent antiterrorist measures prove Schmitt right in his characterization of the state of exception as inscription of the exception in the law. One can even say that the current situation provides the real meaning to his thesis about the maintenance of the legal order by means of the decision concerning the exception.

As with any national State, the United States institutes a double legal system, a rule of law for citizens and a rule without law for foreigners. Classically, for other nations, the distinction between the two legal orders is articulated at the border.

However, for the American State, the border is not a geographic given. The primacy of American citizenship and the organization of the two legal orders do not operate on a clearly delimited territory, but in the whole world. It is not only a question of permitting American citizens to evade the jurisdiction of international courts, i.e., common jurisdictions, but also of forcing other States to acknowledge the right of American authorities to put citizens of these other States on trial in exceptional jurisdictions, specially created for this purpose.

## American Hegemony

The latest extradition agreements signed with the European Union are an acknowledgement by the latter of the American right to decide the exception. They also lead to the practical integration of European judicial systems into the system of suspension of the law set up by the United States. The European countries thus accept surrendering, in conditions imposed by the United States, their own citizens who have been designated as terrorists by the American authorities.

In the elaboration of the imperial legal order, the United States is the driving force. It is the US that decides the exception and transforms the norm, notably criminal law and its enforcement procedures, as a function of the imposed exceptions.

The war against Iraq and the distinction between the camp of good and the camp of evil proceed from a strategic decision that is part of this political management, at the level of domination as much as at the level of hegemony. If the decision is unilateral and thus proceeds from pure domination, it also aims at having other nations legitimize this act. The UN decision to lift the embargo on Iraq after the American invasion is an international acknowledgement of this action. It is indeed a question of a reinsertion of pure violence into the international legal order, of a constitutive act of U.S. hegemony.

The American executive power is doubly constitutive. At the international level, it determines "the fight of good against evil." It is that executive power that establishes the "camp of the good," that grants a democratic label to any country committed to its side and that rejects any non-aligned State as "rogue."

The ostentatious media coverage of the Guatanamo prisoners, captured outside of any declaration of war, is a founding element of the new order. These persons have no legal status, neither prisoners of war nor detainees under common law. The repeated exhibition of these detainees, shackled and hooded, in defiance of all international conventions, demonstrates the desire of the American government to make suspension of the law the cornerstone of imperial organization. The acceptance by other nations of this pure violence, as securing the world order, assures its legitimacy.

President Bush's Military Order also created a zone of non-law for foreigners accused of terrorism. The agreements on extradition between the European Union and the United States are an effective recognition of the right granted to these military courts to try European citizens outside of any judicial safeguards.

*An Inversion of the Relation between Society and State*

The Patriot II Act represents a new step in the construction of the imperial structure. This proposed law, if it is adopted, sets up a generalized state of exception or, in other words, a dictatorship. However, it is more than the suspension of all fundamental liberties. It would allow the American executive branch to change the relation between inside and outside. The possibility that is offered to the executive authority to remove American citizenship from all political opponents involved in civil disobedience activities allows that authority to link the possession of American citizenship and its relative privileges to the acceptance of government policy.

The executive power occupies the position of a magistrate interpreting the law and changing, at any instant, the conditions for implementing legality, determining who is part of the society and who is cast out of it.

In other nations, the expansion of the techniques of exception at all stages of criminal procedure also constitutes a veritable suspension of common law. Justified by the fight against terrorism or organized crime, these measures are generalized, at the inquiry stage, to most crimes.

Criminal codes already contained everything necessary to attack social movements by denying their political character and placing them into the criminal domain. However, antiterrorist laws make it possible to criminalize any manifestation of political opposition because of an expressed or attributed motivation to exercise undue pressure on constituted authority.

The primacy of the procedure of exception gives rise to a change in the law, through which the State establishes society and permanently redefines the borders between the latter and what is outside it. If the antiterrorist struggle entails a suspension of the law and produces a new legal order, at the same time it produces, materially and formally, the enemy to fight. The adaptation of the legal order does not aim, as in the state of siege, at taking on a threat from outside the system, but at part of the system itself. We are witnessing an inversion of the relation between means and objectives. The designated enemy, the terrorist organization, becomes the tool for transforming the legal order and the political system. It is the government itself that constitutes politics in its image.

DICTATORSHIP

The study carried out by Giorgio Agamben, concerning the Roman justitium, allows him to distinguish between the state of exception and dictatorship. The dictator was a special magistrate whose extensive powers had been given to him by a specific law in conformity with the constitutional order. In the state of exception, the extensive powers of magistrates simply result from the suspension of the laws that limited their prerogatives. "The state of exception is then not a dictatorship ... but a space devoid of law, a zone of anomie where all legal determinations—and above all the very distinction between public and private—are deactivated."[17]

For Agamben, the modern forms of exception to the law are indeed part of the state of exception. However, looking a little closer, one notices that things are not so clear. The suspension of the law does not have its end in itself. It is the instrument for the reconstitution of a new legal order. The generalized state of exception, as Agamben shows, is not a stable form. It points to the establishment of a new globalized state structure, the Empire, in which dictatorship as form of government takes shape as horizon, as active strategy of various governments.

Thus the concept of generalized state of exception is in itself a contradiction. A state of exception that is established for an indefinite period of time and concerns all public and private spaces effects a change in the political system. Through all the reforms undertaken at the national and international levels, we find the formal constitutive elements of the establishment of a dictatorship: end of the separation of powers and acquisition by the executive of competences granted to judges, i.e., stating and interpreting the law.

### Subordination of the Judiciary

The augmentation of police powers is simultaneously a suspension of the law and a change in the legal order leading to dictatorship. The increase in the length of time someone can be held in police custody, night searches or close surveillance eliminate the procedures protecting individual liberties. They are also the conditions of a change in the law in which police work and the work of magistrates are assimilated. Special investigative techniques and their spread to almost every type of offense make possible a fundamental modification in the conditions for presenting evidence. The latter is essentially based on a blind confidence in the word of the police.

In Belgium, the secret character of these investigative methods is extended to the trial stage. Not only does the private party associated with the prosecutor have no access to this information, but even the

---

17  Giorgio Agamben, *State of Exception*, p. 50.

judge who is to decide on the merits of the evidence must base his or her decision on an incomplete file. It is the prosecutor alone who must formally supervise the process, but he or she does not even have effective means to do so. The testimony of a police officer thus has the force of proof. Control over the legality of the means of proof is emptied of all substance. There are no sanctions for investigators in breach of their obligations while using these special investigative techniques.[18] There also is a clause providing legal excuses for all offenses committed by police functionaries involved in carrying out a particular investigative technique, when these offenses turn out to be "absolutely necessary." In France, the Perben law permits bringing a person to trial solely on the basis of the anonymous testimony of an officer from the criminal investigation police.

Thus in these two countries, the investigating magistrate, removed from these secret procedures, is no longer the guarantor of individual liberties. This role is entrusted to the prosecutor and, in actual practice, to the police.

The reforms, which grant the police the competences appropriate to magistrates, are accompanied by an instrumentalization of the judiciary by the executive power. The prosecutor is increasingly controlled by a hierarchy established by the executive. Subjected to positive directives and injunctions from the Minister of Justice, the prosecutor carries out the functions of a quasi-judge in the use of the "criminal restitution" and "plea bargaining" processes. The former, continuously extended to new crimes, makes it possible to circumvent the courts. The latter allows the prosecutor to determine the penalties and put pressure on the accused to accept the prosecution's interpretation of the facts and the law. The possibility provided to the prosecutor to determine the offense, not on the basis of the facts, but according to the desire shown by the accused to acknowledge his/her guilt is contrary to the principle of legality. This prerogative is part of the tendency to subjectivize the law, which takes away all substance from the constitutional guarantees provided by the rule of law.

---

18   Damien Vandermeersch, "Un projet de loi particulièrement inquiétant," *Le Journal des Procès* no. 440, Bruxelles, le 28 juin 2002 ; "Les méthodes particulières de recherche et autres moyens d'investigation," *Ligue des droits de l'Homme,* mai 2002.

Because of the enlargement of their prerogatives, the prosecutor and the police, linked to the executive branch, now fulfill functions normally attributed to the judiciary, particularly the judges and investigating magistrates.

These measures do not result only from a real suspension of fundamental liberties, but are recorded in the laws and decrees promoted by the executive structure. They are part of a new legal order.

## Subjectivization of the Law and Politics

The subjectivization of criminal law permits prosecutions on the simple basis of intentions attributed to the suspected person. It also offers particularly weak requirements concerning the production of evidence. In this context, the blurring of the distinction between police work and the work of magistrates appears clearly in the tendency to grant any affirmation of an administrative authority the status of evidence. The antiterrorist struggle permits the prosecution of any person suspected of belonging to an organization on lists drawn up by the Minister of Justice or Attorney General, the Council of the European Union or simply by a police office, such as Europol. (The latter list, moreover, is kept secret.)

The most explicit example of this blurring of different authorities is in the United States, where the President has given himself the power to appoint the judges to the exceptional military courts. The concentration of powers in the executive that would normally devolve to the judiciary allow the President, the Minister of Justice or the Attorney General to act as judges.

The blind confidence in the word of the police, prosecutor or functionaries of the Ministry or Department of Justice in the establishment of proof is part of a tendency that is equally discernible in international relations. A simple declaration by the head of the executive authority suffices to justify the facts, since the latter consist of an intention attributed by this declaration itself to the incriminated person or nation. Thus, in an interview given on December 17, 2003 on ABC television, President Bush said "there was no difference between the possibility that Saddam could acquire weapons of mass destruction and their actual presence in Iraq."[19]

The subjectivization of the law is an inversion of the rule of law, of a form of social organization founded on an objective law. It is the basis of a new legal order in which the rule is entirely adjustable. It is completely dependent on the interpretation that is made of it, that is, of the immediate balance of power.

The subjectivization of the law is coupled with the composition of politics as simple manifestation of the will of the State. This approach denies to the real any existence outside of the interpretation that is given to it.

Imperial power produces a virtual reality that constitutes the only facts justifying its actions. It is no longer a question of simply suspending the law, a measure that is based on the more or less abbreviated interpretation of the objective elements that are partly outside of it. The distinctive feature of this approach does not lie in its interpretation of the facts, but in the production of a reality that is the only world possible. This activity is not only a subjective undertaking. It is an act that produces an identity of possibility and actuality. The path towards dictatorship, be this at the national or international level, is a real possibility. It is an objective of the established authorities and a tendency already underway.

SOVEREIGN DICTATORSHIP: THE EMPIRE'S FORM OF GOVERNMENT

The distinction made by Carl Schmitt between commissarial dictatorship and sovereign dictatorship is also useful to characterize the form of government that is being established worldwide. In the commissarial dictatorship, the power granted to the dictator comes from a constitutional organ. The Constitution can be put aside while continuing to exist. The suspension of the law is a concrete exception that is part of the legal order.

As for the sovereign dictatorship, it does not aim at protecting the existing political order, but at transforming it. "It does not suspend a constitution in force by virtue of a right founded on that constitu-

---

19 "Tony Blair fait état de preuves massives de l'existence d'armes de destruction massive," *Le Monde*, 18 décembre 2003.

tion, that is to say, in conformity with the Constitution. It seeks, on the contrary, to institute the state of things that would make possible a Constitution that it considers to be the true Constitution."[20] Within this context, the action of the dictator becomes constitutive. The dictator's power is not absolute insofar as it is formative of a new order of law. With this intention, it opposes and transforms the existing norm. The dictator's action does not occur outside of any existing legal context, but in relation to it.

Within the current context of imperial politics, it is not a question of replacing one Constitution by another. There is a complex process occurring here: a neutralization of the mechanisms protecting fundamental liberties due to the transformation of criminal law, creation of a body of criminal procedures that have become constitutive, a change in the form of the State, and a reconstruction of a new political order on the basis of anomie. The exceptional procedures proceed from a dismantling of the rule of law, from within the latter. Pure violence, outside of the existing legal order, is reintegrated within it and produces a global change in the system. This double movement is recorded at the level of criminal law, which thus becomes constitutive.

*A New Function of Criminal Law*

The generalization of the techniques of exception, from the investigative stage to the trial, leads to a suspension of the constitutional order. These techniques render the various protections for private life inoperative. New crimes, such as those relating to criminal organizations or acts of terrorism, attack public liberties. They establish a new legal order that makes possible a preventive attack on any project of social reconstruction.

What is more, currently, criminal law is no longer only a mode of State management of a society of individuals. It is also, as the agreements on police and judicial cooperation between the two continents confirm, the internal reorganization of authority and the establishment of a new supranational structure of political command.

---

20  Carl Schmitt, *La Dictature* (Paris: Le Seuil, 2000), p. 142.

Thus, we are within the framework, not of a commissarial dictatorship – a suspension of the law aimed at protecting the existing order – but a sovereign dictatorship that carries out a change in the State superstructure.

Contrary to the commissarial dictatorship, the sovereign dictatorship cannot be considered as a simple form of government. It does not consist only of an internal restructuring of the political level, in a change in the relation between civil society and the State. It prepares a change in the very form of the State, in the existing relation between the political and the economic.[21] What the sovereign dictatorship means here is the form of government appropriate to a new form of the political organization of capital: the Empire. The sovereign dictatorship is the Empire's appropriate form of government and its condition of existence. It is the other face of "good governance," a pure political subjectivity that establishes a globalized "technical" maVnagement of an unprotected labor power, that is, of workers deprived of their political rights and entirely subjected to the imperatives of the world market.

If dictatorship is necessarily a state of exception, it is differentiated from it on one fundamental point. The state of exception appears as a concrete exception. It is a procedure solely aimed at obtaining a definite result. There is an "absolute identity between the task and what is assigned to that task."[22] This is no longer the case in dictatorship, through a reversal carried out between the sought-after goal and the implemented means. The change in the organization of power becomes the objective to attain, while the enemy to fight is the medium of this transformation.

The measures taken within the context of the antiterrorist fight are formally justified by the necessity of resolving a concrete problem. However, the struggle is long term, indeterminate, against an enemy that is constantly redefined. The task is not defined concretely nor is what is attributed to those tasks. The specificity of the current situ-

---

21  On the distinction between form of government and form of State, see Nicos Poulantzas, *Political Power and Social Classes*. Translation editor, Timothy O'Hagan. (London: Verso, 1978), pp. 147-156, 241-245, 247-248, and 317-321.

22  Carl Schmitt, *La Dictature*, p. 19.

ation in relation to past dictatorships results from the fact that the enemy to fight is essentially potential and, in great part, symbolically and materially produced by the established authorities.

## Police State or Dictatorship

Within the imperial context, an identification between two forms of government is carried out, between what Schmitt calls "police State," an exceptional form of the rule of law, established in the absence of a concrete adversary whose elimination would be the goal of such a move,[23] and sovereign dictatorship, a form of organizing power in which all administrative authority, including the police, acquires a judicial competence. The police State is thus a particular form of dictatorship in which the police apparatus, autonomous in relation to the executive structure, plays a central role not only in managing society, but also in the organization of the State apparatus itself.

Through the establishment of an imperial structure, at the national level as well as in international relations, the fight against terrorism acquires a doubly constitutive character. It reorganizes the government around its police function, while giving to the police the prerogatives normally devolving to judges, i.e., the power to apply and interpret the law.

The establishment of such and such a form of government, state of exception or dictatorship, does not depend on formal coherence at the level of the written law, but on the immediate balance of power, on the ability of the population to resist. The American executive power placed the antiterrorist fight within an impassable horizon, the end of history. The legal force of dictatorship fits in perfectly within this perspective. In the state of exception, there is always at least a formal reference made to a return to the rule of law. This scenario is not the one currently accepted by the established authorities.

---

23 *Ibid.*, p. 140.

# CONCLUSION

In an article published in the newspaper Le Monde, Giorgio Agamben argued that the exercise of power in the West rested on the articulation of two relatively separate systems, the legal order and pure violence. "The political system of the West seems to have a double structure, founded on the dialectic between two heterogeneous and, in some way, antithetical elements: law and pure violence. As long as these elements remain separate, their dialectic can function, but when the state of exception becomes the rule, then the political system is transformed into a deadly system."[1] This is exactly the process that is taking place under our noses, the exception becoming the imperial rule. However, there is a double constitutive movement, a suspension of the law and a change in the legal order. The rule, which inscribes the exception into the law, is created as a function of itself.

## THE END OF A DOUBLE LEGAL SYSTEM

It is in the United States, with the Patriot Act, that this double movement can be observed most easily. There is a suspension of the law for certain categories of persons, foreigners and witnesses or suspects belonging to an organization designated as terrorist. But it is above all a transformation in the totality of criminal law that is in question. This change concerns not only particular categories of persons but also the whole population.

The concepts of state of exception and dictatorship, developed by Carl Schmitt as the inscription of pure violence into the law, are much closer to the current form of power than the form of State that was his object of study. While the Nazi regime had suspended the articles guaranteeing individual liberties, it had not eliminated nor suspended the whole of the Weimar Constitution. The inscription of pure violence into the law was not its essential preoccupation. The concrete frame of reference diverged from Schmitt's problem-

---

1   Giorgio Agamben, "L'état d'exception," Le Monde, 12 septembre 2002. See also Giorgio Agamben, Homo sacer: Sovereign Power and Bare Life (Stanford, CA: Stanford University Press, 1998).

atic, who, as theoretician of the Nazi regime, wanted to situate it permanently, therefore in the law.

Upon taking power, this regime prepared for an armed conflict with neighboring countries. The fight against the internal enemy appeared only as a moment in a global war. This situation is, then, formally within the context of a state of siege, in the classic conditions of a suspension of fundamental liberties.

The current context differs from the situation of the 1930s. The Empire has no outside. The conflicts that it pursues are, for it, simply police operations. They are part of the need to maintain order. The limitation or suppression of fundamental liberties is inscribed in the law. Criminal law becomes constitutive. The fundamental change in criminal law is the legal transcription of the change in politics.

The duality, rule of law and organization of pure violence, concealed the structure of a national society that applies the law to what it considers its interior and abrogates it for its exterior. This double system can justify its function in an exceptional situation such as war. However, this legal duality also functioned on a long-term basis, in a relatively stable context, in the relation between the metropolises and their colonies.

Today, the United States occupies a particular place in the imperial structure, since the relation of domination that it exercises is expressed also as the power of a particular nation over the rest of the world, which, although considered as its backyard, remains for it an exterior. The difference in treatment between citizens and foreigners, the suspension of the law for the latter, is there as witness to American singularity in the imperial universe. The contradiction, which has frequently been noted in the foreign policy of the United States, between a strategy of conquering the world and a withdrawal into the nation, represents in fact the two poles of imperial domination. The universality of imperial power is expressed through the particularity of a national State.

As for the Empire as a form of the global organization of power, any movement, any political or military action is internal to it. The dichotomy inside/outside, rule of law/rule of non-law, observed at the national level no longer has any meaning.

The legal organization of the Empire makes the state of exception permanent, as the organizational form of a globalized society. The liberty-killing character of most of the measures taken within the context of the fight against terrorism is not a pure political act, but a constitutive given of the legal order. One can then follow the reasoning of Agamben in which the state of exception represents "a paradigm that is not only currently relevant, but about which one can say that it has only found its true success today."[2] With the Empire, the state of exception has an organic character. It is an internal organization of power. It modifies the entire legal order. The suspension of the law acquires a constitutive character.

REVERSAL OF THE RELATION BETWEEN SOCIETY AND STATE

The reforms circumscribed by the antiterrorist fight give a new dimension to the space of politics. The criminalization of social opposition is not, as in 19th century society, its dismissal into criminal space. On the contrary, it divides politics into two, separating "the good from the evil." Only the constituted authorities can carry out legitimate actions. It is the illegitimate nature of the act of making demands that are not accepted by the government, that destabilize it, that pressure it to take or not take certain actions or that intimidate society, which justify criminalization of social opposition.

Through the fight against terrorism, the constituted authorities attempt to impose a new conception of politics. The latter would no longer be a place for the confrontation and mediation between social groups but a simple space for management, a technical paradigm. Such a construction implies that any process of social reconstruction, of developing a socialized alternative to the market, is preventively dismantled. At this level, the objective of all of the reforms of the criminal codes and procedures is to permit "proactive" action on the part of the police.

This drastic change is the expression of a real transformation in the nature of politics. In the formation of the ruling group as well as in relation to the dominated classes, politics is no longer the mediation of

---

2   *Ibid.*

various rights, but representation, technical management, of particular sectional interests, already established, moreover, as universals.

Furthermore, this process has already been understood as a blurring of the distinction between public and private, as neo-patrimonial management, as privatization of the State. It has also frequently been analyzed as the end of the autonomy of the political in relation to the economic or as absorption by the State of all of the functions of civil society.[3] Even more radically, the problem of the disappearance of civil society into politics can be posed as an inversion of the relationship between society and State, the State now giving rise to society.[4] However, it is advisable to envisage this process, not as an outcome, but as a tendency, as an ongoing strategy of the established authorities. Even though they exclude any effort at social reconstruction, these reforms extend their sphere of intervention into the direct management of private life. The imperial structure thus encompasses the totality of life.

Therefore, with the antiterrorist measures, the relationship between society and State is reversed once and for all. Civil society loses all autonomy in relation to politics. The idea of popular sovereignty, as source of the State's legitimacy, is obsolete. It is the government that grants or takes away citizenship and legitimizes society, that forces the latter to conform to its model or, if necessary, criminalizes it.

As a result of a preventive dismantling of any opposition movement, politics is exclusively positioned as instrument for governing a society of individuals. The specificity of the social is denied, abandoned to the market and its transformation of social relations into relations between commodities.

Organic sovereignty, characteristic of the national form of the State and based on the organization and control of the people's sovereignty, disappears. It gives way to the duality of a globalized civil society, split between the mechanical and external moment of the political order, symbolized by the idea of governance, and a structure of political and military command constructed around the American executive power.

---

3   Norberto Bobbio, *L'État et la démocratie internationale*, (Bruxelles: Éditions Complexe, 1998), p.256.

4   Michael Hardt et Antonio Negri, *Empire* (Cambridge, MA: Harvard University Press, 2000), p. 328-329.

The primacy of the Constitution that characterizes the rule of law implies a relative autonomy of the political sphere in relation to the dominant economic interests. The law is the expression of a compromise between dominant social strata and dominated ones. It is also a long-term method of managing the balance of power between social classes. The dominant role of procedure over law (and, because of the antiterrorist fight, the dominance of exceptional procedures) expresses, on the contrary, a very short-term method of managing political relations and the end of a relative stability, in the formation of the ruling bloc itself as well as in its relations with the dominated classes. If the law records and establishes the equilibrium point of the class struggle, the exceptional procedure calls this stability into question. It is an instrument of managing a situation of permanent crisis.

The fight against terrorism is not only an instrument of dominance, but also a way of exercising hegemony. It establishes a process whereby the population accepts the challenge to their fundamental liberties. This necessity of recognition explains why the various measures restricting liberties, made within the context of the antiterrorist struggle, take a juridical form and, most often, the form of a law. However, it is a question of simple framework-laws that depend on enforcement methods established by the executive authority and that leave all the initiative to the police. In fact, these laws lift the legal obstacles to an expansion of the already much greater powers granted to the police.

## DICTATORSHIP: FORM OF GOVERNMENT OF GOOD GOVERNANCE

In his Political Theology, Carl Schmitt defines sovereignty by the concept of "extreme decision."[5] This concept is intended to establish the theory of the state of exception. In the present context, it acquires its full importance in characterizing imperial sovereignty. The constitutive power of the United States results from its ability to effect a suspension of the law. But this power does not consist only of the possibility of imposing this decision, but also in the ability to legitimize it. Indeed, it is a matter of incorporating non-law into the legal order.

---

5   See Giorgio Agamben's interpretation in *State of Exception.*

If politics is defined as constitutive power, that is, as violence that lays down the law[6] imperial violence carries out a redefinition of politics. The latter is no longer defined by the ability to make war, but as a police function, as the capacity to make proactive decisions in organizing a new social war, a veritable civil war inside the Empire.

The suppression of the law by procedure is the expression of the reduction of the social and the political to the productivist techniques of the company. It is the way in which capital, or at least some fractions of the latter, directly takes in hand the reproduction of the conditions of social production. The power relation is transformed. It expresses the capacity of companies or pressure groups to impose their particular prerogatives directly. The promoters of "good governance" currently defend this type of organization. This modern version of the neo-patrimonial conception of the State denotes an organization of shared life that denies any political character to the latter. Administration is thought of simply as a provider of goods and services to sectional interests or citizen-consumers. That situation makes it possible for international institutions, such as the World Bank or the WTO, to put forward directly political demands under the cover of considerations presented as purely technical.

The idea of governance constitutes the context in which the proceduralization of social relations takes place. The criminalization of terrorism is a new step in this process. It does not create a norm that is intended to evaluate behaviors. The fight against terrorism essentially focuses on presumed intentions, on potential offenses. The most important thing lies in the establishment of exceptional procedures. The latter become the privileged technique of the political management of society.

Governance makes possible a criminalization of opposition movements insofar as it denies any possibility for conflict. Any divergence is supposed to be resolved by negotiations between the parties, as diverse and unequal as local collectivities and monopolist multinational corporations.

The concept of state of exception or dictatorship, conceptualized by Schmitt, as reintegration of the exercise of pure violence into the

---

6   Agamben, *State of Exception*, p. 88.

law, here takes on its full significance, as the political form of world governance. Dictatorship and "good governance" represent the two faces of a form of government for which citizenship is not the expression of rights, but the simple demand for goods and services that have to be integrated into the market.

## THE ANTICIPATION OF A NEW SOCIAL WAR

The antiterrorist struggle is the most advanced point in the establishment of a generalized state of exception or a world dictatorship. It condenses all the elements that characterize this form of government. It effects a restructuring of power by strengthening the supremacy of the executive power. Through the development of framework-laws, enforced by decrees and ministerial circulars or by simple lists drawn up by the Minister of Justice or Attorney General (such as lists of organizations designated as terrorist), the executive power fully exercises legislative functions and strictly instrumentalizes the judiciary.

The deployment of a state of exception traditionally responds to the necessity of maintaining public order following an exceptional situation, often presented as a context of civil war. The antiterrorist fight is presented, moreover, as a global civil war, a long-term fight against a constantly redefined enemy. This situation differs, however, from the normal context. It is not a question of the government having to face existing troubles but of destroying a potential threat. The action is preventive.

The antiterrorist fight anticipates social conflict, it carries out a proactive suppression of any process of political reconstruction. It is necessary to insist on the importance of this anticipatory character in order to understand the effectiveness of this type of legislation. The aim of all these legal tools is less to confront current social conflicts, which are relatively small, than to profit from this favorable situation to prepare for the future. Through the change in criminal law, politics anticipates a new offensive of capital at the economic level.

The significance of the criminalization of terrorism lies in the possibility of criminalizing any form of social pressure on national public authorities or on an international organization. The Framework-Decision on terrorism of the Council of the European Union is particularly explicit since it focuses on the intention of "exerting undue force on public authorities or an international organization to carry out or not to carry out some act or other." This measure acquires its full significance if it is connected to the negotiations taking place within the IMF, OECD or WTO. Up to the present, the treaties signed concerned the liberalization of trade, while the most recent discussions concern investments. The objective of the negotiations that took place within the OECD, leading to the Multilateral Agreement on Investments (MAI), was the free circulation of capital.[7]

National States lose their last prerogatives concerning political economy. For example, they are increasingly unable to direct, through appropriate assistance, investments towards certain sectors in certain regions or to promote the employment of specific categories of the labor force. All regulations not conforming to the principles of the MAI must be gotten rid of. These negotiations were given up within the OECD, but were taken up again in another form under the auspices of the WTO. The fears expressed concerning this agreement remain valid.

In such a context, demonstrations and occupations of or "capturing" public spaces, infrastructures and public transport, carried out with the intention of putting pressure on a national government to take social welfare measures or not proceed with the elimination of the latter, could be considered terrorist acts. Moreover, national States would no longer be masters of their decisions, since a company that considered itself damaged by a legal measure would have the recourse of taking its complaint before an international trade tribunal. Thus we are witnessing a displacement of power that essentially makes it imperceptible and elusive.

In cases where a social movement is defeated, the antiterrorist struggle provides the context within which to criminalize it. In cases where a social movement is victorious, it finds itself facing a national power deprived of the possibility of respecting its commitments. Actions that might directly challenge international organizations could also experience the same situation. The Framework-Decision on ter-

---

7    *Cf.* "AMI : attention, un accord peut en cacher un autre," *Centre Europe-Tiers-monde* (CETIM), 1999; et *Lumière sur l'AMI*, Observatoire de la mondialisation, L'Esprit frappeur, Paris, 1998.

rorism also criminalizes movements that aim at forcing an international organization to undertake or not to undertake an initiative.

*Anticipation of a Restructuring of Capital*

The General Agreement on Trade in Services (GATS), which aims at eliminating governmental measures that impede the total liberalization of services, is another example of the systematic dismantling of all State regulation. Negotiated within the WTO, it countenances the opening of sectors such as health and education to competition.[8] A strong protest movement fighting to maintain public services or to impose regulation on certain services could be considered terrorist.

The existence of discussions leading to international agreements on liberalizing investments or services corresponds to a second phase in the establishment of a structure of integrated power at the world level. In the first phase, the national State still played a determining role. It had to get rid of its prerogatives in economic matters in order to make financial markets the command center over the technical composition of labor power. The globalization of command, under the form of the independence of finance capital,[9] aimed at articulating the interdependence of the labor forces of the countries of the center with those of the periphery. The means was to liberalize trade in commodities and capital. The management of the political component of the labor force remained in the hands of the national States.

The negotiations on investments or on the General Agreement on Trade in Services open a second process: globalizing control over the conditions of production and reproduction of labor power. This time, it is a matter of putting the labor forces of the North directly in competition with those of the South, by profoundly modifying the conditions of reproduction of the former.

---

8  "Alerte Générale à la Capture des Services publics," *Coordination pour le Contrôle Citoyen de l'OMC-CCC-OMC*, avril 2000.

9  François Chesnais, "La nouvelle économie," *in Une nouvelle phase du capitalisme?*, Éditions Syllepse, Paris, 2001.

*A Political Restructuring from Above*

This new step in the construction of the Empire is a revalorization of politics, but in a restricted sense, expressed by the idea of governance. It establishes a direct control over the existence of the workers by setting up structures such as international trade courts.

The intervention of the national State in the reproduction of the labor force resulted in social conflict. The elimination of "social benefits," the change in the organic composition of labor power, occurs first through the preventive elimination of any possibility for political reconstruction. The possibility offered within the context of the antiterrorist fight to criminalize any more or less radical social movement indicates that this process has already begun.

The restructuring of the political from above is thus an anticipation of and preparation for a new offensive by capital on the economic level. The criminalization of social action corresponds to an attempt to be able to determine the terrain of confrontation, but also to create an adversary that would be its match. It is a matter of developing preventive action to destroy real subjects and opposition movements and replace them with a virtual adversary, constructed as a double of the established authorities, as its inverse image: the terrorist organization.

An internationalization of the repression of social movements corresponds to the globalization of control over labor power. The latest agreement between the United States and the European Union is an important part of this plan of action. It allows American exceptional courts to be the exception on which the globalized political command is built. The articulation between laws that authorize the prosecution of any "undue" political pressure on governments or international organizations with the special military courts that are charged with prosecuting foreigners accused of participating in terrorist activities makes it possible to punish any person opposed to the policies of multinational capital outside of any legal protections. The exception is the specific plan of action by which the law assimilates life. The operation of these special tribunals makes possible a reorganization of the whole judicial system on a world level. The judicial system then becomes an asymmetrical organization through which special American courts occupy a determinant position. Indeed, they establish the limits to the normal functioning of the rule of law. Whoever decides the exception to the norm establishes the norm.

# ACKNOWLEDGMENTS

I thank Jean-François Gava for his reading and remarks, and also Christine Pagnoulle for her translations.